Age of Heroes

Henri Keyzer-André

with Hy Steirman

HASTINGS HOUSE
Book Publishers
Mamaroneck, New York

Library of Congress Catalog Card Number 92-074893

ISBN 0-8038-9351-5

Printed in the United States of America

I DEDICATE this book to my dear wife, Mossette, who listened intently to my story and whose keen eyes later sifted through the scattered pieces, helping me to re-create the story of my life; without her participation and strength this book would never have been written.

Acknowledgments

THANKS TO ALL the people who were so kind to me in the early 1980s when I started to put the events together. Their encouragement kept the motor warm for takeoff.

I am indebted to Jerry Perles, my agent/attorney and friend; his guiding hand helped me avoid many pitfalls.

My thanks also to Jesse Newman, adviser and dear friend.

And my gratitude to old friends who helped me along the way and who've been so supportive: Mrs. Arnold Schwartz; Ann Whyte, Pan American Airways historian; Captain Henry Duffy, president of the Airline Pilots Association; John Lindsey, former vice president of Pan American Airways, and retired Pan Am pilots E. R. Banning and Everard Bierer, who helped recall highlights in my life.

Thanks also to: Joan Maier, my loyal secretary, who kept track of everything and who typed and retyped with unflagging interest and good humor; Vallerie Lynn of Hastings House for her editorial assistance; and sincere appreciation to Barbara Harney and Ora Lee Felder.

HENRI KEYZER-ANDRÉ

Contents

This sonnet was written by an American teenager, a volunteer pilot in the Royal Canadian Air Force during World War II. He was killed in action on December 11, 1941, at age nineteen. It has since become a pilot's anthem.

HIGH FLIGHT

Oh, I have slipped the surly bonds of earth,
And danced the skies on laughter-silvered wings;
Sunward I've climbed and joined the tumbling mirth
Of sun-split clouds—and done a hundred things
You have not dreamed of—wheeled and soared and swung
High in the sunlit silence. Hov'ring there,
I've chased the shouting wind along and flung
My eager craft through footless halls of air.
Up, up the long, delirious, burning blue
I've topped the wind-swept heights with easy grace,
Where never lark, or even eagle, flew;
And while with silent, lifting mind I've trod
The high, untrespassed sanctity of space,
Put out my hand and touched the face of God.

JOHN GILLESPIE MAGEE, JR.

Age of Heroes

CHAPTER 1

The Icy Hand of Death, November 7, 1980

A BELL CLANGED twice to get our attention, and the intercom came alive as the pilot said in Russian, "Due to the severe storm, we are experiencing difficulties. We are looking for a place to land. I have flown this area many times and I know of an abandoned military airdrome nearby. Keep seat belts fastened. It will be extremely difficult until we are on the ground."

Being a passenger in a faltering Russian plane, the Ilyushin Il-76 Candid jet, in the middle of desolate Siberia during a winter storm, as we were raked by sleet and snow and buffeted by severe headwinds, was a different experience for me. The Ilyushin was losing stability rapidly as it pitched and yawed erratically over faceless mining villages along the ice-covered Angara River, thirty-two thousand feet below.

I'd survived a half dozen serious plane crashes and numerous near misses with malfunctioning aircraft during my five decades as an airline pilot and aeronautical engineer at Pan Am, and later as a State Department FAA troubleshooter. After thousands of hours of flying, most pilots acquire a sixth sense that warns them when there's danger ahead. I knew all too well the limits of men and flying machines. The Ilyushin, a Soviet version of the American Starlifter, while a rugged aircraft, was struggling against the outer edges of its ability to cope with the ferocious weather conditions. The odds were impossible.

As a religious man, a good Episcopalian, I closed my eyes and said a

3

silent prayer. It might seem strange, but I wasn't afraid. Perhaps I was and didn't recognize it. I had never yet been frightened when confronted with a flying crisis, mostly because God and I had an understanding that went back to my childhood. If He wanted me, He only had to open his arms and I'd come. It was as simple as that.

Suddenly, the plane shuddered. The once-steady drone of the four jet engines began "choo-chooing"—misfiring and then sparking to life again with a bang—like an old Model T backfiring down the street. I was seated on the front seat of the passenger section on the left side, looking at the ice-coated window. Besides the spluttering engines, the raging headwinds were forcing the plane to pitch and bank steeply.

Impurities in the fuel probably were causing the jet engines to cough. It was a perennial Soviet problem. Russian mechanics frequently filtered fuel through a chamois cloth because foreign particles managed to seep into the jet fuel as it traveled from storage tanks to oil trucks and then to barrels before finally reaching airfields thousands of miles in the hinterland. Pilots complained bitterly that it caused their planes to move up and down like porpoises.

Ever since we left Krasnoyarsk earlier in the day, on November 7, 1980, the pilot had been experiencing more than gale-force headwinds of 90 to 100-plus miles per hour. If you consider the nose of the plane twelve o'clock, then the winds were pounding the plane at ten-thirty. With a normal cruising speed of 590 miles per hour, just under Mach 1, the headwinds were slowing our progress. Our destination was Irkutsk, near Lake Baikal. There were various VIPs on board—a cadre of twelve atomic scientists, and me, the only foreigner—fourteen Russian military officers, two members of the KGB, plus the crew of five and two luggage handlers to load and unload the plane. Thirty-six in all.

The stoic silence of the Russian nuclear scientists traveling with me did little to mask an anxiety that stalked the cabin like a ghost. The military personnel, charged with delivering to Vladivostok a cache of naval munitions taken aboard at Archangelsk, exuded a classic Russian fatalism—with good reason. The storm had transformed the Ilyushin and its cargo into a flying ammunition dump waiting to explode. It never occurred to the military bureaucracy that in the expediency of meeting a nonessential military delivery schedule, a dozen of Russia's finest nuclear scientists might be blown out of existence.

Paul Andrei Zhavoronkov, one of the young student scientists who would return to America with me, dropped into the seat beside me. Though it was chilly in the cabin, he was perspiring freely.

"I must tell you, Dr. Keyzer-André, that I am no sky traveler," he said. "In fact, I hate flying."

Zhavoronkov, a brilliant scholar at the Siberian Academy of Sciences, had little faith in the airworthiness of the Ilyushin. "I was not cut out for combat duty," he said. "I hate to complain, but when I do it calms my nerves. Will the plane hold together?"

"I have every faith," I said in the voice I had used for two decades as a Pan Am pilot. I did not mean to deceive him, but a modulated voice creates a calm needed to survive an emergency. But he knew as well as I what the odds were. He excused himself and joined his fellow scientists.

He got me thinking. I'm an old codger of seventy-three. What the hell am I doing here in this remote part of the world two-thirds of the way across Siberia and one hundred miles north of Mongolia? The answer I gave myself was that I was looking for distraction. The shock of losing my beloved wife, Maria, the previous year had depressed me.

But there were other reasons for the trip. Maybe it was the quiet insistence of former President Ford and President Carter to take this final assignment? Maybe it was an inner voice, whispering that the autumn years of my life need not be dull; a call to action and adventure—challenging the daredevil deep inside me. There had always been a need for me to go to the edge, but now there was a chance of going beyond it.

The strain of the seat belt across my lap told me when we were climbing, and my stomach told me when we were falling. The pilot and crew were good, damned good, but I didn't envy them this flight. And there is a limit to what stresses even the best-made plane can sustain. There must have been ice binding the tail section because the plane continued going up and down like a porpoise even when it wasn't misfiring.

The captain switched on the landing lights. Peering through a clear section on the window about the size of a silver dollar, I could see that the sleet was accompanied by heavy rain and snow. It reminded me of those little glass paperweights with tumbling snow.

Through my peephole, I noticed the lights of the airplane dancing up and down. A quick look at my watch told me it was 9:35 P.M., but to be quite honest, I didn't know what time zone we were in.

Engine trouble started on the final leg of the trip about 150 miles beyond the towns of Cheremkhovo, Usolye, and Sibirskoye en route to Angarsk. When the plane first started to shake slightly, I was sitting by myself, reminiscing. Most of the other passengers had full confidence in the ability of the Russian crew and were oblivious to what was going on. They were sitting at tables clutching glasses of vodka and beer and talking. I stared at the three young Soviet atomic scientists seated together, the ones to return to America with me when my year was up the next month.

My breath was condensing in the air and I was feeling the cold. I unbuckled my seat belt and put on my overcoat. The cold numbed my fingers as I fumbled with the buttons. The turbulence made even the simplest chore difficult. As I refastened the seat belt, the insulation panels chattered against the bulkhead as the Ilyushin fought the gusting wind. In a few minutes, the plane would descend to lower altitudes, where the storm was raging with greater intensity. I was forced to consider the possibility that its structural integrity was weakening and might not be up to a battle with nature.

How good was the Ilyushin? This jet plane had been built to replace the turboprop Anatov AN 12EVS, which was the regular paratroop and freight transport of the Soviet Military Transport Aviation, called VTA. The Ilyushin was able to travel a distance of twenty-seven hundred nautical miles without refueling. It had takeoff capabilities to make use of short, unprepared airstrips and a ruggedness to hold up even in the most difficult Siberian weather. It was capable of carrying forty tons of freight (or three personnel carriers weighing thirteen tons apiece). We were carrying almost that much with the load of military hardware and munitions that was being ferried to Vladivostok.

Turning my head, I could see that the right windows were somewhat clearer than on my side, as they were leeward of the headwinds driving the sleet. A stream of hydraulic fluid was splashing against the windows. The leakage meant the landing gears might not be capable of extending fully. The engines continued to backfire and choo-choo as we started our descent.

I put myself in the pilot's position. His Plexiglas windows, no matter how well his heaters worked, must have iced over. Presuming the rudder was frozen, I prayed silently that the wing flaps were working so he could at least guide the plane to the runway. They were. We began to bank one way and then the other. I thought that the pilot must have opened the side window so he could search for the landing strip. We finally straightened out into a long, bumpy descent. The grinding noise of the landing gear going down was a note of hope, but the plane turned sluggish and began to mush. Every second was an hour.

Suddenly, the wheels touched down at the very end of an old, snowy-white concrete runway that was devoid of lights. The plane thumped down heavily, as the landing gear collapsed. The metal of the landing gear scraped along the concrete runway, setting off sparks that immediately ignited the hydraulic fuel on the right wing. It flashed into a blaze. Without thinking, I automatically unfastened my seat belt. I had faced the fact earlier that the plane was a time bomb. The plane was still moving at great speed when the cockpit nose section slammed into something like a concrete abutment on the ground. The skidding plane caromed to the right, as the left wing ripped off.

Simultaneously, the fuselage burst open just where I was sitting and I was hurled through an opening that was laced with jagged metal. I landed first on my rear end and then was slammed onto my back, skidding toward the left side of the runway, hitting water and ice with a tremendous jolt. It felt like crashing into a stone wall, as I slid forward and sideways at the same time. I was moving like a hockey puck, skipping, tumbling, and turning. The momentum kept me going, as the concrete runway ice scraped off my heavy outer and inner clothes while tearing at my body.

It seemed as if I were two city blocks away from the plane, but it must have been closer. There were water burns all over my body. The pain in my spine was excruciating. My body felt as though it had been crushed by a heavy weight. I broke through the ice and ended up on my feet, standing in frigid water up to my navel. My shoulder and back pains were almost more than I could bear.

The plane continued down the runway, and the fire must have reached the munitions as it suddenly blew up. The huge explosion broke apart the plane, shooting flaming pieces high into the air. Some of them fell around me, hissing on contact with the water.

It was still sleeting, snowing, and raining, with a high wind that wafted hot, burning air back toward me. The water was so cold my teeth were chattering. I was dazed and bleeding. Ice was forming all around me. If I wasn't rescued soon, I'd become a statue, frozen in time. The smell of smoke from the burning bodies and the airplane was gagging me.

I could not remain in the water. Despite my screaming body, I forced myself out of the water and leaned thankfully against a tree. I was stunned, dazed, and did not understand how I still could be alive.

I was shivering, my teeth chattering uncontrollably, and I could feel my heart racing. The blood on my face from the many cuts was beginning to freeze. I tried to walk—but it was impossible. I began to lose consciousness. My time was short, and with the flickering part of my mind that was still conscious I prayed to God to take me.

But now was no time to black out. My strong will to live helped me to fight back to consciousness. My head was in turmoil. It was difficult to hold on to consciousness. In the whole struggle, the only element of reality was the light coming from the flames of burning wreckage nearby.

I felt some guilt for those who died, even though they had the honor and comfort of death. Here I was, in a private hell, hoping God would take me, yet trying to hold on to what was left of my life.

The fires burned down and it was soon dark, very silent and getting even colder. My wet clothes stuck to my body as they began to freeze. The only sounds were the falling of sleet and snow, my labored breathing, and the eerie sound of silence after death. Amid all this, I was thinking of survival. If I could get closer to the burning wreckage I might stay warm and alive a while longer. But I was leaning against the tree and couldn't move. It was impossible to get closer.

Suddenly, off in the distance, a small truck with a revolving beacon like a police car's headed toward the crash. The headlights picked me out and they drove up to me.

I could hear one of them shouting in Russian, "Ah. We have found the bastard, the saboteur, who blew up the plane."

CHAPTER 2

"A Stranger in a Strange Land"

—*Exodus*

IT HAD all seemed like a nightmare. The two guards who had arrested me force-walked me to their truck despite my screaming in pain. I kept pleading in Russian that I was injured, but they wouldn't listen. I was their prisoner. After shoving me into the back of the truck, one of them threw a coarse, smelly horse blanket over me. The roughness was like steel wool grating on my wounds.

For hours they questioned me at their headquarters, which smelled like a veterinary hospital. As my watch had stopped, I couldn't tell what time it was.

"He speaks Russian like a foreigner. He has no papers, no passport, no belongings. He is guilty of blowing up the plane."

I begged them to call Moscow, but they shrugged me off. Along with my despair I was dizzy and beginning to lose consciousness. That's when I was tossed into a tiny detention room. By not dying in the crash and then surviving the storm and frigid weather, I just might live long enough to be shot.

My clothes were in tatters, and besides the water burns and scrapes along my body, the pain in my back and leg was excruciating—they were either terribly bruised or broken. Tears wet my face. How many more times could I call on God to save me? I forced my mind else-where, away from the present, to pleasanter times. I thought of my mother and my childhood in the Netherlands, which were the happiest days of my life.

It was a story my mother told me a hundred times. On February 16, 1907, during a second day of heavy snowfall, a freak thunderstorm erupted. A bolt of lightning split the big pear tree in the garden. At that instant, my mother, who had been struggling in labor for hours, gave birth. The baby was not breathing.

Dr. Brooks, standing next to the midwife, picked the baby up by the ankles, holding it upside down as my frightened mother watched. He slapped it once, then a second time. Instead of crying, the baby gasped. This was the beginning for Henri Keyzer-André.

Apparently, I didn't cry much as I grew up, mostly because I was weaned on milk and, when I was cantankerous, it was doctored with champagne. It kept me happy and quiet. I was walking at eight months and talking at nine months. When my nurse, Tina, found me too much to handle, she chastised me in French, German, Dutch, and Flemish—the languages everyone spoke in Holland.

The family always discussed the difficulty of handling little Henri, who was regarded as hardheaded, determined, and a mischief-maker, fiercely independent and requiring surveillance twenty-four hours a day. My mother later confessed that most of these traits were not dissimilar from my father's.

Joseph Keyzer-André was a handsome man with a goatee who ruled the roost as a strict disciplinarian and never spared the rod. He kept the little daredevil locked up inside our garden, forbidden to play in the street with the neighborhood children. I was too rough for them, forever getting into mischief.

My father owned a factory in Maastricht called "Vesta," which made coal briquettes that were used in the new boilers of ships, trains, and factories. He also manufactured these boilers, and the business was very successful. He planned regular trips to numerous European countries, often staying as long as two years at a time. He set up his contacts aided by the advice and counsel of the Dutch ambassador and commercial attaché.

My older brother was August, and three more children arrived after me; a second brother, René John Gregory; a third brother, Carl Francis Joseph; and a sister, Marcelle.

At two, I had an experience that stayed with me for life. I was taken to church for the first time. Later, I was told I must have enjoyed it because I kept talking about the church for days afterward. Some of my observations brought surefire laughter, as I asked questions like "Why did the priest drink so much wine? Was he thirsty? Does God wear a beard like Daddy? How does the priest make the smoke smell so nice and sweet?"—pointing to the incense urn. Most of all, I enjoyed the singing and the big organ. I was determined to one day learn to play the organ.

When I turned three, it became imperative for my mother to hire a new governess to take care of me full-time. She was Indonesian, seventeen years old, with a small Oriental face, a lovely smile, and beautiful raven hair. Her full name was Theodosia Musina Bunga da Hari Natal, meaning "Spring Flower." We nicknamed her "Theo."

Also at age three I started school at the Catholic Brothers and Friars, a Franciscan order. Discipline was stricter than at home, and even at a tender age, I often received a whacking on my bottom when I got into trouble, which was often.

Theo was well educated and intelligent. She saw to it that I learned about discipline, but she also told me stories of the great, strong, brave men in history and their accomplishments. As I grew older, no matter how well I was doing in school, she pushed me to go further. Despite the pressure to do extra work and the spankings she administered, I loved her.

One day, my father announced that he had scheduled a two-year business trip to Portugal and my mother, my brother Gus, and I would accompany him. Also joining us would be Theo and my brother's governess, Lisa.

It was a long train ride to Lisbon, where we moved into an apartment on 24 Avenue de Liberal at Pompal Circle. It was close to my father's office and the Dutch embassy. Without wasting any time, we were enrolled in a Catholic school where our teachers were Franciscan monks. Portuguese is a difficult language to learn, and the monks were always cross with us. They never lost their talent for being hard on small boys, especially on boys' bottoms.

During our leisure time, our governesses, Lisa and Theo, took us to villages where we watched fishermen bringing in their catches of sardines and mending their nets. As the weather was milder than

Maastricht's, the spring came early and the flowers blossomed sooner and seemed more fragrant.

We kept at the task of learning the customs of the Portuguese and sightseeing throughout most of the country. Gus and I eventually became fluent in the language. All too soon the two years were up and we returned home. It was our friends who pointed out laughingly that we now spoke Dutch with a Portuguese accent.

My father's next scheduled trip was to Germany, and once more Gus and I were to accompany our parents. The younger children were to remain at home. Not old enough to realize that war was in the offing, we looked forward to our next adventure.

In Berlin, my parents moved into the Dutch embassy, while the rest of us settled in a large apartment at Strasschens-Weg 328 at the Königshof, about five blocks from the embassy. It wasn't until many years later that I realized my father must have had something more to do with the embassy than selling coal. More years passed before I realized he must have been involved with intelligence work. My father never revealed anything and his secrets were intact when he died.

The Germans were not as friendly as the Portuguese. They could not understand our German and they spoke with a different accent. Gus's governess came from Berlin and spoke Berlinese, which was considered a higher-grade, or snobbish German.

Intense school studies taught by the very strict friars readjusted our accents and "purified" our German, though the emphasis in our studies was mathematics. When it was announced at school in 1914 that war had broken out, I became frightened until I was assured that Germany would win the war quickly. I was only seven years old.

The Netherlands declared its neutrality, though it continued to trade with both Germany and Great Britain. Because Berlin was her home, Lisa took us to wonderful restaurants and introduced us to German beer. There were soldiers everywhere. We went sightseeing, visiting dark old castles and places like the Brandenburg Gate and the Egyptian Museum.

In 1916, we returned home, glad to get away from the fog and cold of the Berlin winters. By contrast, Holland was nice and calm and prospering because of the war. My parents talked about the undercurrent of fear that the opposing armies might ignore our neutrality and send their soldiers, planes, and tanks across the Netherlands.

While my father liked the idea that we were being taught by monks, he was adamant that he didn't want us to be religious. My mother ignored this and we went to church every Sunday. Actually, I was the only one who wanted to go every week. When my father found out about it, he was furious. He lectured me and actually forbade me to go to church. This upset me deeply. I didn't learn till later that he was afraid "the little fool would join the church."

But when Sunday came, off I went with my mother. My father, who was usuually horseback riding on Sunday, came home early and discovered me returning from church. He took me to my room and gave me a fierce spanking. After that, every Sunday, he asked if I had been to church and I would say yes. Again, I got a beating. For a while, I believed rear ends were for beatings and not for sitting.

Finally, one day my father confronted me. "Henri, I am going to give you another beating. Will that stop you from going to church?"

"No, Father."

"Why do you go when I forbid it?"

"Because I believe God is watching over us. I believe in God and that is more important to me than anything on earth."

My father fell silent for a while, then he threw the paddle on the floor and stalked out. It was the last time we discussed religion. A week later, we learned we were going to France. Gus was twelve and I was almost ten. It was Friar Francis de Angelo Chuise who told us, "In your studies and in preparation for your trip to France, you must hold very tightly to the theory that man must use his mind more and his body less. The young man or woman whose mind has been disciplined by a challenging education and who has been taught at school to respect fact, reason, and logic will feel at home in the realm of ideas and abstract concepts.

"The Bible says that where there is no vision the people will perish."

These words made me firmly believe in God.

The trip to France included the whole family this time. It was fun watching the eyes of the younger children pop open at the sights as we went by train from Maastricht to Paris. Because of the warplanes over France, there was a blackout, with no lights shining from the train. We were now traveling with five governesses, one for each child. Our living quarters proved to be an enormous apartment located at the corner of 4 bis Avenue de Ségur and Rue Bixio, just behind the tomb of Napoleon. My parents moved into the embassy, but we saw them frequently.

Besides helping us with our studies, the governesses had other specific duties: teaching us manners as well as the customs and culture of France, for example. Gus and I practiced getting rid of the harsh guttural sounds of the German language that we had picked up in Berlin in order to learn the softer sounds of beautiful, Parisian French, which was a very different French from what we had learned in Holland.

Like the other countries we had visited, we were taken sightseeing. There was the River Seine and the Left Bank, where the artists lived and painted, the Arc de Triomphe, the Eiffel Tower, and the Notre-Dame Cathedral. I kept looking for the Hunchback of Notre-Dame, but he wasn't around.

Once again, the Franciscan monks were severe with Gus and me. They were dedicated to teaching. It seemed to be a fetish with all these monks that one had to learn or watch out! School hours on weekdays were from eight in the morning until noon, and from one o'clock until four, plus a half day on Saturday. If our lessons were not completed on schedule, we received a whacking on our behinds. In the evenings, our governesses saw to it that we completed our studies. We made spectacular progress in mathematics, particularly higher algebra and calculus.

Once we perfected our French, Gus and I enjoyed Paris. We kept abreast with the progress of the war as we read about gas attacks and dogfights between fighter planes in the sky and the exploits of heroic French fighter aces like Fonck. My father remarked long and loud about the stupidity of airplanes. Those that weren't shot down were crashing because of poor maintenance and worse pilots.

At the end of two years, we returned home to Maastricht. As we now spoke Dutch with a French accent, the neighborhood kids treated us like foreigners.

When the war finally ended, Father went away by himself and Mother looked after the business. We were not told where he went. On his return, he scheduled a trip to Spain, but this time only Gus and I would accompany our parents. There was internal trouble in the country—the Basques were fighting the Spanish government and sometimes they would attack foreigners.

We moved into an apartment next to the Fenix Hotel on Paseo de la Castellana 67. Again, we lived close to the Dutch embassy. Our enrollment in a church school was immediate and the teaching monks were the worst monsters of all. They were overly punctual and strict. I was at the age to imagine that the single life and constant celibacy would turn any hot-blooded Spaniard into a tyrant.

Learning Castilian Spanish was difficult. It was spoken with one's tongue between the teeth like a constant lisp. I practiced manipulating my tongue so as not to sputter my words. As I began to speak the language fluently, I would occasionally show off.

The Spanish people were warm and friendly and we got along well. We were taken to several bullfights by young friends, but I was never quite sure I enjoyed them. Large doses of culture were on our agenda and Gus and I visited the Gallerías Preciados, the world-famous Prado, and the Royal Palace at Retiro Park. There were also rounds of parties at the various embassies. In the summer, we vacationed on the beaches of the Costa del Sol.

At the end of two years, we returned home and were reunited with the three younger children. Not long afterward, my father dropped a bombshell on the family. It had been decided that we would leave Holland and emigrate to America.

"It only seems as though the war is over, but it is not," he told the family. "The Germans are already talking about the harsh terms of the armistice. Inflation there is impossible. They will rebuild their army. The Communists in Russia will spread their germs around Europe. And Holland and Belgium are in the crossroads of the coming war. There is no more neutrality in Holland. To save the family, we will move to the United States."

This meant selling our home, the coal business, and the shipping line that my mother inherited when her father died. It also meant leaving most of our friends and possessions. At fourteen, I really looked at it as another adventure.

The hardest part was having to leave Theo, who returned to Indonesia. But I also had to say good-bye to my great-grandmother, who would not be joining us.

We traveled to Liverpool and boarded the *Old Dominion* for the trip across the Atlantic. The trip was unusual in that the seas were very rough around Ireland, which held us up. The captain announced, "For three days we have not made any forward progress because of the severe headwinds."

Everyone was seasick except for our parents, Gus, and myself. In the dining room, dishes kept flying around the room. We were later informed that four passengers had died of dehydration due to seasickness and were buried at sea. At one point, only twenty passengers made it to the dining room for meals. The others were being attended to by a very distressed doctor.

The captain informed us later that we had encountered the tail end of a hurricane. The rest of the trip across the Atlantic was in high seas. Then, when nearing the port of New York, we were diverted to Philadelphia because of a dock strike. We had been eager to see the Statue of Liberty, but it was not to be.

Father decided we should remain a few days in Philadelphia to let the family recuperate from the voyage. The Dutch ambassador to Washington, a friend of my father's, told him about the beauties of Virginia and said that it was a wonderful place to bring up children. So, that's where we went.

After a careful search, my father bought an eighteen-hundred-acre property from Reynolds Realty. It came complete with a homestead farm on it and the price was a dollar an acre. We moved into the Carol Hotel while my parents worked on plans and supervised the building of our new home. Because it was set on a hill and the sun shone most of the time, it was called Bright Hill.

To work the farm, my father hired a black man named Billy Smith. He was a Baptist preacher and my father respected that. Billy's sister-in-law Suzie and her friend Liza also came to work for us.

After Holland, with its low-lying land that was being eroded by the sea and sparse sunshine, it was a pleasure to play out in the sunny air. I took to Billy at once. I followed him around like a puppy and helped him as much as I could. He taught me how things grew and how one got the earth to work for man. Every evening, I still said my prayers and thanked God for all the wonderful things my family had.

My father kept telling us why it had been important for him to emigrate because he didn't trust Germany to remain docile and that it was Germany's intention to acquire more territory. Holland would be swallowed up and who would care? Certainly not Great Britain, as the Boer War in Africa was between the British and the Dutch settlers.

No sooner had we settled into our beautiful home than it was announced that we were to start school. As none of us spoke English, the younger children would have a tutor, while Gus and I would attend Coxie, a small country day school.

English is probably one of the most difficult languages to learn.

Despite our fluency in a half-dozen languages, Gus and I were prepared to have difficulties. My father's Old World ways started us off on the wrong foot.

Our teacher was an extremely large farm woman by the name of Mrs. Bass. She weighed 375 pounds and had large, powerful arms strengthened by farm work. My father prepared us for the first day of school with the following instructions.

"You two dress up in your best clothes, and when you see your teacher, step forward, click your heels, and say, 'Good morning, mistress, we hope you are enjoying perfect health.'" We were each to present her with a small bouquet of flowers, bow, and step back, then wait for her to say something.

We followed instructions and Mrs. Bass almost fell over as the children roared with laughter. Mrs. Bass said, "I hate foreigners. You have no right to live in America."

Embarrassed without really understanding why, we sat down at our double desk and waited for further instructions from the teacher. She deliberately avoided us for four days. Neither Gus nor I knew what was going on. When we tried to speak to her, we got no response. Desperately trying to get some attention, we brought in some sand and began playing freight train at our desk, making lots of noise. Mrs. Bass came down on us like a whale and brushed everything off our desks, then she began berating us in English, which we did not understand.

We learned our first English words from helpful classmates in the playground, listening attentively and practicing diligently. One morning, when we felt comfortable with our limited vocabulary, we came forward, clicked our heels again, and said once more, "Good morning, mistress, I hope you are enjoying perfect health and please enjoy these flowers." Then we added the new words we had learned from our classmates: "Here comes Mrs. Bass with a finger up her ass."

This time, I thought the roof had fallen in. She turned red like a ripe tomato and steam seemed to come out of her ears. Another four days passed without any attention. Because of the boredom, we started playing trains again. It worked for a while as we finally got some attention. She also brought into the classroom a big hickory stick and said, "I'm going to straighten out these foreigners." Of course, we didn't understand what she said.

She approached my desk and suddenly grabbed me by the neck, pulling me up as if I were weightless. Then she bent me over her left arm, picked up the stick, and began whacking. She kept beating me and beating me. What my father and the monks had done to my bottom was nothing compared to this stinging pain. I decided then and there that no one was ever going to whack me again. I lifted her skirt and bit into her fat thigh.

She dropped me on the floor. I got up slowly, went to the stove in the middle of the room and grabbed a poker. My brother kept egging me on in French. As she approached me, I waved the poker in her face. When she finally reached me, she fainted.

Mrs. Bass required thirteen stitches, and thus ended my first encounter with American education. We were expelled and my father had to decide what to do with his two eldest sons. After some research and then a talk with Mrs. Shipley, the principal of the local high school, we were enrolled for our second encounter with teaching in America.

Mrs. Shipley turned out to be a fine, understanding woman. We were enrolled for the next school session. Meanwhile, we had some time to be tutored in English. No more misunderstandings. We worked very hard, as we wanted to be accepted. In the first semester, we did extremely well, except in English. Some of the teachers were patient, others simply did not like foreigners. It was not my place to remind these teachers that some of America's earliest settlers were Dutch.

We already knew calculus and higher algebra, so we were not too popular with the math teacher, as we knew the answers to equations before she got through putting them on the blackboard. Finally, we made good progress with English, and when I could read it more rapidly, I became engrossed by American history.

One day, the principal called our father in and said, "I don't think we can teach these boys much more as they are way ahead of what we are teaching in the high school today." We took our final exam and both of us scored very well. Dad was pleased and decided now was the time for us to try for a university.

I was not yet sixteen, and a new era in my life was about to open up. It was 1923, the year I discarded knee pants, long underwear, suspenders, and high-button shoes. It was a quick conversion to high starched collars and cufflinks. The usual age for such change came after high school graduation.

Of course, my long-pants suit was a hand-me-down from my brother Gus. The pants were too long, the waist too wide, the jacket too small, and the sleeves too short. I never raised or bent my arms to lift the trouser cuffs off the ground, but I wore the suit as proudly as if it had been tailored for me. The suit was an announcement to the world that I was now a junior adult.

My father recognized my adulthood with the fundamentals of this coming of age. He presented me with a box of cigars, three cartons of cigarettes, a pipe, and a pound of Prince Albert smoking tobacco. I was elated when I started to taste my gifts. I tried the cigarettes, but didn't like them and gave them to my brother. The cigars were a mark of sophistication. When I tried a couple, I found them milder, but they made me dizzy and nearly choked me to death.

The pipe, to my way of thinking, was the epitome of manhood. They were milder than the cigarettes or the cigars, but I couldn't understand why one had to endure the hardships of smoking to be considered a man. One evening, when there were female guests in the house, I lit my pipe and started to show off by puffing up a storm. But I soon became dizzy and rushed for the stairs, which fell down on me as I passed out. I was sick for several days, and I swore that there must be other ways to demonstrate my manhood. It cured me of smoking, but not from showing off.

To me, America was still a strange country with a strange language and I promised myself to work extra hard to master English so I could express suitably my feelings of friendship, love, and joy. Meanwhile, I nursed with tender loving care the blond hair sprouting on my face. My voice fluttered between soprano and bass at the oddest moments.

Most of all, by mastering English, I could talk with the opposite sex. With my poor English, I could not make myself understood, so I could not mingle with the ladies. Some fellow once said of himself, "The geometry of girls mesmerizes me." Me, too, for I was jealous of the boys who could talk smoothly with them. By comparison with European girls, the Americans were more flirty, except with me. I began to dislike them. Their presence had acquired a new, bewildering power to dry my throat, muddle my speech, quicken my pulse, shorten my breath, and addle my brain.

As our speech improved, we began to socialize. Sunday-afternoon parties replaced baseball with the boys. Instead of the frenetic black bottom, shimmy, and raccoon, we danced in the style of a semi-embrace to older melodies that one could sing and whistle. Instead of speaking, I smiled a lot.

The real agenda, spurred on by the girls, involved kissing games like post office and spin the bottle. I kissed the girls, and to my surprise, they kissed me back. Being blond, tall, and slim seemed to have contributed more to my progress than my English. Strange country, America.

We moved. Our new home was not another farm but more like a suburban country estate. I enjoyed my father's Pierce-Arrow and dining with my father's associates. On occasion, my father would allow me to pay the check. It was a true sign of manhood. I enjoyed watching things grow, and as I was an early riser, I went out to help the farmhands grow fruits and vegetables and make homemade bread. In the winter, my chores were to light the fires in the house and milk the cows. The farm workers didn't seem to mind.

Despite my mastery of many languages, English was still giving me difficulty. Mostly, it was my speech inflections that made it difficult for people to understand me, not my ability to understand them. The next step to curing the problem was to do what Demosthenes did to cure his speech. I spoke with pebbles in my mouth and then later switched to black-eyed peas. It worked, but even after I grew into adulthood, there would always be a touch of Holland in my speech.

The family continued to be close. We would sit around at the breakfast table swapping stories. Each day, it would be a different language, including English. It was a warm and wonderful time.

Though my father, a graduate engineer, would occasionally make deals to ship coal from Virginia to Europe, he bought a new business that made lawn mowers with the brand name of "The Clippet." For Gus and myself, it was a great experience. We learned to weld in the machine shop and repair engines. From there, Gus and I started a side business, rebuilding automobiles. We'd buy wrecks and then take out the engines and accessories. Father's foundry, machine shop, and woodworking plants were available to us. Besides our skill with welding, we acquired other skills to help us take apart engines, repair them, and then reinstall them in other autos.

On one project, we bought an old sedan that had been crushed on top. We removed the body by cutting it off with a torch, then welded the chassis to support a little truck body. That way, Gus and I each built ourselves a vehicle. It was easy to practice our driving skills on the farm roads.

As I had a natural facility with engines, my father put me in charge of the electric Delco plant on the farm. I also serviced the water pump and all the mechanical equipment on the farm. It was an enjoyable experience. Gus, meanwhile, was in charge of the family cars.

Then came time for university. My father was anxious that Gus and I would follow his career and become engineers. My father made an appointment for me to apply to Virginia Polytechnic Institute in Blacksburg.

CHAPTER 3

How to Fly—in Three
Easy Lessons

WHEN I TOOK my entrance exam to study engineering at VPI in 1924, I was seventeen years old. I passed easily and was accepted. The president, Julian A. Burrus, and Dean Samuel R. Pritchard notified my father. Simultaneously, my brother Gus was scheduled to go to a different university. I didn't find out until months later that he never went.

It seems that Mr. Reynolds, owner of Reynolds Realty, who had sold my father the ranch, had been charmed by my father's business acumen and sales expertise. After he moved his real estate company to Miami, which in the early 1920s was enjoying an extraordinary real estate boom, he wrote and invited my father down for a visit. His sole purpose was to interest my father into buying and selling properties.

My father waited for the summer, when Gus and I would be on summer vacation, and he took both of us along. During our visit, my father became so excited at the prospect of enlarging his fortune that he agreed to a partnership. To prove it, the three of us plus Mr. Reynolds went looking for a house for us to live in. Mr. Reynolds, as a broker, received advance listings of houses for sale. After a week, my father found one to his liking. He bought it, contracted to have repairs, painting inside and out, and some remodeling done, and then left Gus and me in the house to watch the workmen while he returned to

22

Virginia to divest himself of the farm, the garden mower business, his coal export business, and other investments. As usual, he turned a handsome profit on everything.

Left to our own devices, Gus and I took turns baby-sitting the house. I found a local park where teenagers played baseball. I was invited into the game and played every second day. Gus played on alternate days. When there weren't enough kids, I taught the boys how to play soccer. One of the boys was named Charles, and we seemed to hit it off well. He told me he was a volunteer coach for underprivileged youngsters who belonged to the Baptist Church on Fifth Avenue and Fortieth Street. Before long, Charles talked me into being his assistant, even though my knowledge of baseball was limited.

With the farm sold, my father rented a temporary, smaller home on four acres in Virginia. This allowed my father to move to Miami and get the business going while I returned to school and my mother took care of the younger children.

When I entered VPI, Gus was twenty years old, good-looking and full-grown. My father told number-one son he was going into the real estate business with the promise of his own car and lots of pocket money. Gus agreed. It was a grown-up adventure. It was months before Gus wrote and told me about it.

Meanwhile, I had my mind set on finishing college and becoming an engineer. I settled in at VPI, with its twenty-five-hundred-acre campus situated about forty miles east of Roanoke, Virginia. "Thanks" to all the strict friars in Europe, I was spanking good at math, and I took physics and calculus in stride. English was no longer a handicap.

Just before Christmas 1924, a man representing New York, Rio, Buenos Aires Airline (NYRBA) visited VPI. He was Ralph O'Neill and he was accompanied by his attorney, William MacCracken. O'Neill was scouting engineering schools, eager to find students interested in a career in aviation. For the lucky few selected, he was offering a company scholarship. Few VPI students had ever seen a plane.

Most people at that time knew little about aviation except for newspaper stories of early Army and Navy aircraft, or the Wright brothers. And there had been a few headlines about U.S. Navy commander Albert Read, who captained the NC-4, the first plane to fly across the Atlantic; or Captain John Alcock and Lieutenant Arthur Brown, two

British World War I pilots in the Royal Flying Corps, who were the first to fly across the Atlantic nonstop. Aside from these sensational flights, aviation generally was viewed with complete disinterest.

Though history proved the two visitors to be aviation pioneers with vision, students shied away from talking to them. The usual snide comment was "Flying is a good way to get killed." Having lived in Germany and France during the war, I often had seen squadrons of planes flying overhead. I had even witnessed a dogfight between a French and a German plane, and imagined what it would be like to be an aviator. In this respect, I was a little more sophisticated than my fellow students and took the time to talk to O'Neill and MacCracken.

They asked me many questions about my father and my background. When they learned I was fluent in seven languages, including Spanish and Portuguese, O'Neill pressed me to visit him in Washington, D.C., but not before O'Neill, a bald-headed man with a sharp sense of humor, asked me some questions in rapid Mexican-Spanish. His eyebrow lifted when my replies, in the more erudite, pure Spain Spanish, were equally swift.

My trip to the capital never took place. Six months later, O'Neill returned. Apparently, he was a friend of the dean and had been monitoring my progress. He was also advised that I had hands-on experience with engines and woodworking, and had operated my father's maintenance shop.

My academic marks were excellent. Predicated on my school record, O'Neill felt he could exert some pressure on the school and suggested I was eligible to skip to a higher class. The dean said that VPI policy maintained that I must complete all four years. Again, I was invited to Washington to visit the offices of NYRBA.

"Aviation is a new and growing industry, a mere twenty years of age," said O'Neill. "But it's where the future is. It will shrink the world and perhaps one day unite the world. We need bright young men, engineers knowledgeable in aeronautics who understand all aspects of aviation, maintenance and airport control, and who can speak foreign languages. That's why we're offering these scholarships. They will open up the world to airline travel, transportation, and intercontinental mail. Aviation is tomorrow."

I said, "My father will kill me if I go into aviation. He detests flying after what he saw during the war. He promised to disinherit anyone in the family who gets involved."

"Would it serve any purpose to talk with him?"

"No."

"Well, young man, you have the qualifications we're looking for, particularly the languages," said O'Neill, "but the men we seek must be strong-willed and determined, Visionaries. These young men will rise in the company and become wealthy executives. It's an opportunity of a lifetime."

We looked at each other for a while. I didn't let on that I had recently received a disturbing letter from my father requesting that I, too, join him and Gus in the real estate business in Miami. There was money to be made, and if I didn't join them at once, he would refuse to pay my future college tuition.

I said quietly, "I'll come to Washington. The least I can do is listen." O'Neill suggested a date and we shook hands.

In Washington, several executives and some financial backers of the airline were meeting and I was introduced to them. In time, I learned more about my hosts and their supporters.

Ralph O'Neill was a mining engineer who enlisted as a pilot in the American Expeditionary Force. A daredevil during World War I, he became an ace after shooting down his fifth enemy plane. At war's end, with the abundance of returning pilots, he took the job of training the Mexican Air Force. He was fluent in Spanish and he soon saw the potential of bridging North and South America via an airline that would carry mail and passengers.

After five years in Mexico, he talked himself into a job as a flying salesman with Boeing Airplane Company. He flew demonstrator planes to various Latin American countries to sell them on aviation and aircraft. He also made friends as he surveyed the land for potential mail/passenger business. They addressed him as "Colonel," but whether the rank was from the U.S. Army or Mexican Air Force I didn't find out. William P. MacCracken was an attorney out of Chicago, also an Army pilot, who would later become assistant secretary of commerce for aeronautics under President Calvin Coolidge, when Herbert Hoover was secretary.

Consolidated Aircraft Company of California (forerunner of General Dynamics) was run by Reuben Fleet, a designer and builder of aerial patrol boats for the U.S. Navy. He, too, was a veteran of World War I. He had agreed to manufacture and outfit six flying boats called "Commodores," capable of carrying mail and passengers. It was a financial commitment equal to $1.5 million. The last of the group was James R. Rand, Jr., president of the Remington Rand Corporation.

For a young man of eighteen to attend such a meeting as an equal was heady stuff. Some of these men were graduates of Massachusetts Institute of Technology. The university, while it had no formal school of aeronautics, now taught more subjects in the field, and on a higher level, than any other technical university.

Two major hurdles, like twin swords of Damocles, hung over my head: the first, my father's vehement antiflying attitude; the second, if I defied his orders, how could I pay for my education? I wasn't bothered about losing my inheritance, because at the time I was more interested in adventure than money. I was also coming around to the idea that I was ready to make my own way, not my father's.

MacCracken and O'Neill helped me work through these obstacles. NYRBA offered me the scholarship with the proviso that I would work for the company after graduation. If I didn't, I would have to repay the amount of the scholarship. What I now had was a clear course for the future, a chance to attend one of the best universities in the country and a job upon graduation. The first hurdle was to pass the entrance exam. Then another problem surfaced. While my father couldn't force me to work for him, if he ever found out where I was, he could still remove me from school, as I was under twenty-one years of age.

The only way out was to attend school under another name. I enjoyed the shenanigans I would have to go through. It was most exhilarating. But I felt I had to discuss the scheme with my mother. While I was willing to pull the wool over my father's eyes, I was not about to do it to my mother. She listened, asked questions, and while ambivalent about it, was encouraging by reminding me that at seventeen, she had taken over the running of the family shipping line in Belgium after her father's death.

Of the whole affair, the one thing that bothered me the most was the name change. Instead of Henri Adam Ferdinand Keyzer-André, I became Robert K. (Keyzer) Whitten.

Some NYRBA associates were alumni, so my special introduction to MIT was smoothed over. My year and a half at VIP stood me in good stead, as did the training in higher mathematics and science by the monks. Passing my exams with high grades enabled me to get into advanced courses. Because it was obligatory for first-year students to study French and German in order to read up on new technical advances in aviation, after the first complete year, there would be no summer break for freshmen. But as I had already passed language-comprehension tests in French and German, it enabled me to skip summer classes.

It was stressed that MIT was not an institution where newsboys suddenly metamorphosed into industrialists. Here was an opportunity for highly motivated men of intelligence to study new technologies and become winners by making contributions in their fields.

O'Neill got me a job at the university at which I could earn pocket money; it wasn't work I would do with my head or with languages. I became a janitor. The job included cleaning toilets, washing dormitory floors, cutting lawns, tending gardens, and removing garbage.

The Biblical Book of Numbers flashed into my head, "What hath God wrought?" as a fog settled in my brain at the enormity of what I had undertaken. Through this haze of confusion, I heard O'Neill reiterate that NYRBA would lend me $6,000 to make up the difference in tuition. Then he added one more stipulation to our agreement: "We don't want you to have any distractions, so, no girls!"

Settling in quickly, but concerned about the coming years, I learned that MIT originally was called Boston Tech when it had opened as a private college in 1861. It was changed later to MIT, and then nicknamed "tute" by the students, a shortening of the word institute.

Uneasy with fraternity types and more comfortable with non-American students, I made friends with three classmates: Alexander Mikosky from Leningrad, Russia; Jue Ting-hu from Hangchow, China; and Paul René Jacques de Permentier, Brussels, Belgium. In no time flat, they called me "Dutch," though I also answered to the nickname "Klumpa" (wooden shoes).

MIT was mostly populated by wealthy young men who lived in fraternities; the scholarship boys were seldom invited to join, while those Americans and Orientals who were sponsored by Christian missionary funds were seldom pledged to a fraternity. The environment was Anglophile, as England was then the standard of snobbish taste and acceptability. They were trying to be more Oxonian than Oxford. Perhaps it was due to the competition from the other snobs at nearby Harvard.

The first year was a grind. I had no time to myself as I hauled trash, cleaned dormitories, and in between tried to study. Nevertheless, I had no problem making good grades. My father was still angry that I hadn't joined his real estate business. My mother, whom I spoke with regularly in Miami, said he no longer wished to talk with me.

When summer arrived, I went directly to Washington. Even if I had the money, I didn't have time to visit my family in Miami. O'Neill had enrolled me at Brookings Institution and George Washington University to take graduate courses toward a Ph.D. I was registered in advance at both institutions for the next four summers.

Besides my studies, I was being indoctrinated in the general rules and regulations involving aviation. The most important question was "Who owned the skies?" This was an international concern after the advent of airships and warplanes that roamed across borders at will during World War I. Every nation was now vulnerable to indiscriminate air attack unless there was a set of regulations by which all nations could abide. This was further emphasized by longer and longer flights, such as the crossing of the Atlantic by Read in the NC-4, and Alcock and Brown.

In 1919, the Paris Peace Conference convened the International Convention for Air Navigation. It was agreed that the airspace over the high seas was open to everyone, but the skies over each country would remain within the sovereign rights of that country, which could then deny or permit air travel over its territories. But countries were slow in signing the agreement.

NYRBA had earmarked Central and South America for its passenger and airmail routes. But first it had to get operating permits to fly into Latin American countries in order to compete with the French Aeropostale Company already flying mail routes from Europe to various cities in South America. The French used a combination of land and sea routes. The second problem was obtaining routes and subsidized airmail contracts from the U.S. Post Office Department to enable NYRBA to operate on a sound economic basis.

With its financing, advanced new planes, and its political connections, NYRBA should have been successful immediately. It was not to be. The airline had not figured on the devious mind of Juan Trippe, the head of Pan Am, who, with a couple of broken-down planes and close connections in government through his Yale friends, kept managing to outmaneuver NYRBA.

Thus, NYRBA suffered its first defeat when the mail contract it wanted was given to Pan Am. The conflict was turning bitter, but it was just the start of the airline wars. As it progressed, there were constant rumors of graft and political payoffs by Trippe, and a flow of derogatory rumors about NYRBA emanating from Pan Am.

NYRBA tried to make connections with the French interests at Aeropostale in order to make use of their landing facilities. It was soon whispered discreetly into government ears by Pan Am cohorts that any help given NYRBA would constitute help to foreign countries.

The competition could only get worse. Meanwhile, the summer ended and MIT beckoned just as Postmaster General Walter Brown went on record saying that competing bids in the airmail business were of little value. This was contrary to what I had learned at school— that competition was the essence of democracy. I couldn't understand why there was prejudice against NYRBA.

The time was 1927, a mere eight years after the Great War, but aviation was making great strides from the days of the Jennys and Nieuports. Excitement was created by the New York–Paris air race for the Raymond Orteig Prize of $25,000. Air-cooled motors had been developed that were light and reliable. Excitement had increased the year before when Captain René Fonck, the French fighter pilot who shot down seventy-five planes in World War I, set out to win the prize. He crashed shortly after takeoff from Roosevelt Field on Long Island. Two of Fonck's crewmen were killed.

Then two U.S. Navy reservists—Noel Davis, the pilot, and Stanton Wooster, his navigator—also entered the frenzy to be first to complete the trip. Their shiny silver plane was a modified bomber, a Keystone Pathfinder. The two young men took off for a flight test from Langley Field in Virginia, but the plane didn't have enough lift to clear the trees in its path. Davis swerved, missed the trees, and landed in what he thought was an empty field. It turned out to be marshland and both men were killed.

Now, a year later, four other attempts were in progress. It was to be a real race, after all. Commander Richard E. Byrd of the U.S. Navy, the first man to fly to the North Pole; Charles Lindbergh, a U.S. Army airmail pilot; Captain Charles Nungesser, France's second-greatest air ace, with forty-five kills; and Clarence Chamberlin and Charles Levine, the latter an airplane builder.

On May 7, 1927, Nungesser and his navigator, François Coli, took off from Le Bourget Airport near Paris and pointed the plane's nose toward New York. They were last sighted over Ireland and then they disappeared. It is believed they encountered fierce headwinds and ran out of fuel four hundred miles short of their goal.

Two weeks later, on May 20, 1927, Lindbergh took off in a fog from Roosevelt Field and flew solo, nonstop across the Atlantic Ocean, landing at Le Bourget thirty-three and one half hours later. The feat electrified the world. This one historic feat changed aviation forever. Airplanes had gotten long pants.

Everyone in my class was pumped up. Lindbergh, at twenty-five, was only a few years older than we were. We all realized that aviation was here to stay. A few days later, after finishing up my chores of cleaning toilets, mopping the halls, taking out the garbage, I decided to visit the Coke shop and splurge on a five-cent Coca-Cola. There was the usual raucous student chatter accompanied by screaming girls. Though invited, I refused to join in and took my Coke to the farthest vacant table and sat down. A few minutes later, a petite, very pretty girl with dark hair and large, soft-brown eyes stopped at the table and asked if she could join me.

"My name is Minnie—Minerva Morgan—I'm taking courses at MIT. I saw you didn't want to join the loonies, so I think you may be sane. Who are you and what are you studying?" I told her my real name and she wrote it out in her little book.

"Isn't it dangerous for a young woman to sit down next to a stranger?" I asked.

"Students here are never strangers," she said. "Besides being tall, blond, and masculine, you look very much like a hawk with those piercing blue eyes. Yes, you look dangerous, but I like to live dangerously and you are my newest challenge. Besides, I see you in church every Sunday."

I laughed and said, "In Holland, a girl would be punished for being so forward."

"Aren't you glad we're not in Holland?" We talked for a while about what we were each doing at school. When she discovered my interest in aeronautics, she said calmly, "I can fly an airplane."

Now I was shocked. I had never met anyone as bold as Minnie, or as daring. American girls sometimes frightened me, but Minnie and I seemed to be in synch. After a while, she looked me in the eye and asked me to take her to a tea dance the following Friday. Her look dared me to refuse. I didn't answer for a while. "Is there something wrong?" she said.

"No. I have only one dark suit and it's not pressed. Plus, I have chores to do for the school. But, worst of all, I vowed not to date any girls until I graduated."

"Your suit isn't a problem. Place it under the mattress and sleep on it. As for dating girls, if you don't show up, you're going to be in a lot of trouble." I looked at her pretty face and determined expression, and small though she might be, there was a ferocious look in her eye. I had the feeling that this young lady was used to having her own way.

On my way back to the dormitory, I was literally flying when I met up with Marie Loadie, the dietitian for the university. One of my chores was to help clean up after her. I confessed what had happened and she laughed. "You really got yourself into a bind. Don't worry, I won't let you go in a wrinkled suit. As for your pledge of no girls—if you want to be celibate, take up the priesthood. You work too hard, you deserve some relaxation."

On the day of the dance and true to her word, Marie pressed my suit and my best white shirt. When I told her where the dance was being held, she said, "That hotel is only for the very rich, Henri. You're a good, hardworking boy, so I'm going to lend you my auto." She also pressed some money into my hand. It was a $10 bill.

Her car was a Hudson Sensible Six and I arrived at the Beacon Hotel in style. But it was Minerva who knocked me out. She had on a white flapper dress that did wonders for her figure, and with her dark hair and elegant style, she made my heart flutter. I reached over and kissed her on the cheek. She knew I approved and held on to me a little longer than a hello kiss.

I was oblivious of the other young people at the party as we danced, talked, and drank champagne. It was spring, and I told her I would soon be going to Washington to attend summer school. At the party's end, her mother arrived in a Rolls-Royce with a chauffeur. I was introduced to her and she was taken by my European manners, smiling as I clicked my heels and bowed at the introduction. She invited me to spend a whole day with the family on the following Sunday. Minerva kissed me good-bye and her mother kissed me on the cheek.

My only concern was who would do my Sunday work of cleaning up the dorm and finishing the gardening while I was a guest of the Morgans? But "Minnie the beautiful" was also "Minnie the determined." Nothing stood in her way. She called to say, "I'll come early in the morning to pick you up and I'll bring two maids and a gardener to do your garden."

It all worked out. Minerva arrived promptly and I told my temporary helpers what had to be done. I found kissing in a Rolls made me nervous, but it was rather enjoyable. At their magnificent home on the bay, her mother greeted me again with a kiss. Her father was about to shake hands with me when I clicked my heels and bowed. Then I shook his hand.

He said, "You're a nice young man with fine manners."

Minerva was pleased. I later learned from her mother that she rarely brought home young men. She found most of them either too snobbish, too weak, too self-centered, or too interested in her family's fortune. Minerva talked me into playing tennis, which I hadn't played once since coming to MIT. For three sets, she trounced me. I congratulated her and said, "I don't mind being beaten by a woman—if she is beautiful." She smiled. As I was almost a foot taller than she was, she pulled my head down and kissed me. It seems I had passed another test.

After I showered and dressed for lunch, I got the surprise of my life. Her parents had invited a luncheon guest who turned out to be Ralph O'Neill. I don't know who was more startled. At lunch, he told the Morgans how he had found me, literally kidnapped me, and brought me to MIT. I was being groomed for a future executive position with NYRBA. "I also warned him not to date any girls. I guess Henri has proven he has a mind of his own."

Later, eager to exercise her horse, Minerva led all of us to the stables to watch her. Her daring horsemanship amazed me as she began to jump the horse over the hurdles. Her parents told me she was a marvelous equestrian and had done quite a bit of competitive jumping. But the afternoon contained one more surprise.

She later drove me to a pasture on the estate and stopped before a black biplane powered by a big radial engine. A present from her father for her seventeenth birthday, a Waco AG7. She said, "Henri, hop in. I want to show you how this Waco flies."

"I can't, my father forbids me to fly. Besides, he'll disinherit me."

Petite though she was at five foot one, she walked with determination until she was within three inches of me, looked up with her large brown eyes and flaring nostrils, which indicated an iron will, and said, "Henri, you're not a child. You have to learn to make your own decisions, be your own man. How the devil can you study to be an aeronautical engineer and not fly?"

Despite her logic, I struggled with myself mentally. I walked around the plane examining the tail and the elevators, the wings, the struts, and the motor, and I said mentally, What the hell?

"It's a four-seater sedan," she said as she stepped into the captain's seat. She showed me how to strap myself in and then kissed me on the lips. "Henri, you are a man of decision." She started the engine and let it warm up as she checked the magnetos and all the safety items, then taxied up to the starting line near a wind sock, ready to take off into the wind. As she advanced the throttle, the engine revved up. The plane and the wings began to vibrate until she released the brake and the biplane began to skip down the grass runway. She was capable and it didn't take long to overcome my trepidation.

There was a display of gauges on the dashboard. From my classes, I knew about the oil-pressure gauge, the airspeed indicator, the altimeter that indicated the aircraft's height aboveground, the inclinator that showed when the plane was flying level or banking, and the compass to show in which direction we were flying. The stick in front of me was the joystick, which I was ordered not to touch. It moved forward, backward, and side to side as she flew around the estate at three thousand feet. I was enjoying it. My father, to my knowledge, had never been inside a plane. If he had, maybe he'd enjoy it, too.

Minerva flew around the countryside for over two hours after telling me later to put my hand on the stick gently to get the feel of what she was doing. After returning to the estate, she practiced "touch-and-go"s, and "almost" landing in which the wheels touch the ground, then, by giving the engine full throttle, taking off again. After a while, she read my mind. "Henri, why don't you take the controls and try flying?"

She talked me through the basics once more and then let me handle the joystick. It was exhilarating. After a half hour, I got the feel of how to manipulate the Waco smoothly with no jerky movements. Then she put fear in my heart by saying, "I want to see you land this plane." She explained the procedures three times and made me repeat them. The landing carriage was fixed, so that was no problem. The plane would be slowed down to about 80 miles per hour, and I could pretty much glide down and roll along as though I were in a car.

It was later explained that any landing you walk away from is a good landing. The wheel hit hard, but we landed. Then she had me taxi around, and then she made me take off and land two more times. So I had learned how to fly. Then and there I got the "bug."

When we finally ended the flight, O'Neill watched me make a three-point landing. After the motor was turned off, he came over and said, "That was fine, Henri. Learn to fly and practice as much as you can while you have the chance."

After dinner, Minerva accompanied me in the Rolls to MIT to pick up my worker substitutes. I was on a cloud, but I didn't forget to inspect the work done by my assistants. Some of it wasn't very thorough, so I was obliged to work late and do it over again.

Minerva and I got together several more times, and except when the weather was bad, she continued to teach me how to fly. Then she was off to some equestrian meet when the summer holidays arrived. I went by train to Washington for summer school at George Washington University and Brookings Institution.

It was also necessary to go to the NYRBA offices and hear what progress O'Neill was making with the postmaster general. He was spending millions, faster than James Rand could raise the money. It was spent constructing hangars, moorings, buoys, maintenance shops, land-based radio stations, and purchasing radio equipment.

He was assembling a fleet of two dozen aircraft, half of which consisted of Consolidated Commodores, the largest flying boats in existence, with sixty-five-foot hulls, one-hundred-foot wingspans, a twenty-two-passenger capacity, and a 650-mile range. Anticipated payload was 100,000 pounds, ten times that of any competitor. Pan Am, by comparison, had only a few Fokker Trimotors, which were made in Europe, shipped by boat to New Jersey, and assembled there.

I was removed from the airline fight, as I had to spend most of my time at school with a busy study schedule. As I was anxious to see Minerva, autumn was a long time in coming. She'd gone to Europe with her family and was away four months. I was back at school a month before I saw her again. Meanwhile, I continued to do well at MIT, particularly as I was able to bring to the class the details of planning and constructing an airline, which I had picked up at NYRBA. Besides that, I had firsthand knowledge of flying. It supplemented the theoretical with the practical.

At Minerva's urging, I flew frequently and became more adept at takeoffs, landings, and navigation. In the latter part of the fall, Minerva left for New York with her horse to participate in some jumping events. Her parents kept me informed of her progress by telephone while they kept track of mine at school.

That Christmas, Minerva and I knew we were in love and agreed to get engaged. Our marriage would take place when I graduated. Her family was very pleased. From our regular weekly phone conversations, my mother guessed long before I did that I wanted to get married. The Morgans gave us a large engagement party attended by family friends and schoolmates. Because of my father's hatred of flying, my mother insisted my family not attend. I had saved up for a ring. It was tiny, all I could afford, but Minerva loved it.

By Easter, my flying progressed to the point where Minerva insisted that I solo. Ralph O'Neill, a frequent guest of the family because Mr. Morgan was helping him raise money, was present to watch me circle the field, do touch-and-gos and landings. Ralph said, "Now that you have your feet wet, you'll have to study flying more seriously because it's going to be an important part of your life."

That summer, I returned to Washington with new zeal. The work was getting more difficult, so I spent longer hours studying. All my spare time was spent at NYRBA, where I continued to learn the intricacies of the airline business. O'Neill did not like Juan Trippe, and once commented that if Trippe walked into a revolving door behind you, he would come out ahead of you.

Sometimes, the studying made my head feel as if it were filled with oatmeal. What helped were Minerva's visits one weekend every month. That part was heaven.

My fourth year at MIT, which began in September 1928, was a fateful one. The work was difficult and time-consuming, so I had to hire people to help with chores. My schoolwork in the last year included learning the use of all the facilities and tools in an aircraft machine shop, while studying advanced chemistry and all the technical and mechanical knowledge that went into making an airplane.

MIT added a course in the study and use of various woods. The interesting part of building an airplane wing was the selection of different woods of different strengths. Most were spruce. Woods for longerons (the fore-and-aft framing members of the fuselage) and spars had to have certain long grains that ran in one direction. When making the wooden ribs for the wings, they had to have a certain strength to withstand the stresses of the plane's maneuvers. There was also the study of the proper use of rivets to fasten these materials.

How to correct a cracked spar, how to saw it at an angle and glue it together, the study of metals, the strength of high-tensile bolts, the different alclads, the millimeter thickness of the metal to give the wing its proper structural strength, the struts that attach to the wing.

Then there was the use of featherweight balsam wood, which does not add strength but fills voids in wooden wings, wing butts, the trailing edge and at strut ends, the cloth to cover the frame of the wing, the paints and special varnishes.

If that wasn't enough, we had to learn how to use the materials in a variety of combinations—e.g., welding stainless steel and iron for heavy work—then do small, delicate, jeweler-like work with silver solder. And, finally, the construction of landing gears.

Electricity and electronics were taught in basic electricity courses, as electronics was just in the beginning stages of discovery. It became very important later on. Then came motors powerful enough to operate airplanes as well as other units attached to the motor. This was all in connection with the design of an engine, followed by learning stress and working out the pressures in cylinders, as well as determining the power of the engine.

To top it all off, we had to calculate the burning of fuel. How fast does this fuel burn per second? How many miles per second does the fuel burn? Does it burn smoothly or does it detonate? Detonation caused an engine to stutter instead of developing full power.

We also had to master spark plugs. The company that made airplane plugs, the P. G. Spark Plug Company, invited the students on numerous field trips just to see how plugs were engineered and tested.

We also were invited to Pratt & Whitney to observe how engines were built and overhauled, and to study each part of the engine separately. It was imperative to understand what strength of material was needed to contain the power required—particularly the exhaust valves, which worked under intense heat. In order to prevent the heat from burning up the valves, the inside valve stem was filled with sodium to help dissipate the heat and preserve the integrity of the valve.

At this time, I had moved from the dormitory to private quarters on Longwood Avenue, just south of Coolidge Corner. Because of my studies, I could only see Minerva on weekends and holidays. She kept busy practicing her equestrian skills, but we still went flying. I reached the point where I had over ten hours of solo time, most of it doing touch-and-go. I really enjoyed it, and it enhanced my studies, knowing the importance of each part of the plane when your life was involved.

I had written many letters to my mother about Minerva and she wrote back, "Henri, there is nothing more wonderful than to fall in love with a good woman. If you can do this and still master your studies, you have lived up to my expectations of a fine son."

At Eastertime, I was asked to come to Washington so I could be brought up-to-date on the progress of NYRBA. In April 1929, NYRBA was incorporated as the New York, Rio and Buenos Aires Airline. It agreed to provide package, passenger, and mail service between those three cities. But it looked like a knockdown battle for the rest of South America, with a change in the office of secretary of state from Frank B. Kellogg to Henry L. Stimson.

Due to public relations, petitions, and private meetings, Pan Am positioned itself as a 100 percent American company, while NYRBA was viewed, with some help from Pan Am, as being owned by foreign investors. Thus, it was viewed by Postmaster General Francis White as being against American interests. This opinion became policy and was passed on to the U.S. legations in South America. White asked the embassies for proof that nothing further was being done to assist NYRBA in our three key cities of Buenos Aires, Rio, and Santiago, Chile. To counter this, O'Neill left for South America. He was now fighting for the life of NYRBA.

Pan Am claimed, incorrectly, that NYRBA was secretly involved with, and linking up its air routes with, France's Aeropostale in Brazil and a German company in Bolivia. Most of the "information" was conceived by Juan Trippe. His powerful connections consisted of Yale buddies in government and his brother-in-law Edward Stettinius, president of General Motors and a trustee of Brookings Institution and of MIT. The world was getting smaller. Stettinius later became secretary of state.

NYRBA was already running mail routes as far south as Santiago. O'Neill was seeking rights to carry mail from Chile over the Andes

to Argentina, then up the east coast of South America from Argentina
to Uruguay and Brazil, then link up the air route to the United States.
Simply put, Pan Am was paid by the Post Office to fly U.S. mail to most
South American cities; NYRBA had signed up most South American
countries to fly the mail between these countries and to North America. Pan Am flew south. NYRBA flew north.

With a 100,000-pound payload, it would take nearly a full load of
mail and passengers in the Commodore to make it pay. But Juan Trippe
was more astute, as he never spent money to develop an air route until
the signed airmail contract was in his possession. Without a fair share
of mail routes, NYRBA was doomed.

In 1929, Pan American Airways caught up to NYRBA by purchasing
twelve new Sikorsky S-38 amphibian aircraft to add to their fleet of
three Fokker-10 land planes. President Hoover, an aviation stalwart,
suggested to the postmaster general that NYRBA be given the chance
to compete.

The infighting and politicking raged on but was heading for a climax.
From the subsidizing of Pan Am's airmail routes to South America, the
Post Office was bleeding red ink. But it was considered an investment
in the future. This was shaping up to be a fight to the finish and only
one airline was going to survive.

My life at MIT fell back into the pattern of a heavy study schedule
and short visits with Minerva. We discussed our wedding plans, and
while I toiled in Cambridge, she worked hard with her horse in
preparation for a big meet in New York. It turned out to be a disap-
pointing meet as she was only moderately successful.

She went back to practicing with a furious determination. One day,
while practice jumping, the horse didn't clear the barrier and she was
thrown against the fence. Minerva was rushed to the operating room
for an emergency operation to sew up a deep gash in her leg.

When I saw her at the hospital, she was recuperating and in high
spirits. She went home shortly thereafter. Two days later, her sobbing
mother called and asked me to come over quickly. Sensing something
was terribly wrong, I borrowed a car and raced over.

As I entered the Morgan home, they gave me the crushing news.
Minerva had died that evening after an embolism lodged in her brain.
The shock was devastating. I felt so faint I couldn't stand. The next
thing I knew, the family doctor was holding ammonia under my nose.

Mr. Morgan gave me a shot glass full of cognac and made me drink it. Everything was hazy after that.

I had read books in which writers talked about people sleepwalking through difficult situations. It suddenly became apparent to me how true it was. The funeral added to my intense grief, but it all seemed like a dream sequence. I do remember that as the coffin lay open and she seemed to be resting peacefully, I kissed her lips one last time. Later, when I saw her placed into her final resting ground, my whole world collapsed.

CHAPTER 4

My Mother Wants to Fly

MY LIFE had no meaning without Minerva. Her family tried to console me, though they, too, were in deep anguish. I could not sleep or eat. Her parents, realizing the state I was in, reached out to me, asking me to come live with them for a while. I did. It was arranged for me to be driven to and from school, and when I was with them, we spent endless hours talking, going to church, and trying to patch together our torn lives.

Thus, with the help of her parents and prayers, I was pulled back from the brink of despair.

In a gracious gesture, the Morgans gave me her small, white Bible, her locked diary, and other mementos. Finally, they asked me to accept her Waco. I did, but it would be another two weeks before I could bring myself to go to the plane. I touched the wings and it was as though I was touching her. I filled it up with gas from the nearby pump, then flew around for an hour or so. I could swear I could hear her telling me, "Not too much rudder, Henri," or "Lift the nose up, Henri," or "The bank is too steep, Henri, you'll go into a spin." I felt closer to her than ever before, and her soothing voice seemed to comfort me. I landed but could not bring myself to get out of her chair. I simply sat there with my head down, sobbing.

Gradually, I lost myself in schoolwork. There was no separation of days, weeks, and months. Self-examination had a cleansing effect as I finally came to grips with the future. The school year ended and I did well in my finals, graduating with honors. The Morgans were there and they gave me a leather flying jacket, a helmet, and leather flying gloves as graduation presents.

I loaded my bags into the Waco, topped the tanks with gas, then walked to the Morgans' home for a last good-bye. Finally, I took a taxi to the cemetery to pay one last visit and bid farewell to Minerva.

It was now time to go to Miami to visit my family. The last piece of mail I received was from O'Neill, expressing his condolences and asking me to come to Washington as soon as I could pull myself together.

Whether it was foolhardy or sheer ignorance, I decided to fly the Waco by myself to Miami. I had no pilot's license and didn't even know if I needed one, almost no navigational experience, and only a road map to guide me. One bit of advice came from an MIT instructor who advised me to follow the railroad tracks. I did, only to discover that railroads went in different directions. It was totally confusing. The next best thing was to follow the coastline, head east till I reached the Atlantic Ocean, and then southeast as the coastline curved around past Plymouth to Sagamore Beach on Cape Cod, across the narrow neck of land to Buzzards Bay, then west along the coast. I managed it by checking the road map and the compass, while praying for clear visibility.

I continued west-southwest without further incident, looking out of the captain's window every once in a while and watching the waves crash onto the shore. Finally, I saw the lighthouse on Montauk Point, Long Island. I continued west to New York City, turned the nose east again until I saw what looked like a big pasture with a landing strip. It was almost totally surrounded by water, and sitting there was the large Edison gas tank that I was looking for. I watched the wind sock and landed the plane into the wind. The pasture would eventually become La Guardia Airport. Outwardly, I considered myself a hotshot pilot. Inwardly, I attributed my safe journey to Minerva's Bible in my jacket pocket.

I taxied to a small building and was greeted by a man in overalls who helped me tie up the plane, put chocks against the wheels, and then shook my hand. Apparently, he was in charge of the landing strip. He mumbled, so I never got his last name, but his given name was Carl and he was extremely helpful. I told him about the trip. He grinned and said, "You got the bug all right, come, let's celebrate." After he changed clothes, he drove me into Manhattan and suggested I could check into the Blackstone Hotel. Then he treated me to dinner and some Prohibition whiskey at a saloon known as a blind pig.

I am naturally pretty strong, and the hard physical work at MIT had kept me in shape, but that night the body demanded a soaking in a hot tub to get rid of the aches and tension in the arms and legs. Sleep beckoned and I slept the carefree sleep of all foolish young men. Next morning at dawn, I returned to the landing strip. The plane had been refueled and the oil checked and my friend told me there would be no charge. An ex-Army pilot, he handed me an aerial map and told me where to find Hoover Field in Washington. We shook hands, and on that calm, warm summer morning, I took off, waggled my wings, and headed south.

The weather was picture perfect, CAVU (ceiling and visibility unlimited). Once again following the coastline, I passed Baltimore, continued carefully down the coast, then moved inland until I saw the tall Washington Monument. I flew ever-widening circles until I spotted Hoover Field, the place where the Pentagon would someday be built. At this point, I thought I was a real aviator.

When I phoned O'Neill, he asked me to stay over in Washington for a few days. NYRBA would cover the expenses of parking the plane and my hotel. I took a bus to the city.

At our meeting, I was surprised to learn that the company was operating passenger and mail service between Buenos Aires, Argentina, and Montevideo, Uruguay, and when possible over the Andes Mountains to Santiago, Chile. O'Neill was preparing new requirements for his schedule to La Paz, Bolivia. Obviously, O'Neill was building the airline on his own initiative—even scheduling inaugural flights. He was doing this without the Post Office mail subsidies he so often said he needed to keep NYRBA alive. They seemed like moves of desperation.

While O'Neill was about to leave for South America, I found out that operations in New York and Miami were in a sorry state. It was his way of telling me that NYRBA was in bad shape. There was a possibility that the company might have to be sold.

Then he said, "Have you completed your Ph.D?"

I said, "I just have to write my final dissertation."

"We haven't made the final payment to the school. You may have to wait a bit to finish until things straighten out." Left unsaid was the matter of my job.

Then the talk turned to my flight from Boston. O'Neill listened, rubbing his hand over his bald head. When it was over, he simply shook his head. It was his only indication of disapproval. He insisted I meet with a company navigator to brief me on how to get to Miami. The briefing would include a set of topographical maps as well as air regulations to keep me out of trouble.

The navigation briefing took one hour and I was told quite bluntly by this short, stocky man, "You're a damned fool." It seems that I had started out from Boston knowing everything—only to suddenly discover in Washington I knew nothing.

"The clear weather along the coast was a stroke of luck," he said. "If you encountered clouds, it would have been your undoing as there'd be no landmarks. You'd have ended up in the ocean.

"Shifting winds could have thrown you off course. Turbulence, irregular atmospheric conditions, could have torn the Waco apart. Even the dark of night could have forced you to crash."

It was soon apparent that simply getting the small plane off the ground or landing it didn't begin to make me a pilot. The best advice the navigator gave me was: "When in doubt—land! Off course—land! Bad weather—land!—even on a road, a pasture, whatever. At worst, if no landing field is available, land on the beach or pancake on the ocean alongside the beach. Carry an extra pocket compass. Watch your drift and if something in the plane shakes or rattles—land!"

On the map, he circled a series of cities with airfields, short hops averaging two hundred miles with sufficient landmarks to get me from one place to another. My first stop was to be Raleigh, North Carolina. Chagrined, I took off and continued to wend my way homeward.

I flew over the lakes into North Carolina. Raleigh had just a little bit of a station with a small field on a farm. I circled to make sure the cows next to the runway were looking at the plane and not simply grazing, as they might wander onto the landing strip. Finally, I landed, and I considered it quite an epic after navigating across land and not having the shore to guide me.

The next day was partially cloudy and I made arrangements to fly to Charleston, South Carolina. About an hour out, I flew into some light cumulus and headwinds. As I continued, the winds turned gusty and I had trouble keeping the plane level. I started looking for a place to land. Without warning, rain deluged the plane and it felt as if I was flying underwater. I pushed the joystick forward to ease down and find a place to land. Suddenly, a swirl of wind was tossing the aircraft around and it was all I could do to keep the plane stable. The Waco was hurled one way and then another, one second being pulled up, then thrown sideways, then suddenly diving. All at once there was blood rushing to my head and I was being pushed forcibly against the seat straps. The plane was upside down.

Trying to keep level flight while upside down with the wind throwing me around, I screamed. I was terror-stricken. Unable to contain my body functions, I peed in my pants. I forced myself to breathe slowly and try to think. I had to control myself before I could control the plane or I would crash. A thousand questions flashed through my mind. They all echoed my fear. What do I do?

Never having discussed the possibility with Minerva, my first thoughts were to keep calm and keep the upside-down plane level. This I did with my altimeter and turn-and-bank indicator. I had enough theory and aircraft technology in my head to figure out what must be done. There were several solutions, from making believe I was in the top arc of a loop, to diving toward the ground and pulling out of the dive right side up. I finally opted for the simplest solution.

I prayed, made a sign of the cross (did God recognize a cross upside down?), stepped on the right rudder and swung the joystick gently over to one side. I flipped over like a pancake, and before the plane could roll again, I leveled off. It was raining outside and I was drenched inside. I now started flying by compass, trying to stay level at four thousand feet with the wings fluttering in the wind, threatening to break off with each gust. After thirty minutes, the winds diminished and the clouds thinned out. Below me was a large body of water— water with huge waves on it. The Atlantic!

My earlier estimated time of arrival was long gone and I knew that the wind had pushed me off course and eastward. I was guessing now as I altered course 15 degrees and continued to head south-southwest toward land. It was flying by instinct.

Soon I saw what I thought was Cape Romain and adjusted my course again. I flew along the coast to Savannah, only my stomach told me something was wrong. I flew for another half hour, and when the city hove into view, I began looking for the airport circled on my map. It wasn't there!

Then I spotted an airfield with an array of military planes. They looked like Marine F-4B biplanes. It started raining again. I had to get down. With no clearance to land and no radio equipment to contact them, I kept circling the field. "For gosh sake, signal," I said out loud. Someone must have guessed my predicament and started flashing dit-dahs with green lights. I then had to figure out what they were trying to tell me, as I didn't know Morse code. But by guess and by golly I landed on the soggy field in the rain. Only one bounce.

Airmen crowded the plane. I asked for a bathroom and they laughingly carried my bag to the barracks as a warrant officer handed me some towels. I dried, changed clothes, and when I emerged, they had hot coffee waiting for me. One of the maintenance crewmen slipped me two powdered doughnuts. It was the best food I ever tasted.

After telling the pilots what happened, I unashamedly and sheepishly asked how to right a plane flying upside down. Six voices chanted at once and I learned that somehow I had done the right maneuver—though somewhat clumsily. The CO produced a medicinal bottle of Prohibition bourbon and poured drinks, then they toasted my loss of "virginity."

My new friends refueled the plane and told me to follow the river to the coast, then follow the coast to Jacksonville, Florida. It was a simple, trouble-free flight for an hour and then the engine began to sputter. It sounded rough, due no doubt to the rain and dense, humid clouds. I landed and searched out a mechanic. With his help, I bought new spark plugs and he helped change them.

Next morning, after refueling, I took off and followed the coastline to St. Augustine. It seemed to take a long time, as the plane was once more buffeted by winds, this time headwinds. Near the city, I ran into another rainstorm but managed to stay right side up, landing again in hard rain.

I stayed overnight and said an evening prayer for all the nice, helpful people who had made it possible for me to get this far intact. The next morning was bright, shiny, and cloudless. The destination was Daytona Beach, where I circled twice and made a decent landing. Though the Waco held sixteen gallons of gas, about eight hours of flying time, I still topped off the tanks. The plump lady at the coffee shop made me a sandwich to take on the flight. Reverting to my Dutch upbringing, I clicked my heels, bowed, and kissed her hand. American ladies loved it. To me, it was normal.

Taking off smoothly, the fine weather buoyed my spirits. I was heading for Titusville, which boasted a small airfield and very little air traffic. Come to think of it, most of the airfields were small. However, Titusville was really the tiniest. I dropped altitude and circled two or three times to make certain the cows were not close to the landing strip.

Titusville was a town populated mostly by retired people, who didn't get much excitement. They started coming in cars and buggies to see the man in the flying machine. I showed them the plane and answered questions for a while. With several invitations to dinner, I accepted one of them and a night's lodgings.

The next day, most of the town was there to see me off. Two of the men even helped me refuel. I took off and then circled the airfield, waggling my wings and waving at the good folks, then I headed for Merritt Island (Cape Canaveral today). It seemed to be strictly farmland, so I flew on to Melbourne. Once again, the people of the town scooped me up and took me to a club for dinner. I walked around a bit for the exercise and then returned to the airfield.

The people who ran the field wanted to make certain everything was all right. I started my engine and found it rough and spluttering. The first thing was to check the plugs. Sure enough, one was fouled. They helped me find a replacement, though it didn't match the ones I had in my engine. The mechanic said it would do, and true to his word, it worked fine. I kept the bad one, and with the engine running smoothly again, I took off for Vero Beach, after being told exactly where the airfield was located and its distance from town. Probably because aviation was so new and "daring," everyone treated me with great respect and deference.

The engine was acting crotchety once again, so I decided to stay the afternoon and evening. Again, I checked the plugs, cleaned and dried them, and replaced them carefully. I checked the filters and changed the oil. I wondered how clean the aviation fuel was, though that was something I could not control.

When I took off on the next leg of the flight, the engine sounded fine, but before long, it began to vibrate. The closest airfield was Ft. Pierce, so I landed there. Without tools, I could do little by myself.

Searching around town, I located an ex-Navy maintenance chief who agreed to look at the engine.

He listened to the engine for a while and looked at the pistons as the prop idled over. He signaled me to shut the engine and said, "We have to change the oil and put in the correct plugs for this engine. Some of the plugs can't take the high voltage of the magnetos." After agreeing with him, he effected the changes. The motor sounded better immediately. He accepted money only for the plugs and refused anything for his labor. It seemed everyone in aviation was very neighborly. I took off and followed the coast to West Palm Beach. I decided to spend the remaining part of the day there swimming and relaxing on the beach. Though I was told the beach was restricted to residents, I proceeded with blissful ignorance and was not reproached by anyone.

West Palm Beach is close to Miami, and by taking off at 5:30 A.M. I would arrive there early and try to wend my way home. Actually, I headed for Opa-Locka, flying at three thousand feet, well above the antennas that sprouted all over the place. Opa-Locka was a military airport on Fifty-first Street. As I had no clearance, I circled the runway, and on the third circuit, I was flagged in. I learned that the Sunny South Airport, as it was called, was separated, with one part military and one part for civilian aircraft located "next door" on Fifty-fourth Street. It was a simple matter to taxi over.

I stopped at the hangar. One of the problems I hadn't considered was the matter of the airplane. I would have to make arrangements for storage while I was at home. After the maintenance man helped me move the plane off the runway and chock the wheels, I asked directions for the office. That's where I got my next shock. At the counter, drinking a Coke, was my baseball friend Charlie. When I asked him what he was doing there, he said, "My father owns the airport. What in the world are you doing here in that flying gear?"

I told him the story about school and Minerva, including the fact that I didn't have a pilot's license, plus my adventures getting down to Hialeah. Now I had to keep the knowledge of my ownership of the plane from my father and the rest of the family.

"Don't worry, Henri. It's still registered in your girl's name, so you can keep it that way for now and no one will find out." He came out, and with the help of two other men, we pulled the Waco into a corner of the hangar. I put my flying clothes on the backseat and took out my valise, and then I called my mother.

She was so heartbroken at the loss of my fiancée that I could hear her cry. It got me crying, too.

"How was your trip down?" she said.

"Mother, I didn't come by train. I had another means of transportation."

"Henri, how on earth did you come down?"

I spelled it out for her and told her how I got the plane and how O'Neill wanted me to learn to fly as part of my training for work at NYRBA.

"My God. How are we going to keep it from your father?"

"I don't know."

"How many years were you at MIT?"

"Four years."

"Did you learn anything?"

"Of course."

"All right, Son. If you learned anything worthwhile, you'll figure a way out."

Charles drove me home when he was through with work and the family had a nice reunion for the prodigal son. Gus was the one who surprised me the most. He smoked long cigars, dressed in snappy clothes, and had his own car. He was also sparking a girl.

My father really hadn't forgiven me, but he was nevertheless cordial. He knew I had gone to college, but he was too proud to ask me about it as he had not paid my tuition. The girls were getting bigger and filling out into young ladies. My father still had a stern visage and wore a large, gold pocket watch in his vest. My mother seemed to be the only one who hadn't changed.

Over the next few days, with the help of my brother, I was able to acquire an old Ford Skeeter. There was a reason it was inexpensive— the motor needed a lot of work. My dad had the tools, and I had the time, and with Gus's help, we took the motor apart, replaced the worn parts and got the car humming. I now had wheels.

Charles got the Waco transferred to my name, then he told me where to sign up to take proper flying lessons and obtain a license. When I applied, I was told that although I was of age, an adult member of my family would have to co-sign my application.

Again my mother came to the rescue. "If you believe that strongly in flying, I'll sign the application—on one condition." I looked at my mother quizzically, wondering what she was going to say: "I want to learn how to fly, too." My mother never failed to amaze me with her determination and daring. If her son was that interested, she wanted to know all about it. I guess if my mother were ten or fifteen years, younger she'd have been another Amelia Earhart. There was no question in my mind that she would master the art despite the dangers involved. It solved another problem for me. I was low on funds and my mother offered to pay for both of us.

While we didn't want to deceive the family, Mother said that she and I were going to tour Florida in the old Skeeter, a different place every day. We would return home at night. She hadn't had a vacation and, besides, she hadn't seen me for so long. We promptly headed for Hialeah and my ever-faithful Waco.

I checked out the plane and discovered that the last set of spark plugs were functioning perfectly. Just as Minerva had done with me, I strapped my mother in the co-pilot's seat and took off for her first trip. She loved every minute of it as I described the function of each instrument, the joystick and rudder pedals.

Minerva's voice seemed to whisper advice in my ear, coaching me, and I in turn repeated everything. My mother was quick and daring. She flew amazingly well. Then she learned touch-and-go landings and within a week she was flying solo. We kept on flying until she was really proficient, then we both registered for the written exams.

To my chagrin, Mother completed her test first, but we both received high grades. Now it was a matter of getting checked out in actual flight. My pilot's wings were awarded immediately, but nervousness caused my mother to fail her first checkout. Back we went for more practice and flying for several days. When her confidence returned, she reapplied for a checkout and passed.

CHAPTER 5

My Mother and I Go Crop-Dusting

WE HAD great times flying together and, between flights, talking. Mother kept encouraging me to tell her about Minerva and I did. Before long, all the pent-up emotions inside me poured out—like in a confessional—how much we enjoyed each other, what we did, our plans for the future, how she enjoyed life to the fullest, and my deep, deep feelings for her. And then I told her of the ache that didn't seem to go away. Unconsciously, I even admitted something I hadn't shared with anyone but Minerva. During our prenuptial medical tests, the Morgan family doctors discovered that though I could enjoy sex, I would be unable to father any children.

I looked at my mother, but she didn't act surprised. She said, "What did Minerva say to that?"

"She said it didn't matter."

"Henri, she sounds like a wonderful woman. Now I think it's time to tell you a family secret." She brushed a wisp of hair from her forehead and added, "On your father's side, going back many, many generations, some of the male descendants were unable to father children. It is heredity, not an illness. Your father told me that and I said I would marry him anyway. We were more fortunate—or you wouldn't be here now." I laughed at that and she added, "Son, there are many children in this world who need loving parents. Some day you will marry and God will find children for you." My mother's words touched me deeply.

The heartfelt talk unburdened me, and it seemed as though a page in my life had turned over. After a time, I said, "I'm ready to start working at the airline. I hope Father won't be too upset."

I called NYRBA in Washington to get word on when I should start. O'Neill's assistant told me Pan Am was winning the battle on all fronts and that O'Neill was raging like a wounded bear. He spoke to O'Neill while I remained on the phone. The word came back that I should wait a few months, possibly until January 1930, to see what developed.

Mother returned to family life. Nevertheless, once a week we went flying and she improved remarkably. Sometimes when I think back, I can never figure out if she truly wanted to fly or if she was consoling a troubled son. Of course, she claimed her inspiration was Amelia Earhart, who had become the first woman to cross the Atlantic by air in 1928, though she wasn't the actual pilot. To keep her reputation as an aviatrix intact, she entered the Women's Air Derby in 1929 and finished third. Earhart then organized the Ninety-niners, an organization of women pilots with ninety-nine charter members.

My father didn't invite me to his office, a sure sign I wasn't forgiven, so I marked time by flying, stripping the engine and overhauling it, repairing tears in the fabric of the Waco, playing tennis, and helping Charles teach youngsters baseball. My funds were low, and I couldn't expect my mother to keep giving me gas money for the Skeeter and the Waco. It was time to find a temporary job.

Charlie, spending all his time at the airport, passed along to me pupils who were eager to learn flying. The going rate was $10 a half hour, using my plane, and I discovered quickly that not everyone was cut out to be a pilot. After one bone-crushing landing by an uncoordinated college student and a broken wing tip by a nearsighted, though amorous, young lady, I decided to change jobs.

Also, I had to think about the unthinkable—what would I do if NYRBA didn't need me? I began wondering about Pan Am. They had an office in Miami, but I dared not approach them, as my indoctrination made me feel as though it was forbidden territory. The other options were the few existing airlines and a limited number of plane manufacturers.

I wrote down everything I was qualified to do, from pilot to car mechanic, to welder, to aeronautical engineer two inches from his Ph.D., to janitor/gardener. Suddenly, I thought of the pipe organ. One

of my hobbies was music, and I could play several instruments passably well, but my favorite was the organ. But who needed an organist?
There had been a great need for them before talking pictures were
born, when every silent movie house had an accompanist, either on a
piano or organ. But times had changed, and I thought there surely
must be a surplus of organists. Nevertheless, maybe I could practice
and earn money playing the "Wedding March" at weddings. On a
hunch, I started walking up and down the streets in our neighborhood
talking to priests, ministers, and rabbis, and leaving my name and
phone number should they need my services. Our own church had a
large pipe organ, and it took a lot of fast talking and an organ checkout
consisting of "I Love You Truly" and "Für Elise" before the priest
granted me permission to practice.

On October 29, 1929, without warning, the stock market in New
York City crashed. *Variety* summed it up with "Wall Street Lays an
Egg," as the market dropped $26 billion. It was called "Black Tues-
day," and heralded the beginning of the Great Depression.

In that same year, the *Graf Zeppelin* airship flew around the world
in twenty days, and on St. Valentine's Day in Chicago, six mobsters
were machine-gunned by a rival gang—the St. Valentine's Day
Massacre.

It turned out that 1929 would also be my worst year. Minerva died,
the common stock of NYRBA sank on Wall Street, O'Neill was forced to
resign his position by the board of directors, and MacCracken became
chairman. Within a few months, Pan Am acquired all the assets of
NYRBA, including the brand-new Commodores and its air routes. Not
only was I jobless, but I was reminded that I owed the company
$6,000. The final blow fell when my father's business collapsed as the
real estate market in Miami evaporated, along with my father's assets,
mostly speculations in high-priced houses.

My family needed my help to survive. Against my better judgment,
I was obliged to once again teach students to fly, and along with a half
dozen "Oh Promise Me"s on the organ, I saved $200. I desperately
needed a decent-paying job. I decided to invest in a trip to New York to
try to land a job as an aeronautical engineer with Pan Am. The cheap-
est and fastest way to get there was to fly.

When I told my mother, she insisted on accompanying me. I was in
no position to say no, so two days later, we simply took off. The flight
north was different from my solo trip down, as we were both licensed

pilots and I had acquired correct maps and proper equipment. If we got lost, Mother could fly while I studied the terrain and our maps.

We returned to the same New York airfield and bused into New York City. It was early afternoon when I swept into the Pan Am offices. Juan Trippe was not in and neither was André Priester, the chief engineer. But I was able to speak with John Steel, deputy chief engineer. and John Leslie, an associate. Mr. Leslie, when he heard my un-American name, told me his son had been one grade behind me at MIT. Pan Am had no openings for aeronautical engineers, but he tipped me off confidentially that since I lived in Miami, I might try to see Priester on his next visit six weeks hence.

We stayed in New York two days: one day and night to see the sights with my mother, then one day to try and find a job with other airlines, and the last night to see the new Gershwin show, *Show Girl*. The next morning at dawn, we headed for home. My major worry was for my family, as they had run out of luck and out of money. The only asset I owned was the Waco, and if it was necessary to sell it, I would.

Once we landed at Hialeah, Charlie ran out to see us. "There's a man in the office looking for a couple of pilots to fly dusters." He dragged us to his office to meet Mr. Tyler.

After the introductions, he said, "I need two pilots to dust vegetable crops in Clewiston, Florida."

Behind me, my mother said, "What are your rates, and if we agree, do we get a contract?" The startled farmer agreed, and he told us he had two Delta crop-dusting aircraft. We offered to go out the next day to look them over.

The planes were not old, but they had seen hard service. I ran up the engines and they were running rough. Mr. Tyler was looking over my shoulder. "Neither my mother nor I will fly either of these planes without the engines being serviced. They're unsafe and will never pass inspection."

"There's no one around who can do it," Mr. Tyler complained.

"I'll put the engines in shape and do the maintenance at the same rates as flying." He agreed, and we shook on it.

He had some tools and bought the ones that were missing. Then Mother and I went to work. Luckily, the planes were stored in a barn-cum-hangar, along with a metal tank filled with pesticide.

I set up an old rickety kitchen table, which I propped up, and began dismantling the engine. I tested every part against the maintenance manual with a micrometer, then double-checked it against the *Air Service Engine Handbook* that I managed to scrounge from Charlie. Every so often, I would write down the parts I needed, from special spark plugs to oil filters, and my mother would take the Skeeter and scoot to the dealer in Miami to buy them. In two days, we each earned over $120. The decision was to always have on hand $25 for emergencies. The rest went toward family expenses.

At the same time, I did my homework on the plane, studying the maintenance manual to learn the cruising speed, rate of climb, stalling speed, and so forth, and how to release the poison to dust the crops. When I had it down pat and the engines were purring, I took up one plane and put it through its paces, then did the same with the second, testing its idiosyncrasies in flight. Only then, did I take up my mother and let her handle the plane and land it. A half hour later, we took up both planes and checked out the dusting releases. We were ready to start the next day.

On our ride home, we worked out some hand signals indicating when I would take one side of the field and my mother the other, another for a coffee break, and still another signal for crisscross, always flying over the telephone lines, which were the house rules. My mother let me take the lead without question in all flight instructions—except one. She flew her plane with great precision, but being a daredevil at heart, she insisted on flying under the telephone wires. When she did it, I would become almost apoplectic. She was a disaster waiting to happen—and it did.

We worked at the job for several weeks before I realized that after a lot of low-level flying, the boredom made my mind wander. If it happened to me, it happened to my mother. When it came on, I would dip my wings, a signal to my mother to land for a stretch and coffee. Once, after a fifteen-minute break, we took off. Mother, going first, went under the wires again and didn't see the old Ford coming up the highway. She was looking the other way, oblivious of the traffic, and flying maybe ten feet or less above the ground.

Her wheel took off the soft top of the touring car, along with several ladies' hats. Frantically, I signaled her to land. She signaled back that we had just had a coffee break. I signaled to her again, as the Ford was heading for the airfield and I could plainly see four violently angry people.

Not realizing what had happened, she landed her plane next to mine. The driver, a man, and three lady passengers, without hats, were screaming, waving their fists, and demanding payment for damages. All we could scrape up was our emergency fund of $25. Though unhappy, they took it and went off in a huff to repossess their hats and the car top. When I told Mother what had actually happened, she simply laughed.

When we took off again, I was sure my mother had been cured once and for always of recklessness. How wrong I was! As I flew above the wires, she once more flew under them. Then she poured on the fuel and began to climb, and at one thousand feet, she leveled off and made a slow roll. My mother wasn't going to kill herself—she was going to kill me just watching her. As time went on, she became a better pilot, more aware and more cautious. We earned good money to put into the family coffers. As this job was not going to last forever, there was a need to look for other opportunities.

A couple of days after Mr. Priester's arrival in Miami, I arranged to meet with him. When I discovered he was from Holland and spoke with a Dutch accent, I spoke to him in Dutch. It cut no ice with him and he continued talking in English.

"I have enough aeronautical engineers from MIT."

"Mr. Priester, I was being trained to work with NYRBA and took graduate courses toward a doctorate. I will take any kind of job with Pan Am."

"I'm not interested. I want only people who have been through Annapolis and Pensacola. They are disciplined and have better knowledge of Pan Am planes, as these pilots have nautical training—and the Commodores are seaplanes.

"If you want to work at Pan Am, go to New York. There may be something—some small job. But don't bother me with your training. It doesn't mean anything. Now I must inspect my planes. Good-bye."

My disappointment was almost unbearable. The way he told it, my four years of work at MIT were worthless. I stopped off at the church to pound out my sorrow on the organ. Neither did I forget to light a candle and pray. Alone in the church, I thought about all the other people in the country without jobs, homes, or money, with nothing to look forward to but a bleak future.

Everything seemed to be falling apart. With the stock markets closing down, the banks forced out of business, the unemployment lines stretching, what kind of future could I look forward to? I had only a few months' work to complete my doctorate, but I was reading how teachers, professors, and Ph. D.'s were driving taxis in New York. And, besides, I couldn't afford to take off the time nor could I scrape up the money to do it.

My father was in terrible straits. Not only had he lost all his money, he was depressed by the amount of money he owed. All Gus knew at this point was real estate, and he was not qualified for anything other than inconsequential work.

With the dusting job completed and Mother ensconced at home, I trudged the streets looking for work—any kind of work. Flying lessons were now scarce. My plane was put up for sale, but it seemed as though nobody could afford it. Bridal couples went into retreat. They got married, but opted for smaller church weddings and saved a few dollars by not hiring an organist. Once I heard that I was undercut by a youngster who played the "Wedding March" on his mouth organ for 50 cents.

I did have some luck on one job. In the industrial area, where I prowled regularly, a shop foreman was putting up a sign for a welder. No sooner was it up, then I took it down and applied for the job. The foreman tested me and I passed. For the next six weeks, while the job lasted, I was able to help support my family. Near the end of that job, Gus and my father sold some property and it helped straighten out some of my father's affairs.

I kept in touch with friends in Washington, but the story was always the same. Even Bill MacCracken told me there was nothing available and the whole country was looking for work. "Lie low for a while until things perk up," he said.

The next job hunt centered on my languages, but nobody seemed to need translators or language teachers or tutors. Just for something to do, I decided to clean my closets. There were a number of musical instruments, including a battered banjo. I'd forgotten all about it, as I hadn't played it since my VPI days. A couple of strings were broken, but I remembered I'd had extra ones in my all-purpose drawer. With nothing better to do, I set about cleaning it up and putting it into shape.

With the strings back in, I tuned it to the old minstrel rhythm of

"My dog has fleas," then I began to pluck away with the ivory pick. The warmth of nostalgia came over me and I must have played for over two hours. All I needed was a straw hat, a rowboat, and a girl. Then I thought of Minerva and a depression came over me. I knew I had to shake myself out of it.

It was my mother who suggested I put an ad in the paper for anyone looking for a banjo player. Sure enough, there was a combo, the Opa-Locka Three, looking for a banjo player. It was a group of young college graduates, and I tried out, first as a banjo player, then as a singer. They were great musicians, but none of them had more than an average voice. My choir practice in church now came in handy. I sang the two or three songs I knew and we became the Opa-Locka Four. We played music at night, whenever anyone would hire us, and learned more songs. During the daytime, I found odd jobs, but it took a lot of effort. Mowing lawns, clipping hedges, and, finally, setting fence posts.

One job was setting fence posts around a cow pasture in Opa-Locka. I figured the man must have heard me play. There were a lot of fence posts and I was expected to plant one concrete post every half hour. Whacking those posts down real tight was a backbreaking job, as they got heavier as the day dragged on. Eventually, I began to enjoy the exercise—even the hardship.

With my father not quite able to support the family, it was necessary for me to make a bigger contribution. I also thought it was time to look into my future. Mr. Priester did say that if I wanted to find a job with Pan Am, I would have to go to New York. Now was time to go there and talk turkey with those people. I had too much training to let it go to waste. It had to be Pan Am. I was determined to get a job with them or bust.

This time, I didn't have enough money to fly my plane there or take a train or bus. I was left with a final transportation choice—my little topless, fenderless Ford Skeeter. I needed sweaters and a yellow rain slicker and hat to keep warm and dry, but I also needed a trunk on the car. I scavenged around and found a discarded oil drum. This had numerous possibilities. I took it to the welding shop, where I cleaned it out. They let me use a torch to cut an opening in the side of the drum and put little leather flaps on it. Then I welded it to the back of the Skeeter. It was large enough to store my suitcases, my collection of tools, and my banjo. And with $25 in my pocket and a load of food prepared by my mother, I went to New York once more to seek my fortune.

The trip through Florida in warm weather was pleasant. At night, I could sleep on the beach and in the morning bathe or swim in the ocean. A couple of rainstorms forced me to don the raincoat and hat. There was no windshield, so the rain kept sweeping over me. When it got too wet, the motor would conk out. I couldn't always find parts for the Skeeter's two continuing trouble spots, the ignition and the carburetor. Strangely enough, the farmers kept two or three old Fords around for parts, and whenever I ran into trouble, that's where I went for help.

The people I met were always nice and helpful, for which I was grateful. I tried to repay them by offering to do some work or chore, then I would get rolling again. Thus, I got to Washington and saw some old friends and classmates. I spent two days with the MacCrackens, but I made no progress in finding a job.

Anxious to get going again, I took off for New York City. Locating lodgings was a problem, but after a few phone calls, Ed Keeland, a school chum, invited me to spend a few days. He told me the job market was the worst in the history of the country.

Preparing to assault Pan Am, I had to find out their new location. I tracked it to the Chrysler Building. I was shown Mr. Priester's office, and when I entered, I saw a small man with a bald head behind a desk. The light, from the window behind him, kept his face in shadow, so once again, I told him about my school background, my language skills, my flying experience and my aspirations, and my desire for a job with Pan Am. He said nothing, and by now I was too embarrassed to stop—and, anyway, I had nothing to lose. When I stopped talking, it was as though a freight train had come to a crashing halt. He still said nothing, so I walked out of the office.

Priester's secretary winked at me and said, "How was the old man? Was he hard on you?"

I was embarrassed and felt the blood rushing to my cheeks. "No, he wasn't. He didn't say anything." I guess I failed the interview, so I would know better next time, though deep down I knew there'd be no next time. The secretary told me to sit down.

A few minutes later, she showed me into Mr. Schildhauer's office, the man in charge of operations. But he wasn't in. The secretary smiled at me and told me to come back after lunch.

Wandering around Forty-second Street and Lexington Avenue, I wondered why they wanted me to come back. Maybe they were going to let me fill out an application?

After two hours, I went back to Pan Am and spoke to the secretary. She said, "Mr. Priester will see you now." Then she held her finger to her lips. I wasn't certain what she meant, but I took it to mean "Keep your trap shut."

André Priester waved me to a seat, so I nodded and sat down. Then this genius/engineer of Pan Am started talking about airplanes, the huge ones that would someday fly across the ocean with mail and passengers, with their captains running their ships as masters of ocean liners. He spoke of the responsibilities of these commanders and the problems of international aviation. He touched on navigation, the need for excellent weather forecasts, fuel consumption and conservation. I had heard of Juan Trippe being a visionary, but this man had laid out a course for aviation for the next fifty years.

This dour Dutchman with his sober, simple manner had a vision that was almost poetic. Then I heard him say, "*Snel wie lang Jan met de bloote Kont.*" Translated into English, this meant "Lickety-split as bare-assed John," in other words, "Get to work quickly."

He said, "Talking too much is a form of verbal diarrhea, and all Dutchmen talk too much. It is a common weakness in all of us." He got up and left. I stood there mystified. Did I or did I not have a job? When I went outside, I asked the secretary.

"Did he say he wouldn't hire you?"

"No!"

"Then you have a job. Anyway, he winked at me when he left, which means you're in. I think he liked your persistence. Get your tail down to Miami and report at the administrative office. They'll be expecting you."

So, as fast as bare-assed John, I hopped into the Skeeter and started back to Miami, but not before I bought three roses for the secretary. I don't know if that little car could go more than 25 miles per hour, but I got every ounce of speed out of her. The only problem was a bad case of sunburn. My nose was swollen and I looked like a drunkard when I walked into the little administrative office on Thirty-sixth Street in Miami. The trouble was I had no name to report to, so I reported to everyone who walked, talked, or looked at me. Finally, I met Mr.

Aires, who said he was expecting me. Since it was close to Christmas, Mr. Aires suggested I start the first of the year. This would give me time to unpack, rest, and enjoy my family for the holidays. It was a joyous Christmas at home, and my long years of training as an aeronautical engineer were going to pay off—or so I thought.

CHAPTER 6

"Through Labor to the Stars"

THE DAY my job started was nervous day. I wore a new suit, shirt, and tie, and I was washed and scrubbed to the point where a doctor could pronounce me germ-free. When I walked into the hangar at Dinner Key, my path was strewn with discarded spark plugs, oily rags, grease guns, Coke bottles, and littered pages torn from manuals on how to disassemble a seaplane.

The first thing Mr. Aires said was "Do you have engineering tools?"

"Yes, sir, in the car."

"I'll give you a locker to stow them." He handed me a pair of new, white overalls, size forty-two. After putting them on, I stowed my tools, and when I faced Mr. Aires again, he said, "On instructions from Mr. Priester, this is your job." He handed me a large broom. "I expect you to sweep the floor clean." He walked away, leaving the mechanics and engineers snickering.

I swallowed my pride, my college degrees, and my embarrassment, and began to clean up the mess, which was no different from sweeping up the MIT dorms. When the others saw that I didn't bitch, they slapped me on the back and made jokes. A few promised not to throw garbage on the floor.

Mr. Aires inspected the hangar's concrete floor twice a day, and when he'd notice me, he merely nodded his head. This went on for six weeks. On Monday of the seventh week, Mr. Aires confronted me, taking the broom out of my hands. "You have a new job. Scraping bilges of Commodore and Sikorsky seaplanes until they're clean."

61

Working with mechanics and engineers, at least now I had someone to talk to. Part of the job was learning how to splice cables and tie proper knots with ropes. And when there was free time, I voluntarily assisted in servicing engines. Later, I was shifted to another hangar. When I got there, I found total disaster—everyone was working at cross-purposes and no one seemed to know what was going on. It turned out that Mr. Priester was coming down for an inspection tour and Foreman Richardson was adding to the confusion by storming around like a whirling dervish. He wanted everything in that hangar that wasn't moving to be scraped, painted, or polished.

Someone finally admitted that if Mr. Priester found something wrong, the person nearest to the problem was fired. Mr. Priester was a perfectionist who repeated countless times, "The lives of the crew members and the passengers on Pan Am planes are in your hands."

On the fateful inspection day, I was standing by the engine of an S-36 seaplane, one that I had worked on with great diligence. He came up to me and said, "I hear you have your license."

"I have a pilot's license, an airframe license, and an engine license," I told him.

He blinked and then rather sternly said, "Have you completed your correspondence course?" Because the seaplane was a watercraft as well as an aircraft, it was recommended that some of us take a course where you had to rig a large sailing ship from top to bottom. We learned to name all the sails of the fully rigged ship and learn to say in Spanish, "Are there any rocks in the harbor?" Then you had to learn tidbits like *ropa interior* and *rop exterior*, meaning "outside clothing" and "inside clothing," and the Spanish for "Do you have any United States money?"

I told him I did. Then, in a staccato voice, he fired some difficult questions at me. I answered them all. He suddenly switched the subject to planes by saying, "Do you understand the clearance of the valve in the right engine?" I gave him the answer to the nearest thousandth of an inch and the timing.

He looked at me and said gruffly, "Come to my office this afternoon." My knees didn't stop shaking for ten minutes.

When I arrived, he introduced me to Mr. Schildauer, the new operations manager. Priester now talked a blue streak in Dutch about the work he did for Europe's oldest airline, Holland's KLM Airlines, and the time he spent in the Dutch East Indies, particularly in Djakarta. Now I understood why his Dutch speech sounded different from mine.

In English, he said, "Sweeping floors and scraping may seem like menial jobs. But as they say in the Army, 'You must learn how to take orders before you can give orders.' Henri, you are now assigned to training under Mr. Schildhauer. You will accept whatever task he gives you."

My first job was to become a welder, and I was assigned to a man named Rittenhouse. It was 4:00 P.M., and he wanted me to be ready for work by the time we started that evening. I was surprised to discover he was also a pilot.

Though I knew how to weld, I now came under the scrutiny of a master welder—a perfectionist. The job was to weld the aircraft exhaust pipes that were cracked. Chromalloy, the metal we used, was difficult to weld, so what seemed simple at first turned out to be difficult. Rittenhouse was patient and kind, so after a few hours I caught on to the metal's idiosyncrasies.

We took the damaged exhaust pipes off each plane, welded the cracks, and replaced them on the engine. Next day, the plane was flying again. This went on for two days. When there was spare time, I kept practicing welds with Chromalloy I took from the stockroom. On the fourth day, Rittenhouse took ill and didn't show up at work. Now I was the lone welder.

When I went to the stockroom for supplies, there was no more Chromalloy. I had carelessly used up all the stock practicing welds. As the planes' exhausts continued to crack in flight even after repairing them, it was necessary to keep rewelding. There was no one to witness my embarrassment. Having worked so hard to get this job, I was now in danger of losing it.

Think! Think! Pray! Pray!

The last prayer that worked for me happened when I was flying upside down. How often could He come to this dummy's rescue? I looked around the hangar frantically. What other metal could be used to weld the pipes?

Nothing struck me as a possible source. I sat down, staring at the empty oil drums stacked in the corner. They seemed to be telling me something, but what? The drums! Was it possible to use the metal in the steel drums?

Taking a chisel, drill, and saw, I cut out a large piece, then cut it into metal strips of the correct proportions. Each drum was painted on the outside, but the inside was clean and shiny. With the painted section on the inside, the resulting weld was excellent and the work progressed faster and easier than with Chromalloy. I remembered Priester's anecdote, "Lickety-split as bare-assed John."

Though my background told me that the weld would be as good or better than Chromalloy, the test of the weld was in the flying. What would be the condition of these pipes when the planes returned? If they failed, how could I confess to anyone in authority that I had tackled the job on my own? I couldn't eat or sleep for two days until the first of the repaired planes returned. The welds turned out to be a great improvement; there were no cracks or damage to the pipes because the metal was more malleable and would expand and contract in the heat and cold and not split like the Chromalloy.

The maintenance engineers and the pilots were amazed as they continued to ask, "How did you weld those exhaust pipes?"

"Engineering training at MIT."

For the eight days that Rittenhouse was away, I continued the Henri welds. Because I was alone in the hangar each night, I was at liberty to cut up empty oil drums.

Then word came in that Rittenhouse was returning to work. By now, the stock of Chromalloy had been replenished. My decision was to keep quiet and hope everything would return to normal. Another message came in for me that he was giving a student pilot a lesson and would be late for work. However, he arrived early and I watched them take off. He was an excellent aviator and once airborne, I saw him turn the controls over to the student. I returned to the hangar and prepared the material needed for the night's work. Later, a maintenance man rushed in.

"There's been a crash," he yelled. He waved me along and I followed him onto the crash truck with some of the others. The plane had come down somewhere in Opa-Locka. We headed toward a high plume of black smoke.

It was Rittenhouse and his pupil, but we were too late. The flames and smoke had burned off their clothes and seared their bodies to a crisp. Nevertheless, we all took fire extinguishers to spray the bodies and the plane. The fire was finally killed when the fire truck arrived and blasted out the fire with streams of water. All that was left intact was Rittenhouse's toolbox.

I stared at the debris. The great unspoken factor of flying was the ever-present possibility of sudden death. The reasons for crashes were varied, but the result was always the same. A plane in trouble that landed safely was lucky. And I was pegging my life on this will-o'-the-wisp existence. But I didn't want it any other way.

An hour later, the police chief came back to the hangar and asked, "Who worked with him?"

"I did," I said.

"We're unable to reach his supervisor, and we must inform his family at once. Since you know him, you can represent Pan Am. Please come with me." We left at once in his car to tell Rittenhouse's wife. Over the years, it was never a task I welcomed, but it was unavoidable.

A month later, I was transferred out of the welding shop to a new job—scraping the bilges of the Commodore while getting ready for my training as a "wheel-holder," a euphemism for co-pilot.

My replacement welder was a feisty little fellow with experience. I had removed all traces of the sliced-up oil drums and now the work bin contained only Chromalloy. In a few days, the cracks in the exhaust pipes began to appear once more. It was back to normal. I vowed never to overstep my authority again and gave God an oath on it. But I couldn't leave well enough alone. My last act was to suggest he experiment with a plain steel weld.

Scraping seaplane hulls was tedious work, but scraping bilges to make them clean enough to pass inspection was much more difficult. After finishing my first bilge, I inspected it carefully, and noticed deeply embedded corrosion. It was a disaster waiting to happen. I notified my supervisor that the plane was not serviceable.

"What do you know, you young twit?" he said angrily, puffing on the butt of a Pittsburgh stogie.

"Isn't it part of my job to make that determination?"

"Well, you snot-nosed kid, scrape it clean—or find another job."

The next day, before I could get started, the CAA inspector came around investigating the Commodore against his checklist. He slapped a U/S (unserviceable) on the plane and brought it to my supervisor. By the time I arrived, a new stogie was belching fire and so was my boss. "All right, big mouth. Everybody in the joint heard what you said. You may be a hotshot engineer—which I doubt—so you get the job of taking this plane apart and fixing it. When you're through, if it don't pass inspection, you're fired." It was a heads-you-lose, tails-you-lose situation.

Actually, there were two men in charge of disassembling and assembling the plane: Walter Morgan and his foreman, Mr. Field. They asked me questions, but everybody seemed to be afraid to agree with my answers. Then I thought I'd get their attention by suggesting some engineering principles.

"The corroded parts have to be sandblasted, then the assembled parts must be rigged and trammeled," I said. Everyone looked at me. They didn't know what "trammeling" meant, so I added, "If you remove corroded metal then you're grinding it down and the thickness specifications change, so you use gauges, replace the fragile sections, and then adjust the parts so they fit."

Now they were looking at me askance. "Look, if I'm in charge, I'll take the responsibility. This is no quick fix. We'll approach it from an engineering point of view and overhaul it to the highest standards—the way it should be done."

We brought in the fuselage and with a group of helpers, punched, marked, and drilled out all the rivets. With the hull disassembled, we sandblasted each part to remove the corrosion. Many parts were salvageable, some were not. The unusable parts had to be replaced, and if they were not available, parts were made. After a while, the older workers began to resent being instructed by a twenty-three-year-old blond kid with an accent who shaved only once a week.

So I had to face some meanness—like petty sabotage, missing parts, parts not cut to specs, misplaced work, and other delays. I overheard one oldster say, "We'll teach that college kid that experience is more important than book-learnin'."

When the fuselage was ready, everything was assembled, then covered with electric tape and Helldite, a French-manufactured solution to prevent corrosion. The job had taken four months. We measured the keel and it was straight. So was the whole assembly.

I got no praise, not a single comment from my fellow workers, my supervisors, or their bosses. To me, the hull was as good as when it was built and fit to fly again. Suddenly, Mr. Priester, who obviously knew what was going on, made a surprise visit to see the fuselage. He checked everything out minutely and then said in his nastiest voice, "Who is the person responsible for this job?"

Everyone pointed to me and I came forward, shaking in my boots. "I am," I said.

"Doctor, this is what I consider a perfect job," he said. "After you write out the procedures on how to do it, I'm transferring you to engines." My supervisors listened grudgingly while I prepared the procedures and selected the most reliable workers to be in charge of each aspect of the job.

A week later, like Hercules, I was facing new challenges. When not working on engines, I was officially scheduled to practice flying on Pan Am's seaplanes, the Sikorsky S-36s, and later S-38s and S41s, as I had to earn my seaplane and transport licenses. Compared with my trusty old Waco, the planes were more cumbersome and "heavy." I had trouble adjusting, but the Pan Am captains were understanding and generally helpful.

To paraphrase Will Rogers, "I never met a pilot I didn't like." On the other hand, my mother told me more than once, "You're a kind man, Henri. You think everybody is nice. You're too soft. Be careful or one day you will get hurt."

Engines were something I understood, so I spent time disassembling and assembling them. Then I worked on disassembling and assembling magnetos, learning how to set clearances properly. The most important lesson I learned was how to recognize the problem. As Freud once said, "Recognizing the problem is halfway through solving it."

Sometimes it was the sound of the engine, sometimes a holistic look or an intuitive sense based on experience that resolved problems quickly. I learned various approaches from people who worked on the engines constantly. And they were helpful in adding to my knowledge. This was hands-on problem-solving, but I had no trouble relating it to schoolbook engineering.

By the time I took my examination, everything on an engine was like second nature to me. Then I was shunted over to the propeller department. Here I had only limited knowledge. Propeller blades, setting up proper angles (indexing), and the two positions: takeoff (fine) and cruising (coarse). These were necessary to obtain greater power or to develop greater efficiency, that is, to save fuel.

The last step was inspecting the propellers with a magnifying glass to be sure no cracks from stress or fatigue disabled the "lifeblood" of the aircraft before it was considered airworthy.

When my last maintenance course was over, I knew a lot about flying, but more importantly, I knew how to take a plane apart, repair it, and get it back in the air. Seaplanes in distress often landed on the ocean, sometimes hundreds of miles from help. The nearest mechanics were the captain himself and/or the co-pilot. For some reason, I seemed to have been selected for special, intensive training. I doubted whether other pilots-in-training had the background to do what I was doing.

This training came in handy in the years ahead, when Juan Trippe, or André Priester freely offered my services to numerous world-famous pilots like Lindbergh or Amelia Earhart to check out, prepare, or repair their aircraft prior to their attempting record-breaking flights.

The S-38, an amphibian aircraft created and built by Igor Sikorsky, the Russian designer who had emigrated to America after World War I, was small and ugly. It looked ungainly as it huffed and puffed along the ocean's surface, throwing waves of water as it took off. But once I mastered it, I found it to be the sweetest flying ship of its kind. It cruised at 100 miles per hour and carried ten passengers. Eventually, one hundred S-38s were built; they would fly a total of twenty-five million commercial air miles for Pan Am before being retired.

The wheels under the S-38 hull allowed it to land on a runway, but once in the water, it took forty turns on a metal handle to raise the wheels. To get it into the air, loaded with passengers, mail, and fuel, it was necessary to apply full throttle, gain enough speed, then yank the wheels into your belly. From the captain's position, the plane appeared hidden behind a waterfall until suddenly it was airborne and as graceful as an eagle.

Inside the twin-engine plane, the crew and passengers were separated by a thin partition called a bulkhead; the lavatory, located in the back, was usually filled with mailbags and luggage. Because of the noise of the engines, talking was out of the question and communication was managed by hand gestures. Even the pilot and wheel-holder had difficulty talking above the noise of the engines. As there was only one, centrally located control wheel, seated on a pedestal that swung right or left, for the pilot and co-pilot to switch controls was a matter of sign language.

In the beginning, Pan Am flew to Cuba; Kingston, Jamaica; Barranquilla, Colombia; and Cristobal, Panama. But Juan Trippe dreamed of more than that. He had his eyes on South America as a major market. But land airports were scarce, hence the need for seaplanes, which could find an airstrip wherever there was a decent-sized body of water.

To get my license as a co-pilot, I flew with a number of great captains. The first one was William Grooch, who took me out and let me try my hand on the Commodore. When he was satisfied, he worked with me on the S-38. He talked to me about the tendencies of some planes to yaw, while others flew smoothly. I landed, took off, taxied around the ocean, learned about the flotsam and debris in the water that could crush a hull. Later, I learned about weeds, floating tree trunks and hog pens, particularly around the Magdalena River in Barranquilla.

At Pan Am, I was still regarded as a peon of sorts. As if pilot training wasn't considered work, I was transferred to a barge for my next assignment. I finally located an office, and when I entered, I was confronted by a huge man with a hard face and the look of a Marine sergeant.

"My name is Henri Keyzer-André and I was told to report here."

"Your name's too complicated. Do you have a nickname?"

"Yeah, Dutch or Klumpa."

He wrote on a clipboard and shouted to someone outside who I later found out was the beachmaster—the person in charge of beaching aircraft. A man popped his head in the doorway. The big man said, "Walt. Got another college punk here. Put him in the bilge and show him what to do."

The beachmaster, Walter Richards, was a gruff man. He said, "Before they put you in a cockpit, you have to polish all the rivets in the bottom of the plane. Every college wonder that comes here has to go through this maneuver. You sound Dutch, like Mr. Priester and Mr. Schildhauer. This place is filling up with squareheads." He tried hard to sound irritated, but I soon found out he was decent man.

There were four in this class—Brock, Ford, Leffingwell, and myself. Our job was to lift the floorboards of the S-38s and remove all the trash and stagnant water from the bilges to prevent the aluminum material from corroding. The toxic cleaning materials used were turpentine and sometimes a solution of ammonia. The smell of noxious fumes never seemed to leave the small plane.

We worked in turns, as no one could stay down in the bilges for more than fifteen minutes at a time. Under these conditions, we became fast friends, so much so that we were soon making bets as to who would make co-captain first.

We went from the ridiculous to the sublime. From the bilges, we had to complete the study of celestial navigation and learn the Morse code, international law, and meteorology. We continued to practice Navy knots, so we could tie ships to moorings or tie up anchors when we landed in some remote river.

We were more childish than grown up, as one of our pranks was to beep Morse code messages on our car horns on the way home. It got to the point where annoyed neighbors called the police and we were each given a dressing-down.

The time came for me to be checked out on the Commodore and the S-38. The captain in charge was Grooch. I passed without trouble and I became a certified wheel-holder. My first flying job was to be co-pilot/ engineer on a Commodore taking Priester to Paramaribo, Brazil. I was supercautious and doubly aware of each sound, the plane's rattling in flight, the noisy engines; the crew didn't mind the noise, as Pratt & Whitney engines were generally trouble-free. Flying meant facing danger, so if you wanted to live on the edge, fly cantankerous planes through sleet, rain, lightning, perverse winds and typhoons, the pilot's seat was the only place for you—this was the glitz and the glamour of flying.

To pick up a mooring line from a buoy, it was necessary to maneuver the seaplane by "blimping," which was to keep the propellers spinning slowly by blimping the magneto switch on the off, or speeding up one engine or the other to move into the direction you wanted to go. If you didn't time it correctly, the plane would keep spinning around like a man rowing with one oar.

After awhile, it all became second nature. I was generally a cautious person and took no hazardous chances, so I had no trouble mooring the aircraft. The beaching crew would dash out to secure the plane front and after and let the passengers disembark.

Priester ordered all aircrew members to wear regulation Pan Am uniforms of navy-blue-serge with white caps. In public, the uniforms had to be clean, pressed, and immaculate. Ranks were a modification of air forces around the world, that is, wings on the left breast with Pan Am grades determined by stars on the wings: one star for co-pilot, two stars for captain, and, later, three stars for master ocean pilot, which began when a captain flew China Clippers.

When I returned from my first flight as co-pilot, my friends were waiting for me. I was the first one checked out and the first to be initiated—thrown in the bay fully clothed.

The serge suit cost $25 and was made by Bill the Tailor in Miami. When he finished, you ended up looking like a rear admiral. A new uniform called for a $5 tip, which was a fortune at the time. The hats were made separately by Harry the Hatter.

My next flight was as wheel-holder to Captain Johnny Rogerson, who, if he had his way, would have been a professional golfer. He got me into a Commodore on a test run and watched how I handled the ship, while asking me questions about the length of the wingspan (one hundred feet) and the type of engines (525-horsepower Pratt & Whitneys) and directing me to perform certain maneuvers. Then he asked me to land the seaplane by myself as he watched. After we moored, he simply nodded his head.

We loaded up with passengers and mail, topped off the tanks with fuel, including the outrigger floats that also served as gas tanks. With my checklist, I assisted Rogerson with the preflight inspection, after which we revved up the engines full power and headed into the wind and took off. Our destination was Recife, in the province of Pernambuco, on the northeastern tip of Brazil.

On reaching our altitude and a cruising speed of 100 miles per hour with the engines synchronized, the captain began talking golf. And more golf. There were a thousand questions I wanted to ask about flying, but he only talked golf.

We took turns flying the craft, and she handled as sweet as whipped cream. There were several short stops along the route to unload and pick up mail. As this was a thirty-hour trip, we stayed overnight at Belém, Brazil. It's incomprehensible today to think there were no meteorological reports about the weather ahead. If we were lucky, there would be a telephone at the port and we could call ahead and ask about the weather.

Preparing for takeoff at Belém, the captain insisted on going over takeoff procedures with me. When he was satisfied, he handed me the wheel and said, "Go."

I took off smoothly and proudly and flew the plane. It was a great thrill. I did not want to muddle my thoughts with the fact that this was originally an NYRBA plane, built by Reuben Fleet for O'Neill. The preliminary part of the trip was calm and pleasant, but it wasn't long before we ran into rough weather. First there was upheaval within the aircraft as we flew through several fierce squalls. Rogerson continued to watch me closely. Then we popped into a genuine, mind-boggling, ear-deafening South American thunderstorm. It was a monstrous cumulonimbus, the daddy of all thunderclouds, with gale winds, drenching rain, horrendous thunderclaps, and fierce lightning.

"I'm not checked out for instrument flying," I told the captain, clutching on to the cross on my chest.

"This is the best way to learn," he replied, "and say a prayer for all of us while you're at it."

I was having second thoughts about earning my captain's wings as the Commodore was tossed around by the wind and pelted by heavy rain. Nevertheless, the aircraft behaved admirably. Rogerson stopped his chip shot, golf chatter and talked to me about how to read the instruments when there was no visibility. When we passed the worst of the turbulence, we took turns flying the plane and going back to calm the passengers, who were now white with fright. Thank heavens I never looked into a mirror to check my own appearance.

There were no longer thoughts in my head about the dangers of flying, the fickleness of the weather, and the untried builders who designed the early aircraft. Along with the fragile wings, there were then a thousand other things that could go wrong with the instruments. The engines were the only things I had confidence in and felt they would not cause problems.

An hour's flying time from Recife, we hit the same thunderstorm, or its first cousin. It felt as if we were in a submarine moving through the ocean. It was during this flight that I made a major pact with God. There was no use getting scared every time. I encountered a problem in flight. If God wanted me, all he had to do was ask me politely and I would go to Him. So I flew through God's own handiwork, a thunderstorm. Lightning flashed across the sky and though it was still daylight, the flashes and booming thunder could wake the dead.

Rogerson was at the controls when he waved for me to take over. He was going for a pee. I took the wheel and said, "Have one for me while you're at it."

It was a wonder the wings weren't ripped apart as rain pounded at them. When I could hold her steady, the compass heading was 110 degrees while the wheel bucked in my hands. To say I was perspiring was to put it mildly. My arms ached from the strain. Rogerson returned and strapped himself in and waved for me to continue flying.

There was too much noise for him to talk about golf, but it didn't stop him from making practice swings. Then I had a flash of insight—it wasn't golf he was interested in as much as giving me confidence in myself.

We were near land and we could occasionally see it. It was twilight and getting darker, with the rain still pummeling the seaplane. "Better get down, we can't go into Recife now."

"Land in the ocean?"

"Sure—unless you have a better idea."

Which way was the wind blowing? I had to land into the wind. I started to bring her down when the port engine began sputtering and finally quit. "The rain got to the spark plugs," said Rogerson.

"It couldn't be—they're covered with grease."

"Argue later. Bring the damned ship down."

When the sea is calm, it's difficult enough to gauge where the surface is, but in the choppy, rain-drenched ocean, I could see the waves and, from the spray, which way the wind was blowing. I banked around in a wide circle and headed into the wind toward land. I eased her down as gently as I could on one engine, fought gusts of headwind plus the downpour and the darkness. In the cabin, I heard people praying out loud. I recited my prayers in my head.

Most pilots said that under normal circumstances, it was extremely difficult to make a bad landing in the Commodore. These were not normal circumstances. Rogerson was smiling as I struggled to keep the aircraft level. No question, his nerves were made of steel. We came down hard into the water and retained an even keel. I still consider it the best landing I ever made. We finally slowed down when we were approximately a quarter mile from land. The waves were smaller, but the rain was just as fierce.

We threw out an anchor and Captain Rogerson went back and told the passengers and crew that the staff would prepare a meal for us. We would spend the night on the plane. The food was good, but the plane bobbed like a cork until about midnight, when the rain slowed down and then mercifully stopped. That's when I finally fell asleep.

Next morning, the sun was shining and it was warn. After coffee, Rogerson said, "Well, Dutch, take a look at the spark plugs." I took my toolbox along and removed the cowl from the engine to examine the spark plugs. Rogerson was right. The hard rain had poured into the engine and washed off all the grease. I removed the plugs, wiped them down carefully and put them back. Then I covered them with an extra-thick coating of grease.

When I was back in position, Rogerson said, "All right, Dutch, you got us down, you cleaned the engine, so check the motors. If they work, let's get the hell out of here."

The engines started beautifully. The wind had shifted, so I taxied into position and the passengers and crew were notified. Then I gave her the gun and we took off. We arrived over Recife fifteen minutes later. Rogerson then signaled to me that he was taking over. I gave him the wheel and he began to talk about how to use a mashie and a niblick. When I finally could get a word in, I asked, "Weren't you afraid that the plane might ground-loop when I landed on one engine?"

"No. You have to understand your aircraft. Commodores seldom ground-loop. Unless you crashed into the ocean, there was no way you could botch up that landing. You're a cautious pilot, Henri. I knew you wouldn't foul up."

This was the first of a series of lessons I would learn from the great captains. Only from their experiences could we learn about flying through extremely rough weather, uncharted oceans, jungles infested with wild animals, uncharted mountains, and sometimes fickle air-craft. These captains were part of a rare breed, men with nerve, a ruggedness that was unique, with an ability to keep their cool in crisis situations. There was a warm camaraderie among pilots whose hero-ism was an everyday occurrence. Their friendship had to be earned—it was never given freely.

I was honored just to be there.

Captains came in all shapes, sizes, and from assorted backgrounds. When he had confidence in your ability, Captain Shorty Clark would say, "Take over. I'm going to take a nap." Dutch Schultz (no relation to the famous gangster) was a big, former Marine pilot who was always in control. He had a million wonderful anecdotes and rarely repeated himself. Basil Row came to Pan Am from a pioneer airline. He had an ear problem, so he put plugs in his ears. It was difficult to communi-cate with him over the engine noise, but you learned just by watch-ing him.

Captain Swinson smoked the biggest Cuban cigars I'd ever seen. Being wheel-holder to him was like flying through smog. Slim Extrone was Swedish, a former Army pilot who was jovial but intense. His only problem was that he stuttered. Communication was difficult.

Flying with Cubby Cobleson was like flying with the Sphinx. He seldom spoke. The top captain at Pan Am was Edwin Musick; he also didn't speak much but was very compulsive about making every flight perfect. An old Navy pilot called Red Williamson was a chain-smoker. He was another silent man; he was slow and deliberate about making decisions, but once he made them, the co-pilot had better follow instructions or all hell broke loose.

There was only one pilot of Russian background among the captains, Leo Terletsky. He was the resident philosopher and once told me, "The earth is the cradle of mankind—but man cannot stay in the cradle forever."

Co-pilots were treated like plebes at West Point. We were called all sorts of pejorative names, like bilge rats and college wonders. But we were a new breed of recruits. We were being molded into Pan Am pilots by old-timers with limited schooling—ex-Navy/Army/Marine pilots and some barnstormers were breaking in the college boys with graduate degrees or with engineering specialties.

We had so much studying to do when we weren't in the air that the joy of flying was beginning to lose its luster. Priester was behind it all, setting higher and higher standards. It was hard work. It's difficult to believe now, but we flew one round-trip, then returned to base—not to rest, but to study semaphore (signaling with two flags). Fly another round-trip, then study to qualify for a second-class radio license. It was hard work, but upon completion of the course, the radio license permitted you to operate a radio station in flight as well as on the ground. There was also the requirement to speak at least one foreign language. That was the least of my problems.

Then came navigation by dead reckoning, followed by celestial navigation, which included shooting the stars with an aerial sextant. Our instructor in navigation was Fred Noonan, at the time acknowledged as one of the country's greatest navigators. He was tall and slender and looked like Jimmy Stewart. He would later find his niche in history as Amelia Earhart's navigator; both vanished in 1937.

But of all the things we had to learn, the most frightening was landing in a calm sea. The sun reflected off the water, and it was difficult to judge where the descending seaplane would make contact. There were a variety of methods and each captain preferred his own.

Many captains preferred the antenna method. Each ship had a "trailing antenna," which was a spool of wire that was let out once you were in flight to allow the radio operator to communicate. At the tip of the antenna was a lead ball that acted as a weight when unraveling. The antenna was to be pulled in before a landing, but if the sea was calm, the captain allowed the antenna to trail down. When the lead ball came in contact with the water, it started to bounce. The captain then eased back on the throttle until the plane settled on the water.

Another system was to have station personnel put flare pots on the water and you would land next to the pots. Still another captain swore by his own system, which was to throw shredded paper onto the water to gauge where the surface was.

Finally, the system officially adopted by Pan Am was to have station personnel take a boat over the water to make waves, thus helping the pilot locate the surface. A forced landing on calm water necessitated the antenna method. This landing on becalmed water caused many a wheel-holder to fail his final test.

By 1932, the wheel-holders flew five days a week and worked two in the hangar. The forty-hour, the forty-eight-hour, and the sixty-hour week were unheard-of. We were expected to dedicate our lives to Pan Am. Priester quoted the Army bromide: "If you look after your rifle, your rifle will look after you." He said the same was true of the plane: "If you look after your plane, your plane will look after you." Though there were mechanics to service the aircraft, you spent more time away from base than on it, so you had to learn to depend on yourself.

By now, most of my associates knew about my late fiancée, Minerva. They tried coaxing me to date again, but it was difficult for me. They took me to the local country club, but first they dragged me to Bill the Tailor, where we all borrowed Bill's tuxedos. This was the Depression, but we were pilots, and we felt like dashing movie stars. My friends tried fixing me up with girls—friends of friends, sisters, and cousins—but to no avail. They danced while I hung around the orchestra listening to the music.

One Saturday night, a substitute musician in the band turned out to be a compatriot from the Opa-Locka Four. He invited me to sit in with the band and I played a little banjo with them. My friend coaxed me to stand in front of the microphone and sing my old songs like "The Boulevard of Broken Dreams" and "My Blue Heaven." Though my voice wasn't special, I had had enough practice to fake it.

One Saturday, a very tall, lovely blond girl came up to me and said, "I understand you're a pilot with Pan Am. Well, to me, you look like a hawk."

I was so startled, I couldn't say anything. She introduced herself as Gracie Greer. Only Minerva had ever compared me to a hawk, so I took it as a sign from above and asked her to dance. We stayed together all evening. I was our group's tallest wheel-holder, at six feet, but at that I was only a few inches taller than she was in high heels. It might have been the reason she approached me.

When I had a chance to talk with Gracie, she told me she was seventeen and was expected to win the Miss Miami beauty contest, even though she was from Dublin, Georgia. Unfortunately, her mother chaperoned her everywhere. I was disappointed to learn that her mother refused to let her go out frequently with me. Mama wanted a wealthy husband, and obviously I wasn't on the list.

So, I plunged back into my work. My ambition now was to complete five thousand hours flying as a co-pilot so I could qualify for captain. But Pan Am had other ideas.

CHAPTER 7

Charles Lindbergh

WITHOUT QUESTION, the most famous aviator in American history was Charles Lindbergh. His close friendship with Juan Trippe was such that sometimes Lindbergh worked for Pan Am or did consulting work for the company. On occasion he was in business for himself, while at other times, he became so bored that he sought out flying adventures to spice up his life. Lindbergh and Trippe served each other's purposes. For Lindbergh, it often meant searching out new air routes for Pan Am; for Trippe, it meant the continuing publicity and the ease of getting more government contracts.

Trippe's not-so-secret ambition was to own all the foreign routes from the United States to all parts of the world. At the time, this was a mind-boggling ambition. Regular commercial airline flights to Europe and Asia? To this end, Trippe's suggestion that Lindbergh might want to explore air routes to China triggered a delightful response. Recently married to Anne Morrow, Lindbergh thought it might be a nice adventure if they made the flight together. While he selected a plane, his wife would study navigation, learn how to operate a radio, and study Morse code.

He mapped out a route to Asia via the Arctic. This meant crossing Canada to Alaska to Siberia to Japan and China. For some unknown reason, Lindbergh decided to make this flight under his own auspices and pay for it himself. Many thought it was because he enjoyed making headlines and hungered for more.

Early in 1931, Juan Trippe had a meeting in Miami at the Thirty-sixth Street Airport. All the principals of Pan Am were there, including William MacCracken, now attorney for Pan Am who suggested to Trippe that he get to know a new employee, a multilingual young man with a Ph.D. in aeronautical engineering who was also a licensed co-pilot at Pan Am.

Trippe, a "seeing-is-believing" sort of man, checked me out with several captains, including Grooch as well as André Priester. I discovered later that Priester somehow knew every single thing I had accomplished with the company, from the day he ordered me to sweep out the hangar. He must have said some nice things, as Trippe finally asked to meet me. When we were introduced, we chatted a bit, then he said, "Since you have all these blankety-blank credentials, why don't you come to New York? There are enough pilots down here. I have some special duties for you." He turned around and walked away.

MacCracken sought me out for a drink after work and filled in some of the blanks. "Trippe has a one-track mind. Nothing—and I mean nothing—stands in his way. Which is why he will succeed where O'Neill failed. Lindbergh has asked Juan for some help on his Arctic trip and Juan agreed. I think you may be it."

"But, Bill, Priester tells everyone I have a doctorate."

"How far are you from it?"

"Just a dissertation away."

"Henri, let me give you some fatherly advice. There's a moral to it, because it's a story I heard Will Rogers tell.

"A new widow went to a Gypsy to try and find out if her husband had gone to heaven. The Gypsy looked into her crystal ball and said, 'The crystal is cloudy. Cover my palm with silver and we'll see what happens.'

"The widow gave her some money. 'Ah, the crystal ball is clearing up. I see your husband. He looks just like his picture. Yes. He's walking toward heaven. He's about three miles away. Ah, the crystal is clouding up—please come back tomorrow.'

"On the second visit, the Gypsy gazed into her crystal ball and said once more, 'The crystal is cloudy, cross my palm with silver.' Money changed hands and the Gypsy added, 'Ah, it is clearing up. Your husband is still walking on the road to heaven.'

" 'And how far away is he?'

" 'Two miles. Ah, it is getting cloudy.'

"This went on for several weeks, as the late husband marched toward heaven. He grew closer, a mile, then a half mile, then a quarter of a mile, until he was ten yards away.

"On the next visit, the same litany took place. The widow crossed the Gypsy's palm with silver. The crystal cleared. 'How far away is he?' she cried out.

" 'Your husband is now three feet away. Ah, the crystal ball is getting cloudy. Come back tomorrow.'

" 'I will not.'

"The startled Gypsy asked, 'Why not?'

"The widow said, 'If John can't jump three feet into heaven, he can go to hell.' "

MacCracken looked at me and said, "Henri, you're three feet from heaven. If you can't jump into your doctorate, you can jump into . . . well, oblivion."

"Okay. But when I have the time, I promise I will finish it."

"It's fine with me—Doctor."

So I packed up and went to New York in my Waco. I wasn't sure yet what I thought of Trippe. He seemed a pleasant-enough, chubby type of man with blazing eyes and snake oil charm. But I had no complaints, as he paid my salary on time. It was Lindbergh whom I held in awe.

Lindbergh had already decided that for the China trip, he would use a Lockheed Sirius. It was a land plane, and he had already flown it across the country testing it. He had discovered that flying at about 12,500 feet, you could escape a lot of bad weather and increase the speed, performance, and fuel efficiency of the engines. He had come to the same conclusion as Juan Trippe about overseas travel. Airports were scarce, so it would be wiser to convert the Sirius into a seaplane.

When we met on Long Island, I was impressed with this tall, slender man with fair hair. He was now twenty-nine years old, and he looked the part of the all-American hero. It was hard to believe he was five years my senior and was already a household word around the world. He told me about a few engineering courses at a university, including some classes in aeronautical engineering. But his technical education was quite limited.

He wanted to know about my background, everything I had worked on at Pan Am. My Waco interested him, so I let him take it up for a spin. After that, he was all business. We discussed his ideas for converting the Sirius into a seaplane. He insisted that the plane should have a range of two thousand miles. I told him this meant larger gas tanks and a more powerful engine.

It seemed that I was becoming his sounding board. He wanted to discuss ideas with me and was attentive to any comments I cared to make. After three hours, he thanked me and we shook hands.

At Lockheed, Lindbergh made up a list of modifications. The engine he selected was the newest, most powerful Wright Cyclone, 600-horsepower engine. It was also light. Meanwhile, Anne Lindbergh studied navigation and Morse code, the latter under the instruction of Mr. Leuteritz. The same gentleman advised me what radio equipment was to be installed in the plane, because Juan Trippe put me in charge of all the safety equipment for the trip.

The Sirius was a monoplane with a single engine, a two-blade propeller, two open cockpits over which Lockheed placed sliding glass canopies as protection in case of bad weather. The pontoons now carried most of the gasoline needed for its two-thousand-mile range.

Lindbergh planned to navigate a Great Circle route. The long-range radio and wireless transmitter included a loop direction finder, an invention perfected by Leuteritz. For about ten days, while waiting for the proper weather conditions, Anne Lindbergh pressed me into service to help her practice sending Morse code.

On July 27, 1931, the Lindberghs took off from College Point, Long Island, and headed for Ottawa, Canada, the first leg, 425 air miles away. The newspapers were filled with stories about the adventurous couple, and were impressed with Lucky Lindy and his literary wife, Anne, who could quote French poets. The Lindberghs christened the little Lockheed Sirius, *Tijustilatog*, the Eskimo equivalent of "One who flies like a bird."

The flight took them across Hudson Bay to the Amundsen Gulf to Point Barrow above the Arctic Circle, the northernmost tip of Alaska. The now famous story has it that the fur traders presented the Lindberghs with fresh trout. In exchange, the Lindberghs gave them their roast beef sandwiches, which the traders, not having had meat in months, gleefully devoured.

The last part of their trip within continental North America was the most harrowing. From Point Barrow they circled down the coast of Alaska so that they flew over Wales Island. To the west, they could see Siberia fifty miles away. They continued on to Nome. Because of their side trip, they didn't get there as scheduled. It was almost nightfall as they neared the city, but it was also a mountainous region. Lindbergh decided to land in a lagoon to spend the night.

Because they didn't arrive as scheduled, the world's newspapers bemoaned the fate of the "lost" Lindberghs, who had simply moored their plane, burrowed in the back with the luggage, and fallen fast asleep.

When they landed in Nome the following day and were "found" again, the world breathed a sigh of relief. Their next stop was Japan and another brush with death. Their plane ran into a dense fog and it was impossible for Lindbergh to descend. He spotted a volcano rising above the fog, and on a hunch, he followed it down into the sea and landed. The luck of Lucky Lindy was holding up.

The strangest adventure took place in China. Here's how it was related by Paula Austin in a book entitled *The Clipper Heritage*, written for the Air Line Pilots Association of Pan Am.

"In China the Lindberghs found fewer natural hazards, but instead they had to worry about people. At one point the plane was mobbed not because the Chinese were wild about the great Lindbergh or even because they were fascinated by a flying machine. They grabbed the plane's pontoons and jumped on to its wings because they were starving and wanted food. Lindbergh fired his revolver in a warning shot. The mob backed off, and before they pressed forward again, the Sirius was racing across the water and into the air."

Just after Thanksgiving in 1932, Juan Trippe asked Captain William Grooch and me to attend a meeting in his New York office. There were a number of people in the office besides us. Trippe was excited as he rattled on about another great opportunity that had just opened up in China. He had Lindbergh's report on the need for an airline in China, where it took a letter one month to travel five hundred miles.

Just as he had swallowed NYRBA and the Cuban Airline, Trippe was interested in another distressed airline that had come on the market—the China National Aviation Corporation (CNAC). Trippe wanted the group of us to know what Pan Am was getting into, that somehow we were going to be involved.

"A national airline can easily be converted to military purposes," said Trippe. "The Nationalists are asking for bids from other airlines. I'm going to bid on 45 percent of the stock and end up taking over the airline. The way to do this would be to assume a large portion of their debts in exchange for future equity if they can't pay."

CHAPTER 8

Getting China off the Ground

JUAN TRIPPE'S New York office featured a large globe of the world on which he planned Pan Am strategy. Crisscrossing the globe was a network of strings spanning the oceans between major cities, tying countries together. One critic said Juan Trippe was a spider spinning his web around the world. Nevertheless, Trippe could never be accused of not planning ahead.

Thanks to Lindbergh's report on Alaska, Trippe knew that it held the key to shorter, safer flights between the United States, Russia, Japan, and China. Even before Lindbergh's flight, Trippe had tried to penetrate the air routes in Alaska, but without success. Now, five years had gone by, seaplanes were bigger and faster and Asia beckoned.

The stock market crash hampered the progress of most airlines, some still reeling from lack of cash. Trippe, seizing his opportunity, purchased both the Alaskan Airways and Pacific International Airways of Alaska for $90,000.

It was obvious Trippe's next step was China, a land of over 400 million people and growing. Despite the fact that Chiang Kai-shek was the head of the government, China was not really united. There were numerous fiefdoms, where each warlord ruled his dynasty with an iron fist and Chiang Kai-shek's policies were often ignored. There was also a growing ferment of communism under the leadership of Mao Tse-tung, who now controlled two provinces, Hunan and Kiangsi. At that time, Japan began its incursion into China by annexing Manchuria, a province in northern China.

Considering "the enemy from within" a greater threat than the
Japanese, Chiang and his Nationalist army continued to battle the
guerrilla war of Mao while he left the Japanese to his lieutenants. Some
suggested that while this turmoil in China continued, it was no place
to travel by air, particularly when the warlords often held planes as
hostage. But Trippe saw it as an opportunity.

China National Aviation Corporation, started in partnership with
the Curtiss Wright Group, with CNAC owning 55 percent. The airline
had poor equipment and poorer management. Though it was in desperate condition, it took six months of negotiations before CNAC
agreed to discuss Pan Am's interest in acquiring Curtiss Wright's 45
percent of the company. CNAC wanted the airline to operate strictly
within China, but Trippe's grand scheme included international flights
from the United States to China, with fuel stops in Hawaii and the
Philippines.

There were other possible stops on intermediate islands, like Wake
Island and Guam, but that's when Juan Trippe ran headlong into his
most formidable foe—Japan.

About the time it swallowed the mineral-rich, fertile province of
Manchuria, success had given Japan a voracious appetite. It was the
beginning of such Japanese edicts as "The Pacific is a Japanese lake"
and "Asia for the Asians." These were ploys to keep the Americans and
the British out of their sphere of influence.

Earlier, China, Japan, and several other Asian nations had signed an
international treaty, an open-door policy, saying that if China granted
commercial landing rights to any nation, Japan and the other co-
signers of the treaty would be granted similar rights. Why China
worried about this treaty when it was at war with Japan was never
quite clear.

Pan Am also was seeking landing rights in Hong Kong, then a British
protectorate, but Great Britain was still the world's mightiest colonial
power and it did not relish competition from an upstart American
company. Trippe reasoned that if Pan Am planes could land at Hong
Kong, it was feasible for CNAC to form a link between Hong Kong and
China.

Selected to head the team to China was a forty-two-year-old former
banker from St. Louis, Harold M. Bixby, who was no stranger to
aviation. He was the man who raised the money to finance Lindbergh's
flight to Paris and he remained a close friend. Trippe hired him on

Lindbergh's recommendation. His job was to put the jigsaw pieces together to create a Chinese air world according to Trippe.

Though I was part of the group in New York learning about the Chinese airline in preparation for going to China, I honestly didn't know what was expected of me. All I knew was I was going to China. So I listened to background lectures on Chinese politics. Finally, we were sent home to wait until Trippe recalled us for further instructions.

Back in Miami, Grooch, myself, and some designated technicians were plunged into work immediately. It consisted of hurricane duty—that is, bad-weather flying—checking storms and wind turbulence, all the standard conditions we would encounter in China. We were brought up-to-date on the latest meteorological technology and wind patterns and we flew in the small amphibian planes we would fly in China, the Loening air yachts. If everything worked out, they would be supplemented with S-38s. As I was not into heavy socializing, in my spare time I did extra homework.

Finally, we were called back to New York to have a special meeting with Vilhjalmur Stefansson, the noted Canadian explorer born of Icelandic parents. Pan Am had sponsored some of his Arctic expeditions in order to accumulate data for future use in cold-weather flights. He briefed us on flying conditions in the far north as well as means of survival. It gave me nightmares to think of landing a seaplane in freezing northern waters, and after standing a few hours to discover your pontoons were encased in ice.

Then, at one session, I was called in to meet privately with Juan Trippe. "Henri, with your command of languages and your background in foreign countries, you could be a great asset to Harold Bixby to get this operation going. I want you to work closely with him and assist him all you can. Do you think you can learn Chinese?"

I blushed and said, "Mr. Trippe, one of my former flying students is Chinese. He's been teaching me to speak Mandarin while I was in Miami."

He looked at me for a good long time, then said, "Do a good job, as I will have other special projects for you to handle for me personally. Meanwhile, help Bixby. Keep your eyes and ears open on how everything comes together." Then, paraphrasing Priester's favorite expression, he said, "Be as fast as bare-assed John and get to work lickety-split."

Before leaving for China, Priester got Gooch, myself, and another pilot together and lectured us on safety first and methods of operating an airline. He presented us with books on the quality of leadership, Pan Am rules and regulations, brochures on operating an amphibious airport, and how to conduct ourselves in a foreign land.

Two air yachts were disassembled and placed in crates, and we all took off for San Francisco, where we left by ship for Shanghai.

Flying in China was the most dangerous I had encountered up to that point in my life. The weather was unbelievably bad, CNAC (nicknamed the People's Kingdom Family Machine) lacked even the most elementary navigational aids. Single-engine planes were not equipped with radios, so pilots were obliged to find their destinations by visual contact. Despite this, Bixby flew around China on a Loening air yacht trying to convince the government to support the airline.

Finally, the Chinese government agreed to raise the funds by holding nationwide lotteries for the construction of airports along the coast and to finance the necessary equipment to aid the airlines. While I didn't speak fluent Chinese, I understood more than most the concerns of the Chinese pilots; rugged mountains created fierce thunderstorms, typhoons, and wind shear. And if the dense fog, wind currents, and mountains didn't get you—there were always the pirates. Even flying along the Yangtze River was frightening, and we learned from the Chinese that you followed the shoreline of the river, not the fog on the river. If you didn't see land, the safest course was to return to base.

Checkpoints were set up with codes about weather conditions. Even then, it was the pilot who had to decide on the accuracy of the "meteorological" information. Within a span of five months, two Pan Am planes crashed, killing the crews. The cause was the weather, but the Chinese were becoming skeptical about our ability.

Being religious, every time I took off in an airplane, I asked the Lord for guidance. I was always prepared for a catastrophe. There were close encounters too numerous to mention, often because the Chinese radio operators were confused by American terminology. Luckily, I understood enough Chinese to catch the nuance of sounds uttered by the radio operator. It helped me avoid disasters.

One of my jobs was to visit the University of Peking and try to find students interested in aviation. They were very polite, but the answer was always the same: "No, thank you." Meanwhile, Bixby and the Chinese government continued negotiations.

In July 1933, Pan Am's purchase of the 45 percent stake was approved. Operations of the Shanghai-Canton mail route was scheduled to start on October 24, 1933. Then the fun began. The government imposed a 30 percent tax on revenues, while petty officials in local post offices refused to hand over mailbags for the service.

Further negotiations by Bixby reduced the tax to 10 percent, and some mail for service trickled through. When the inaugural flight from Shanghai to Canton was to take off, coolies began dropping gas cans deliberately on the Loening's bow to tear the metal skin; they also shoved their feet through the wing fabric and threw rocks, shattering the cockpit window.

The decision was made to abandon the coastal routes along the Pacific and switch to internal routes. Floating bamboo passenger terminals were built, about thirty-five feet square, which included a waiting lounge, offices, and storeroom. The one coastal route that remained was the Hong Kong extension.

Flying may have been hell, but outside of flying, life was great. We all lived in a building called the Pan Am Staff House. We ate Chinese food, and there was plenty of recreation from tennis to bicycle riding to horseback riding. We became friendly with the university students who could speak English, and some of us had girlfriends.

In order to remove the fear-of-flying syndrome from the students, with the aid of the university, I set up a series of lectures and symposiums on flying, navigation, engineering, and radio communication. My fluency in Chinese improved through the simple-usage words such as yes (*dui*), no (*bu dui*), please (*ging*), thank you (*xie-xie ni*), and so forth—on to more difficult words. But I had to be alert and diplomatic at all times. The Chinese had their own slow, stubborn way. It revolved around the Oriental trait of "saving face."

To face the probability of poor weather conditions, Grooch advised us always to start out with a full load of fuel, thus giving us additional opportunity to fly out of bad weather or to head east over the ocean to more stable air and then try to find familiar landmarks.

As a sort of assistant to Bixby, I was given the job of trying to resolve personnel difficulties. First, I had to write a set of aviation rules to establish safety. I now better understood Priester's indoctrination. Pan

Am (China) would then give out licenses to Chinese mechanics, inspectors, and maintenance workers. These were the people responsible for certifying if a plane was airworthy.

Then the problem was to move up to pilots, flight engineers, radio operators, and meteorologists. Finally, there was a set of rules to certify licensed engineers to build navigation facilities, as well as a national Chinese code of identification for Chinese-owned airplanes.

There were very few railways in China, so Pan Am's successful reorganization of CNAC led to dramatic improvements in communications and with trade within its own borders. Labor was never a problem in China. Thousands of people could be called on to hand-build a land airport or anything else. I was always amazed at how much could be accomplished without machines.

Bixby's Loenings were replaced by two twin-engine Douglas Dolphins, capable of flying 150 miles per hour, with a range of 740 miles, plus four Sikorsky S-38s.

Frequently, the government held formal functions, and we were obliged to wear starched uniforms to these gatherings. One month before the formal opening of the Shanghai-Canton service, I was recalled home by Juan Trippe. Bixby expressed his gratitude for my help and my attitude during his endeavors. That company of men continued to fly and build a successful enterprise without me.

I had made many friends at the university, and they surprised me with a ceremony at which I was awarded the first of my honorary Ph.D.'s.

CHAPTER 9

I Save a Dictator's Neck

AFTER MY LONG boat trip from China to San Francisco and train ride to Miami, I was able to have a reunion with my family. My father was interested in my diplomatic encounters, and while he knew I worked for Pan Am, he still didn't know about my flying. My mother listened to my stories, but with a different viewpoint.

Suddenly, I was ordered to see W. O. Snyder, chief of the South American Division, and Jimmy Walker, chief of operations and chief pilot. Based on my experience, they were sending me to South America to set up Pan Am's newest procedures for building and docking seaplanes. I wasn't sure if I was brought from China for this specific job, or if Juan Trippe, who had recalled me, really wanted to talk with me.

Unexpectedly, I was put on hurricane watch until I was scheduled to leave because a major hurricane was heading toward Miami. By the time the roaring 90-mile-per-hour winds and the slashing rain began, I had everything at the station buttoned down. I was to remain on duty in case anything broke free.

It was comfortable in the hangar, and as it was getting dark, I took out my banjo to practice some picking. Naturally, I began playing the biggest tune of the year, "Stormy Weather," when I heard a noise. I couldn't believe my ears. It was the sound of airplane engines. I dropped the banjo and ran to the hangar door. Landing at the far end of the runway was a twin-engine S-36. It couldn't be a Pan Am plane, as we had none at the time.

How the plane survived I'll never know. It was aligned with the runway one minute, then blown across it the next. It was insane to fly in this weather, yet here was a pilot fighting his way down. It couldn't survive; it would surely break up. It finally hit the runway and kept bouncing up and down like a rubber ball. It was impossible to figure out who could be desperate enough to fly in this weather.

The plane taxied toward the hangar and I saw the pilot and passenger get drenched as they left the plane. I opened the door slightly, allowing the rain to sluice into the hangar. Then I recognized the roly-poly figure of the passenger: General Gerardo Machado. Obviously, he and his pilot had just escaped from Cuba, where Fulgencio Batista's armed forces had overthrown President Machado's government.

The general and pilot entered the hangar and the general, speaking in rapid, frightened Spanish, said, "Please hide us, *señor*, there are agents everywhere who wish to kill me. We are in great danger. They will be looking for this plane."

I decided to help, and the pilot and I swung open the doors as everything outside began blowing in and everything inside started blowing out. Then the three of us pushed the plane into the hangar and closed the door. "There are saboteurs waiting to shoot us. Batista has sent word for the Cubans in Miami to kill us on sight. Please hide us!"

As I saw it, I couldn't have the death of this man on my hands, even though Batista was another dictator. It was the same old game of Latin politics in the banana republics.

I went into action immediately. From the locker, I got my sou'wester, a shiny yellow slicker, and went inside to fetch my Dodge roadster. It was a two-seater with no top and a large rumble seat. The pilot helped me remove the tools and rumble seat from the back, then I put the pilot in the rear and Machado in the passenger seat. I searched out a tarpaulin large enough to cover both men and hide them from view. There were enough pieces of rope around to tie the tarp so the wind wouldn't blow it away. I kept wondering why I was putting myself in harm's way to protect a dictator. But his fate was in someone else's hands, not mine. My last act was to streak my face with grease.

I cranked up the Dodge and drove the car outside. Then I came back to lock the hangar. The general kept up a running stream of Spanish, cursing me for stopping while his life was in danger.

"*El presidente*," I said in Spanish. "If you don't shut up your enemies will discover you. If they shoot you, they will shoot me as well, so from now on I don't want to hear a peep out of you."

I eased onto Thirty-sixth Street as the wind picked up in intensity. The general had given me his destination, a secluded place on Star Island. If I remember correctly it was supposedly the hiding place of the Chicago gangster Al Capone.

Under my slicker, I was still in work overalls; that, plus the grease on my face, was the only disguise possible. Nobody, but nobody, ventures outside in a Miami hurricane. Nevertheless, there were cars cruising the street and fierce men holding rifles out windows. I drove slowly so as not to arouse suspicion, but a large passenger car came up beside me. A gun was pointed at me and I was asked questions in Spanish. I shrugged and said, *"No hablo español."* I waved at him, smiled, and drove on.

Pieces of roofs and tree branches came hurtling down on the street, and though I won't swear to it, I think I heard gunfire. I drove cautiously down central Miami, my knees shaking from the rain and wind, interspersed with fear. I turned onto a smaller causeway that led to Star Island. When we arrived, there were four police sergeants with drawn guns guarding the entrance. I didn't know what to think. Were these good guys or bad guys in disguise? They waved me down. I stopped the car and said, "I just left work and I'm trying to get out of this hurricane."

"Do you have anyone hidden in the car?"

"Take a look."

"Naw, the weather's too lousy. Proceed."

I put the car in gear and heard one of the men in rapid Spanish saying he should have searched the car. I increased speed and skidded around a corner. Then I accelerated and headed to the address the general had given me. I told Machado, still hiding under the tarp, where we were. He told me to drive around the back to the guesthouse. Then I untied the ropes, and the two men huddled under the tarp got out. I retied the ropes exactly as before.

Machado said, "Please do not mention the name of Machado to anyone." Then he and the pilot thanked me and ducked inside the house.

Now I had to get off the island without arousing the suspicions of the police sergeants and drive back to the hangar. In my head, I cooked up a story of having to go back to close the hangar doors or I would lose my job. Luckily, there was a burst of traffic and I slid through when the gate was up and scooted back to Miami. The streets were flooded, as

the water could not be absorbed into the ground. I began to fishtail
down the road, with the wind aiding and abetting the skids.

By the time I reached Flagler Street and started up Biscayne Boulevard, I came up against roadblocks. Men with guns stopped to inspect
my car, back and front. Altogether, I was stopped four different times,
once by a cruel-looking man with a scarred face who kept jabbing me
with his rifle, as though he could read my mind and would ask me
where I took Machado.

As I drove down the causeway, the wind was driving the rain so hard
I couldn't see ten feet ahead. My family lived on Northwest Fortieth
Street, and I inched my way there, my windshield wipers no longer
working and a worn-out battery causing my car lights to flicker. Somehow, I made it.

The hurricane lasted two days before it subsided. I returned to Pan
Am. About four days later, a letter from the deposed dictator arrived.

Please turn my S-36 back to Pan American. Thank Juan Trippe for the use
of this plane. I want to thank you for helping me return it into the hands
of the person who was gracious enough to give it to me. Also, I want to
thank you for the courageous way you drove me to safety.

A very grateful
General Machado.

I wrote a letter to Juan Trippe, enclosing Machado's letter that
explained the return of the plane he had given Machado for favors
granted to Pan Am in Cuba.

CHAPTER 10

I Chart a Pan Am Air Route
Across Siberia

ON NOVEMBER 12, 1933, I received my orders to meet Juan Trippe in
New York. As I was traveling by train, I stopped off in Washington for a
few hours to visit with Bill MacCracken, who by now was a vice
president of Pan Am.

"You seem worried, Henri," he said.

I told him about China and how I was suddenly called back. Then I
told him how I was scheduled to go to South America but nothing came
of it. "I don't know if I'm going to be fired," I said.

"You have nothing to worry about. Juan told me he's been keeping
an eye on you. You're a good pilot, a fine engineer, and a helluva
linguist. I think he wants you to handle some special jobs for him."

"What kinds of jobs?"

"More like a troubleshooter. He needs someone he can trust implic-
itly."

I was no closer to understanding what he was talking about than
before—except to learn I wasn't about to be fired. I traveled to New
York and checked in to the Blackstone Hotel, where most Pan Am
crews stayed. I met some of my co-workers, and it gave me an opportunity to catch up on the gossip of the day.

Trippe was out of town, but the moment he returned, he called for
me. When I walked in, he treated me like an old friend. "Come in,
Henri, and close the door. I want to talk to you in private."

93

When I sat down, he added, "Bill MacCracken and I talked about having a special person with international diplomatic training—with a mastery of languages—to survey an air route through Russia for possible airports for round-the-world travel.

"He also has to be a pilot and an engineer with enough meteorological background to detail a clear report on weather conditions en route, report on prospective places for airports near prominent cities, and also, if necessary, to deal with the Russian aviation interests on behalf of Pan Am."

I was completely flabbergasted, though, in retrospect, I shouldn't have been. Some mysterious hand—unless I missed my guess, it was Bill MacCracken's—was manipulating my career and recommending me for just such a job.

For a moment, I lost my concentration. Then I tuned back in as Trippe spoke: ". . . An international airline could perform certain strategic services for the Soviet government—something the government cannot do on its own now, nor could it fund. Pan American could provide such services, a route from Alaska, over the Aleutians and across Siberia, following, pretty much, the Trans-Siberian Railroad. The emphasis here will be on winter flying.

"You could take photos of flat areas near cities, where airports could be built as well as radio towers. So the trip has to be done in winter as a feasibility study. Remember, this is land flying. To be able to fly east to west from North America to Europe by a northern route over land would be extraordinary."

He paused and looked at me, his eyes piercing through my skull. "I know what you're thinking. Why should Pan Am put so much responsibility on a twenty-seven-year-old man? Well, remember that Lindbergh was only twenty-five when he flew the Atlantic. He is now Pan Am's technical director. He thinks highly of you, too, as do Priester, Bixby, and MacCracken."

We kept talking for a few more hours and finally he said, "Well, Henri, would you tackle this trip? Do you feel up to it?"

"Yes," I said as positively as I could.

"There is a handsome bonus in this for you. Get together with Ann Archibald for your visa, and she'll tell you the people to see for a briefing. It will be up to you to order everything you need. There will be no publicity. Tell no one where you are going.

"This is one trip I wish to evaluate myself, personally, with Mac-

Cracken, but without the knowledge of anyone else in the company. The purpose of this trip is to be kept secret. It is strictly between you and me. Go to it and good luck."

What I didn't know until years later was that I was walking into a stew of diplomatic intrigue. In 1931, Juan Trippe had tried to establish a relationship with the Russians, who turned him down until the United States officially recognized the Soviet Union. After Roosevelt took office in 1933, the United States did recognize the Soviet Union. The Russians then made overtures to Juan Trippe about establishing an airline from Nome, Alaska, to Moscow. But now the United States government refused to sanction any deals until the USSR resolved its pre-Revolutionary debts to the United States.

On one side was the angry Russian bear, on the other side was an angry Uncle Sam. And me, I was in the middle—the little Dutch boy with a finger in the dike.

With only ten days for preparation, I enrolled in a crash course to learn Russian at a nearby language school. It was one-on-one instruction from 4:00 P.M. until midnight. During the day, I met with a variety of Pan Am people. I met with Arctic explorer Vilhjalmur Stefansson regarding the heavy clothing required for Arctic travel. Trippe's secretary consulted with me to work out a schedule and travel arrangements such as passport, visa, and letters of introduction to ambassadors. I took along a new 35-millimeter Leica camera with an extra-long-range lens, plus two dozen rolls of high-speed Kodak film. I was stuffed with foreign currencies and methods for obtaining more through U.S. consuls along the way.

On the evening of November 21, 1933, I took the Pennsylvania Railroad from New York to Columbus, Ohio. There I boarded a Trans Continental Airways (now called TWA) trimotor Ford and flew into Tulsa, Oklahoma. The following day, I rode the Santa Fe Railroad to Clovis, New Mexico. There was a twenty-four-hour delay until I boarded a Los Angeles Airways twin-engine plane to the City of Angels, where I had dinner with Howard Hughes.

The last U.S. leg was a train trip to San Francisco to board the *Mariposa* of the American-Australian Steamship Line. The date was November 25. The cabins were tiny, and I sometimes felt I had to back into the room just to fit next to my luggage. We traveled in fine weather to Hawaii and after a two-day stop, headed into rough seas for the trip to Yokohama, Japan.

There wasn't much to do except study Russian or keep a log about the weather. Unfortunately, no one on the ship spoke Russian, so I couldn't practice my pronunciation. As one of the few passengers who didn't get seasick, I usually dined with the captain or one of the officers. In order to keep the plates of food from falling off the table, the stewards kept the tablecloths wet.

At Yokohama, the weather was still awful—a mixture of snow and sleet was falling. During my two-day stopover, I could do little shopping or sightseeing, so I stayed snug at the Hotel Marumitsu until I could board the Russian ship *Amursky*. It was another small ship, with even smaller cabins. But the crew made up for it with plates of steaming hot borscht, caviar, and stew.

The Sea of Japan was even worse than the Yokohama trip, and the pitching and rolling ship in windswept high seas was frightening. The one good aspect of this leg was that most of the passengers and all of the crew spoke Russian. We spent Christmas Day aboard the *Amursky*, and the captain threw a party. Unfortunately, a rolling ship and vodka don't mix and many passengers left in a hurry. The seas were now so bad that the captain announced we might have to dock at Nakhodka instead of Vladivostok; weather conditions were worse at Nakhodka, so we made it back to Vladivostok.

Once more, luck and faith were on my side as we sneaked into Vladivostok on a pitch-black night and finally docked. I had learned two sets of idioms; one was how to curse in Russian when we bounced like a cork on the high seas, and the other was a prayer of thanks when we made it to safety.

By morning, the decks were crawling with immigration and customs inspectors, and all the foreigners were checked inside out. Every suitcase was opened, checked for false bottoms. Bottles were opened and examined. Next, my papers went through close scrutiny.

It was the following evening when we were finally taken on a little old, decrepit bus to the Vladivostok Hotel. No one smiled much. It was too cold. Water froze on those men with mustaches. The bed was smaller than a youth's bunk and my legs extended beyond the mattress. And there was no heat. When I pleaded in Russian to the chambermaid, and aided by a few kopeks, I was given a torn comforter. The bathroom felt like the inside of a refrigerator.

Next morning when I awoke, there was a pitcher and bowl to wash in. The water was frozen. Luckily, with my blond beard, I could avoid shaving for a few days, but to wash, I had to break up the ice in the pitcher.

My first morning's breakfast was simple and hot, and just when I was enjoying my *chai* (hot tea), I was called to the immigration office. The guards were courteous but thorough. In appearance, they looked more Mongol than European-Russian, but that was to be expected, as this part of Siberia was sitting on northern China.

Hearing different dialects, I was informed there was no "true" standard Russian language—it was a variety of languages and dozens of dialects. The Russians were always gracious in helping me with their language. A few spoke English, but nobody spoke Dutch, Hungarian, German, or Spanish.

It turned out this was one of the worst winters in Vladivostok history. My trip was on hold, as the Trans-Siberian train had been delayed by mountainous snowdrifts. But Vladivostok, though bitterly cold, was navigable. I went sightseeing with some of the other ship's passengers who were also awaiting the train.

At the time, Vladivostok, with a population of just over 100,000 people, was the largest Russian city on the Pacific coast. It was surprising to find any industry there, but we soon learned of a furniture factory and a pharmaceutical manufacturing plant, which made products from trees, spotted deer antlers (for special health cures), plants and roots indigenous to the region.

Because of the large number of commercial fishing boats, there were stores and kiosks catering to their needs, from boats to nets to sails to anchors. Established in 1860 as a city, Vladivostok was obliged to become self-sustaining, as Moscow was some 5,780 miles away.

While having breakfast on January 2, 1934, I was told to prepare to leave. The train totaled nineteen cars and was pulled by three engines. We were told to expect fierce weather all the way. Aboard the sleeping car, I had my own table, which, surprisingly, held a vase with a fresh flower in it.

The train traveled north and then, after several long stops because of high winds and heavy snowfalls, moved to Khabarovsk. It curved around the River Khor above the northern section of China, heading west-southwest, moving toward Irkutsk on the southern tip of Lake Baikal, the largest freshwater lake in the world.

Not forgetting the purpose of the trip, I took copious notes and photographs. The horrendous weather made it an unsafe place to fly in the winter. The train had many working women, each pushing a rolling table holding a large copper samovar. They dispensed tea to passengers, and the tea was kept hot by smoldering coals around the samovar. There were cookies as well. It was indeed friendly.

The one or two times I left "first" class to visit the working-class quarters, everything was downgraded—except the hot tea. In third class, just the bare necessities were available. But the people, once they learned you were a foreigner and not with the OGPU (secret police), welcomed you with *Da comrade* and hugs and kisses. Having been tipped off by my Russian-language teacher, I came prepared with small gifts from the States. The people loved "their generous American friend" and they answered all my questions about the rivers, lakes, mills, mountains, the weather, and the general lay of the land.

I knew that Lindbergh had flown across Siberia on behalf of Pan Am, but this had been done in the summer under different weather conditions. He was hailed as a hero. I was here disguised as a sightseer who in reality was—what? An advance man? A commercial spy?

At Irkutsk, the train stopped to give passengers a chance to stretch and shop. I bought some gifts for my family, warming up at the stoves along the aisles. The locomotives were at the rear of the train, so I went back to take a look. They were puffing huge clouds of steam; while inspecting them, the train began to pull out. I had completely forgotten it was a ninety-minute stop. Just like a Keystone Kop comedy, I began to chase the train in the snow, and when I reached the rear locomotive, I started to climb into the cab. "*Nyet*," said the fireman, giving me a shove.

"I'm a passenger," I shouted in English. The train was gathering speed and hot cinders from the other two locomotives were singeing my face. The engineer got into the act as they tried to push me off. I clung on desperately, speaking to them in ten languages, forgetting for the moment I could speak Russian. Suddenly, I shouted in Russian, "*Ya iz Nyoo Yorka*" ("I'm from New York"). They smiled through smoke-stained faces and let me stay.

The engine was burning wood, so I pitched in to keep the fire going. The engineer was looking ahead, then looking at me and laughing. He took out a mammoth black bread sandwich, broke off half and handed it to me. We were comrades for the next thirteen hours and snow-bound three times until we reached Cheremkhovo, where I got off. *"Balshoye spasiba,"* I said. "Thank you".

At Novasibirsk, I saw something unusual. Local people were climbing onto the train. It seems that some cars were stocked with food items and novelties and the locals were the customers. Each local carried an *oyoska* (a bag) to carry purchases. The fastest-selling item was a special sausage. To mark the end of the visit, a special "people off" bell rang several times to clear the train.

Then new passengers came aboard. A beautiful woman in her forties, with her two look-alike daughters in their twenties, came into my compartment and sat opposite me. They were bundled up in sables with pert sable hats. The women's features were exquisite: high Slavic cheekbones, flawless skin, black hair, and coal-black eyes, eyes with a slight almond shape to them. The girls were slender and cut from the same cookie mold as their mother.

I said nothing and just watched them get settled. This was a Communist country, with everyone supposedly equal, but I doubt if many elegant women in New York or Paris or London dressed better than the mother and daughters. We were well on our way when the mother invited me to join them. They spoke only Russian so I stumbled along and they laughed charmingly,

I ordered *half-chai* (tea with whole grapes added plus jelly) and cookies for all. The mother did have a few halting English words, and we tried to introduce ourselves. For the next eight days, we played cards and games on the little table. During the day, we shared the same compartment, at night they had the room to themselves and I went next door to my upper berth. It was a wonderful way to pass the time and increased my understanding of Russian. They told me of the history of Siberia, its people, the wars, the cultures and the sorrow of the poorer classes, and the cruelty of the Cossacks. I enjoyed their company for three weeks.

Throughout the train, there was warm informality. Women dressed comfortably in housecoats, men in a variety of coarse-woven but comfortable clothes. Some, particularly young soldiers, ran up and down the aisles to exercise their muscles. Besides the shopping for the locals, there were several doctors on board, and at every long stop, the villagers visited them for their ailments or to get medication. The railroad, started in 1891, was the only link that tied the country together. Trippe was right. This country could use an air passenger service—if it could survive the weather.

On occasion, the train was delayed because of a major snowdrift and snowplows were called in to free us. My lovely Russian ladies were perfect as they cooperated in letting me take pictures of them against important backgrounds or flat areas near large cities. In all, we stopped at 120 towns and cities.

The Trans-Siberian Railroad was a modern miracle considering the conditions under which it existed. It played a major role in developing mining, timber, and fishing industries, as well as supplying food and manpower to build the cities and explore for more rich ore and oil fields. Siberia's greatest resource was Lake Baikal itself; it contained 20 percent of all the fresh water in the world.

With it came the permafrost (where the ground never thawed out) and the extremes of weather with long winter nights and icicles that formed around your breath. This was a country for hardy people only—but I could see that an airline under these conditions was not feasible. Nevertheless, I did my duty to Juan Trippe and continued my scouting.

The food consisted mainly of sausages, herrings, wonderful breads, borscht, cheeses, and kumquat pickles. Near the railroad stations, there were *stolovayas* (workers' cafés), where the main fare was hot soup, potatoes, and vodka. Prices seemed high.

Other than my lovely ladies, few of the other passengers got too friendly. Perhaps they were afraid of me, a stranger who spoke a foreign tongue. I did make the acquaintance of one man whose name I've long forgotten. He was about thirty and he was returning to Omsk from Vladivostok. During our one conversation, he attributed the popularity of the railroad to the amount of leisure it offered.

"For many days [he counted off on his fingers], I can do exactly as I please. I don't have to answer to my boss. I don't have to answer to my wife. The train stops at Omsk and I can have a visit with my brother. And I can play all the chess I want."

I didn't play well enough to interest him, so he studied his chess manual and played with the other passengers. He was planning to teach the game to his son. Toward the evening, he treated himself to two carafes of cognac and, I presume, slept soundly.

The chief conductor on the train was an amiable, ex-soccer player who spent his free time fussing with his extensive coin collection, to which I contributed some American coins. I learned from him that another railroad was being built from Baikal to the Amur River, approximately two thousand miles long. It was intended to open up large resources of iron ore, gold, diamonds, and oil that had hitherto been inaccessible. The railroad was called the BAM, and had just been started. It was scheduled to be completed in 1985. He told me that airplanes were used in the summer only, but the railroad would be the mainstay source of supply.

During my trip, I seldom saw the sun, but there was no shortage of snow and ice. The windows were frosted over and I could only take pictures when the train stopped or was stuck in deep snow. I discovered there was some kind of radio communication when we got stuck and a snowplow on a locomotive arrived to free us. Once, we were stuck for forty-eight hours when the snowplow itself was snowbound during a blizzard.

Conditions were below what were considered minimums for safe flying. While it's true that a plane flying at ten to fifteen thousand feet was usually traveling at 40 below zero, the blinding snow, the gale winds, and lack of visual landmarks made land flight virtually impossible with the current equipment.

Six weeks later, on February 16, we arrived at the Leningrad station in Moscow. After my luggage had been carefully packed, two customs/immigration officials (or secret police) entered our compartment and asked for my passport and visa, then went through my belongings. One of them put some of my aftershave lotion on his face. I said in Russian, "Well, you look better now."

They laughed, and asked where I was staying: "Khastimitz Hotel." "*Kharasho*" ("Okay"), said one, and off I went.

Again, the hotel room was small and freezing, not quite Siberia but not far from it. Wearing two pairs of long underwear plus my overcoat and a blanket provided by the hotel, I managed to get some sleep. In the morning, the chambermaid brought in a pot of *chai* to fill up my teapot. As there was no hot water, I drank half my tea and shaved with the other half.

After breakfast, I tried to contact William C. Bullitt at the American embassy, but he would not arrive for another two days. I was anxious to get his help to meet the officials who could grant Pan Am permission to fly across Siberia on a round-the-world route. After I obtained that letter, it would be up to Trippe to fight it out with the U.S. government officials.

I decided to wander around the GUM department store and pick up some gifts for my family. The store was crowded, and like most American department stores, the toy department was the most popular. There was little variety, but they had plenty of tricycles and other toys.

At the perfume counter, I got a pleasant surprise, for there were my "three ladies" waiting to be served—Olga, the mother, and her two daughters, Khatanga and Gulmira. *"Zdrahz stvooite"* ("Glad to see you"), I said.

As we began to wander around, everyone seemed to know them and bowed to them. This puzzled me. They wore beautiful dresses and furs, so these were not underprivileged peasants. It was while we were having *chai* and cookies that I was informed that the mother was Olga Shostakovich, a relative of the famed composer.

Olga had suspected that I was no ordinary tourist. She hinted at it once but made no further comments. I did not admit anything. I was dragged along to their house for dinner and an after-dinner musicale. There were numerous other guests and luckily none spoke English, so I would not be questioned. I struggled with my Russian, but offsetting that, I had a beautiful girl on each arm.

The next day, I did get to meet Bullitt, who went out of his way to make me welcome. I told him vaguely about my mission (as advised by Trippe) and that I was merely an emissary to set the stage for the time the situation would be resolved. He was encouraging. He called in his staff and asked them to make arrangements for me to visit the Kremlin's "Union of Aviation"—the Civil Air Fleet.

The ambassador was kind enough to ask about my welfare and what I was doing to keep occupied in Moscow. When he heard about the Shostakovich family, he warned me to be careful about whom I met and where. "If they invite you out, be careful what you say. The city is loaded with government agents spying on foreigners. Don't get into any arguments about the merits of democracy over communism. You're a guest here."

The staff at the American embassy briefed me on the letter Juan Trippe had written to the Union of Aviation Air Civil Fleet in 1931. One aide also briefed me on Washington's official position regarding the debt Russia owed to the United States. Then the staff inquired as to the real reason for my visit. They made it clear that Trippe was not trusted in Washington and President Roosevelt was not overly fond of him.

The situation was tricky. I didn't want to get Pan Am into trouble, so I stuck to generalities. In other words, I was trying diplomatically to find out what the status was about future cooperation.

The intensive briefing lasted three hours. The group of three men and a secretary must have been satisfied as they arranged for an official visit four days hence. Once more, I was warned to be careful with whom I talked, as the secret police were everywhere—even at my hotel, which was staffed with informers.

Afterward, Ambassador Bullitt had staff members squire me on a guided tour of Moscow, from the museums to Gorky Park, the Bolshoi. Though I love music, the only event that put me to sleep was the opera *Boris Godunov*. On my free evenings, I spent time preparing Pan Am's conditional proposal and being comfortable with all salient points.

The day of reckoning came and the embassy staff informed me that I would be accompanied by a senior aide to Ambassador Bullitt and an interpreter. We drove over in an embassy car and made our way into the Kremlin, to the people involved in aviation matters. There were three desks and four people present.

I presented the letter and advised them it had not yet been approved by Washington, but I came with a proposal describing Pan Am's intentions. I emphasized again that this was not a negotiation but an agreement of principles—a sort of basis for working together in the future.

They agreed to study my letter and asked us to come back the next day at four o'clock. I had been warned several times that the Russians could be difficult and stubborn. I sensed this immediately. During the second meeting, I put Pan Am's cards on the table, much to the chagrin of the ambassador's aide. I proposed Pan Am cooperation with the Russian commercial air service in exchange for technical data, as well as radio guidance systems and accurate weather information stations.

I gave them Trippe's usual speech that Pan Am's air systems were a community effort on the part of the United States aviation industry, stressing the most productive aspects without going overboard. The golden key to Trippe's dream was the Northwest Passage—the passage across the Kuril Islands and Siberia.

After several more meetings with give and take on both sides, they came up with an official document. It approved Pan Am's original agreement if certain concessions that Russia wanted could be handled through the American embassy and okayed by Washington. This was way beyond my mission. All I wanted was an agreement to talk in principle. Instead, I had the final agreement.

My secret prayers were more than answered. The only worry was that the agreement, when revealed, would expose Trippe's "chosen instrument" program; in other words, Pan Am would be the sole foreign air system for the United States. I was obliged to seal the agreement by drinking with these men—a tumbler full of vodka. The staff carried me back to the hotel, 175 pounds of snoring deadweight. While I slept, they were considerate enough to prepare the papers I was to bring back. Next morning, a light-headed Dutch-American teetotaler was carted to the railroad and put on a train to Warsaw, Poland. The tiny compartment had a bouquet of roses and a touching letter from the Shostakovich ladies.

There was a great amount of snow, and the weather had not let up. It was still bitter cold. What bothered me most was the noisy clickity-clack of train wheels over the rails. Steel rails shrink in freezing weather, and there were gaps between them like in Siberia. It was driving my hangover crazy.

The stops in the big cities, like Minsk, attracted many people to the train. Everyone was looking to buy "special cooked Moscow sausage." But I never did get to taste it. Finally, we reached Warsaw and my headache abated. When I was young, I had been there with my mother, so I checked in at the hotel where we had stayed. Later, I discussed my trip with U.S. ambassador John Cudahy.

That next morning at breakfast, I ran into a group of German businessmen who had taken the same train from Moscow and with whom I had shared a soft drink and a general discussion of aviation (in German). One of them had commented that KLM was the oldest airline in Europe—if one could ever find out where the airline operated. It was a big secret.

By coincidence, we were all headed for Berlin, so we changed trains together. They must have had something to do with aviation as they kept talking about it. I made doubly sure not to expose myself or my Pan Am connection.

"People are still afraid to fly," said the oldest man.

"It would still be nice if one could fly around the world on a plane—"

"—in eighty days?" Everyone laughed.

"Machines would have to be more reliable."

"It would increase business if things could be transported rapidly—like flowers, perishable foods, sorely needed medicines . . . and businessmen in a hurry to conclude deals."

It was an interesting exchange, and they pointed out things I was not yet aware of. We talked of the possibility of flying from Warsaw to Berlin by KLM, if only the weather would clear up.

"Germany is starting Lufthansa, an airline like KLM, and soon there will be connections across Europe." It was a bit of information that would interest Juan Trippe.

In Berlin, I transferred to the Paris train, and this time met up with Frenchmen returning home from a business trip to Frankfurt. We discussed aviation (in French), and they were just as interested in the expansion of aviation as the Germans and Americans.

When I reached Paris, the weather was beginning to warm up. At the travel agency, I learned that the French ocean liner *Normandie* would be leaving from Le Havre for New York in four days. I purchased a ticket and went to Le Havre to wait until the ship arrived and was ready for boarding. Unfortunately, the weather kicked up again and I boarded the ship during a downpour.

The ship may have been the last word in luxury, but when we sailed across the turbulent English Channel the following day, dishes started jumping off the tables and crashing to the floor. The Atlantic was not as rough, but it was nevertheless rocky. Still, I enjoyed my twelve days on board, eating exquisite French food, tasting (not drinking) classic wines, and enjoying the company. Flying was still in its infancy, so I would not betray any loyalty to say I enjoyed myself.

Though I sent a wire to Pan Am specifying when I would arrive, there was no one to greet me when we docked in New York Harbor. We disembarked around 6:00 P.M. and I taxied to the hotel. Because getting around Moscow, Warsaw, and Berlin was so difficult, I thanked God for New York taxis. I was bursting with news, and when I phoned and found the offices closed, everything had to remain bottled up.

Next day, Trippe's secretary told me the boss was in Washington negotiating some new routes and would be back next day. I bumped into Vilhjalmur Stefansson and we spent an afternoon discussing weather and clothing. Priester found me and got me into discussions on the new plans for a China Clipper. I wasn't certain he knew about my mission, so I said nothing to him.

Next morning, I was called to Juan Trippe's office and found Stefansson there. Trippe closed the door. He said, "Good morning," and then he started a harangue about competition. He said the Europeans were gaining in the Orient very quickly and the French were in Indochina, the Dutch were in Java, and British Imperial Airways had flown to Port Darwin, Australia, in partnership with Qantas and had agreements for landing rights in Cairo.

"Now Europe will soon be eight days away from Asia by air," said Trippe. An opportunity will be lost if Pan Am, with the finest planes ever built, is not there to take the lead.

"Dammit! The northern route through the Orient is still blocked. My dialogue with Japan Air Transport Company about landing rights has fallen through—the air minister has denied access to Japanese territory and its waters to foreigners.

"Now our State Department won't let us move in Russia until the debts are satisfied. So, what I am proposing to do is make a route from California to China through the mid-Pacific."

It was common knowledge, that Trippe got angry if things did not proceed according to plan—his plan. Therefore, no one in the company challenged his "one man rule."

I read my report, explaining in minute detail that there was little or no possibility of making a profit without special equipment and extraordinary personnel to operate in 40-to-60-degrees-below-zero weather.

"Some time in the future, when planes can fly at higher speeds at higher altitudes above the weather, it might become more economically feasible."

"Okay," said Juan Trippe, "we'll talk about it some more. Now let's get to work, we've got an airline to run." He made no comment about my seven months of travel around a frozen world and the agreement I brought back. It was the first of many secret, impossible missions I would undertake on behalf of Juan Trippe. Not once did he ever say, "Thank you."

CHAPTER 11

My Funniest Moments in Flight

MY HEART was set on becoming a captain in the shortest possible time. It required five thousand hours as co-pilot in the right-hand seat on scheduled flights before I would be eligible. While I confided in no one about my Russian trip, word had somehow gotten out that I was the new "troubleshooter" for Pan Am. At the same time, my buddies, who earned their co-pilots' wings long after I did, were now amassing hours in their logbooks faster than I was. They would make captain before I did.

Though I had been scheduled to work in South America, it had been canceled because of my trip to Russia. Now I found myself back on the line. My friends, who had buddied up with the captains in my absence, were being selected for trips before I was—that is, unless one of them took ill or had a hangover. A couple of them had been fired for being caught smoking cigarettes while on duty and in uniform. This was a no-no in Priester's book.

To make up hours, I told the operations manager I would be available for any trip I could clock as official hours. This led to some dull trips to Cuba and South America, but for countable hours. But not all of the "special" flights were dull, particularly those where the call of nature had to be answered.

On one, I was assigned to an S-38, where a young couple, related to the Gautier Funeral Home in Miami, wanted to get married in an airplane at five thousand feet. Not anxious to get involved in a publicity stunt, I inquired whether it really was a stunt or a genuine desire to marry at five thousand feet. I was assured it was the latter.

There were some rain clouds on the wedding day, so as a precaution, I brought along some red ribbon from my sister's sewing box. When the minister, the bride and bridegroom, and the wedding party were seated in the tight quarters of the plane, I insisted that the groom tie the ribbon through the wedding ring.

"You're weird," said the young man.

"Sure, all pilots are wacky," I replied. I wasn't going to spoil his wedding day by telling him I expected turbulence. And turbulence we got. As we worked our way up to five thousand feet, somebody brought out a bottle of champagne, though I had warned them to leave all liquor behind. Confiscating the bottle was irksome.

When we reached the right height, the bridal couple and minister rose. Suddenly, there was a downpour and the plane began to bounce around. The couple, swaying in front of the minister, had no choice but to sit down. When it calmed somewhat, the ceremony started all over again. And the turbulence started again. This time the minister got violently ill—all over the plane.

My co-pilot took him to the john to clean up. I flew out to sea, hoping to find calmer weather, when the plane began to bounce around the sky. Now everyone was throwing up and there was a line in front of the toilet. Then the bride screamed, "Why do we have to get married in a plane? I don't even want to get married."

Her friends tried to calm the hysterical woman. I went still farther out, looking for calm air. With full tanks, the plane could stay aloft for three hours, but we were now down to half tanks. I knew we had to get this ceremony over with and still have enough fuel to get home. I finally found a patch of sun and calm air. I flew in a lazy circle to port as the minister performed the ceremony. As the bridegroom was about to put the ring on her finger, we again hit turbulence. The ring flew out of his hand, and before it bounced into the bilge and was lost forever, the maid of honor grabbed the red ribbon. A scowling groom put the ring on the bride's finger ribbon and all.

Then the bride threw her flowers. The bouquet hit me in the back of the neck. The plane took an unexpected dip. I tossed it back minus some blossoms. A young bridesmaid caught the second throw.

We hit more bad weather on the way back, and everyone was pale and sick and finally happy to be back on the ground. Except the bridegroom. "You sonofabitch, you did that on purpose. I'm gonna sue you. Wait till I get you into the funeral parlor."

And, of course, the "nonpublicity" wedding turned out to be a front-page story featuring the funeral parlor. But I did get to kiss the bride.

My second threatened lawsuit came on another special flight. In May 1936, Mr. Critchley, Pan Am's operations manager, tracked me down and told me he could help me add a lot of time to my logbook. With Leffingwell as co-pilot, I was assigned to fly a number of speleologists to Yucatán, Mexico, where they would explore the famous caves of Mérida. Because there were only ten in the group, we decided to use the Sikorsky S-41, NC-784Y. It was the same as the S-38 but with bigger engines and capable of carrying more passengers.

The members of this cave explorers' group turned out to be between seventy and eighty years of age, all very knowledgeable and charming. The plane could accommodate twelve passengers; they sat on wicker seats, and as the cockpit was open about halfway, the captain and co-pilot were visible to the passengers.

Our flight plan was to fly to Havana, refuel, and go on to Yucatán. The passengers requested that we fly low so they could spot marine life. This we did, as I pointed out schools of fish and turtles. In Havana, the airport manager gave them piña coladas and the airport hostess presented everyone with red-and-white-speckled roses. So far, so good.

After we were airborne, one of the passengers went back to the toilet, which was quite primitive. It was constructed so that when you sat down, little flaps would spread open like the shutter on a camera lens. Then, when you stood up, they would close. Basically, they were not much better than small rural privies—that is, the little house behind the big house. If you weren't careful, the flaps made it a bear trap. And when you hit an air pocket, the water in the toilet shot through the top. There were no stewards on the flight, just the captain and co-pilot, who were not only required to fly the plane, but to look after the needs of the passengers.

Suddenly, there was an animal-like scream from the toilet. "Captain, Captain! What's wrong with this toilet? I got my testicles caught." Leffingwell said with a big smile, "He wants the captain."

I charged back down the narrow aisle to investigate. Meanwhile, the victim was shrieking like a banshee, using the most awful language. He was snared by the flaps, and the harder he tried to free himself, the tighter the trap. I said, "I'll hold down the toilet and keep the flaps open. When you're free, jump up."

He wasn't listening as he continued struggling, unable to escape. His derrière was stuck to the toilet seat like a suction cup, his pants down, his face red while he screamed. Again I held the toilet down and told him to push off. Finally, I pulled him up with a tremendous yank and freed him.

He began screaming, "YOU DECAPITATED ME, YOU DECAPITATED ME!"

Meanwhile, the toilet action reversed itself and my nice, crisp white uniform was drenched with everything in the toilet. Calmly, I said, "You are not emasculated, sir, you're still intact."

"I'm going to sue you," he shouted. "And you stink."

I had a change of clothes in my overnight bag up front and I managed to exchange clothes while sitting in the wheel-holder's seat, listening to Leffingwell's hysterical laughter. In the background, over the noise of the engines, I could hear screaming, "I'm suing Pan Am, I'm suing that goddamn pilot."

The remainder of the trip was not exactly pleasant. Upon our arrival at Yucatán, I approached the passenger and apologized for his inconvenience. "After all," I said, "you're too well hung for our little toilets."

He laughed so hard he told me to forget it. Of course, I reported the incident when I returned to Miami and was called to account by Priester. When I told him what had occurred, he said, "I guess we need a new toilet design for our passengers. Henri, investigate the matter and draw up designs for a new toilet. After all, you already have the experience."

There is another story about toilets that took place a few years later, but which I was reminded of recently. I was attending a dinner in Palm Beach at which Monsignor Maestrini of the local church was to make a speech. I didn't recognize him, but he remembered me—in his speech. He opened up with the anecdote of a trip he made as a young priest in the thirties on a Pan Am China Clipper ship bound for China. After eight or nine hours of flying, he wondered why the captain hadn't passed down the aisle to use the toilet facilities.

"Being a curious man, I went to the flight deck and asked the captain how come he didn't use the toilet on such a long flight. Was he, in fact, a camel?

" 'No,' said the captain, 'I use a peepee tube, which is up front for that purpose.' He showed it to me and I asked if I could use it.

"The captain said, 'Of course—but are you allowed to spread Holy Water on the Pacific?' "

When the howling stopped, he pointed at me and told the audience that I was the captain on that flight. This was forty years later.

CHAPTER 12

Bigger, Better, Faster, Higher

WHENEVER I RAN into Priester, he'd always spend a few minutes chatting with me. In my eyes, he was no longer a "tyrant" but a meticulous engineer with a penchant for perfection. For a couple of years, he'd been mentioning a new era of Pan Am planes that would fly higher, faster, and farther than anything on the line.

Of course, the driving force was Juan Trippe, who would come up with some impossible aircraft idea and it was up to Priester to fulfill the impossible dream. The same held true for mind-boggling (at the time) air routes. One day, Trippe looked at the world globe in his office and figured out that the safest way to Europe was with short hops to Labrador, Greenland, and on to Europe. He discussed it with Lindbergh, who not only concurred but offered to pioneer such a trip. He and his wife, Anne, made careful plans and then took off in their Sirius seaplane on a successful, five-month, thirty-thousand-mile trip that proved the route was feasible.

Besides extending the limits of new routes, Trippe also extended the performance of his aircraft. The minute he had the most advanced aircraft in the world under construction, he extended the range and speed of the next design and promptly put it under construction. If Juan had a secret motto it would be "Bigger, better, faster, higher, and farther." Then he would negotiate a contract to have the next design in production.

Thus, Trippe and Priester worked out the next generation of aircraft beyond the current Sikorsky S-42s, and sent specifications to all the

112

major aircraft manufacturers. The proposed plane was to be amphibious, with a minimum cruising speed of 145 miles per hour and a minimum range of twenty-five hundred miles. It would carry a crew of four, with twelve passengers, and carry three hundred pounds of mail. He had his eye set on foreign travel.

But Trippe's hidden agenda was to have a virtual monopoly, be the only American airline to control all foreign air routes. He wanted Pan Am to be America's "chosen instrument," and what better way than by owning the most advanced planes in the world?

Most American aircraft builders thought Trippe was crazy, the plane he wanted was impossible. It would be unable to take off with that payload, let alone reach the airspeed he demanded. Two builders didn't scoff at the idea. Pan Am was already using Sikorsky planes successfully, so Sikorsky was confident that a redesign and upgrade of his S-42 would win. His new seaplane would have a nineteen-ton hull and four 750-horsepower Pratt & Whitney engines designed into the wings. Additional gas tanks would be placed inside the aircraft, and his price would beat any competition.

But Glenn L. Martin felt his design of the M-130 was a bigger and better plane. He was renowned for being the third man in the world to fly a heavier-than-air machine.

Martin's projected craft would be the first one built to carry a payload equal to the plane itself. The twenty-six-ton plane, with four 800-horsepower Pratt & Whitney supercharged Wasp engines, had a range of thirty-two hundred miles nonstop and would buck 50-mile-per-hour headwinds at a speed of 130 miles per hour (the engines were later upgraded to 950 horsepower, so the Clipper, in an emergency, could fly on two engines). This was a plane that could span the Pacific nonstop with a full load of freight and passengers. While previous flying boats carried fuel in the pontoons, Glenn Martin designed "sea wings" from the hull to the waterline, which not only stabilized the seaplane but could carry 1,999 gallons of gasoline.

Always concerned with safety, he designed a double hull with watertight compartments. In the event the hull was damaged by a submerged obstacle, the plane could still remain afloat. (Fifty years later, oil companies, after numerous oil spills, would be compelled to do the same thing with their tankers.) Martin also added lockers for emergency equipment like fishing tackle, flares, shotguns, life rafts, and an emergency generator.

Trippe was excited about the Martin aircraft until he heard the price: three planes for $2 million. Reluctantly, he turned it down. It was during the Depression, and Martin, with a modern plant in Middle River, Maryland, had to have the order or face bankruptcy. His associates also knew that if he lowered the price, he would lose money and ruin the company.

Martin made the decision to stave off the banks and after some difficult negotiations with Trippe, agreed to build the plane for $417,000 each—a $1.25 million contract, with a promise of more orders to come. They went through eight different contracts before the final one was signed in 1932. Trippe also signed a contract for three Sikorsky S-42Bs, each one at half the price of the M-130.

Trippe, an avid reader and nautical history buff, named the planes "Clippers" after the old, speedy, American clipper ships that roamed the world engaging in the tea, tobacco, and silk trade; then he would append the country or city of destination before it, so a China-bound plane became the China Clipper.

Before the Clippers could span the Pacific Ocean, there was an incredible amount of work to accomplish. Pan Am purchased a fifteen-thousand-ton steamer as a supply ship. The *New Haven* was to be loaded with enough matériel to outfit three villages, complete with motor launches, diesel generators, water-distilling plants, and thousands of items from food to diesel oil, plus 500,000 gallons of aviation fuel. There were enough supplies to equip and sustain five air bases and 118 people, including construction workers, to build and equip them.

The ship left San Francisco and set sail for Honolulu on March 27, 1935. It reached its destination at the end of April. It took one month to build a terminal there, as well as a barge that was able to carry a load of four thousand gallons of fuel to refuel the seaplanes.

Later, the *New Haven* would go on to three islands—Wake, Midway, and Guam—after Trippe had convinced the U.S. government that an American presence in the area would serve not only civilian endeavors but the military as well.

Trippe never realized the consequences of his actions. The Japanese, considering the Pacific their own private "lake," were furious. But Pan Am plunged ahead, first on Wake, gaining momentum one day and suffering setbacks the next. Fresh water was usually nonexistent and deep wells only brought up seawater. The distillation plants didn't work and new systems had to be reconfigured on the mainland

and brought back to the islands. Also, it was impossible to grow anything on coral reefs and sand. Later, tons of topsoil were shipped to the islands to create gardens to grow fresh fruits and vegetables for staff and passengers. Five tons of dynamite were needed to clear away the coral reefs and make a channel for the seaplanes to land.

Guam was a different story. It was two hundred square miles and was already occupied by the U.S. Navy. Situated six hundred miles off the equator, it had once been used by the U.S. Marines and their flying boats, so there were existing hangars, workshops, and storerooms.

The next port was to be in Manila, in the Philippines. Docks were constructed of redwood poles set in oil drums filled with concrete. An effective solar water-heating system was built that worked well.

While this was going on, I was assigned to the Martin plant in Maryland to assist on the Clipper. I was startled by the size of the plane. There was a spacious lounge with three divisions: sleeping rooms, dressing rooms, and lavatories. The flight crew slept in bunks in the tail, so that five were always on duty while two slept. There was a modern galley to prepare hot meals, with sink, refrigerator, and electric grill. It was apparent that even though Martin was losing about $700,000 on the deal, he didn't cut corners. His reputation was that of a man who always pursued excellence, which is why the Army Air Corps selected his plant to build bombers.

Van Doozen, the Martin business manager, always referred to Juan Trippe as "a dirty red fox" because of his crafty way of trapping everyone to do things for him against their will.

I was fortunate to be on the plane for the trial runs to see how the various installations functioned. At that time, the plane was so advanced that we had to do our own proving as the CAB was not equipped to do it. Upon completion, the CAB approved the airworthiness of the Martin and we received the CAB number N14716.

True to form, after the three planes were built, Trippe infuriated Martin by telling him there would be no reorders. Martin faced bankruptcy, but the Army came through with a defense order and the factory was saved.

The Martin M-130 heralded in the new era of Clipper ships. Around this time, as I prepared to return to Miami, I received a hurry-up call from Priester to get to New York ASAP, where he gave me new orders.

"The Hawaiian and the Philippine Clippers are in Alameda, California. You were in Baltimore to certify the M-130, so you know how they're supposed to handle. Do some pilot training up and down the coast in the Philippine Clipper. When you're through there, I want you to go to the state of Washington and work on the new Boeing seaplane."

Boeing had built the B-15 for the Army Air Corps and believed it could be adapted to a seaplane for the relatively low cost of $550,000 each. They received a contract from Pan Am to build six.

The surest way to San Francisco was still by train. When I arrived there, I found about 150 people on the island of Alameda, many of them acquaintances or friends who worked at Pan Am. Of the pilots, I knew Terletsky and Lodeseen, and we generally got along well together. We flew up and down the coast of California so that in an emergency, if we had to return to San Francisco, we would recognize the coast from any angle.

Author's parents, Joseph
and Alice Keyzer-André,
on their wedding day,
April 5, 1905 in
Maastricht, Holland.
(*From author's files*)

Author, 22, on the 43rd floor,
Chrysler Building in New York City
after he was hired by André
Priester, chief engineer at Pan Am.
(*From author's files*)

Author at work at Pan Am in the early days. (*From author's files*)

Speaking at a Palm Beach affair, Monsignor Maestrini, right, spotted author, left, and told audience how forty years earlier Captain Henri Keyzer-André had flown him across the Pacific in the China Clipper. (*Photo by Mort Kaye Studios*)

Author in front of his home in Trinidad, 1942. (*From author's files*)

Charles Lindbergh, left, and Juan Trippe with their wives.
(*From author's files*)

William P. MacCracken, the author's mentor and close friend. Herbert Hoover appointed him his assistant secretary of commerce for aviation. When Hoover offered MacCracken pilot's license #1, aviation pioneer Orville Wright urged him to accept it. (*From author's files*)

1930. Juan Trippe, center, president of Pan Am, flanked by chief engineer, André Priester, left, and deputy chief engineer, John Steel, right. (*From author's files*)

Howard Hughes standing beside a plane he flew in air races. (*Courtesy of the National Air and Space Museum, Smithsonian Institution*)

The exhaust pipes on the Fokker F-10's flown by Pan Am often cracked. Author used oil drum steel to repair them. (*Courtesy Pan Am*)

A twin-engine Consolidated Commodore of the type used by author to practice flying. (*Courtesy Pan Am*)

Inspection team watching a new Martin aircraft being built at Twin Rivers Plant near Baltimore. Author is fifth man from left; Howard Hughes is at extreme right. (*From author's files*)

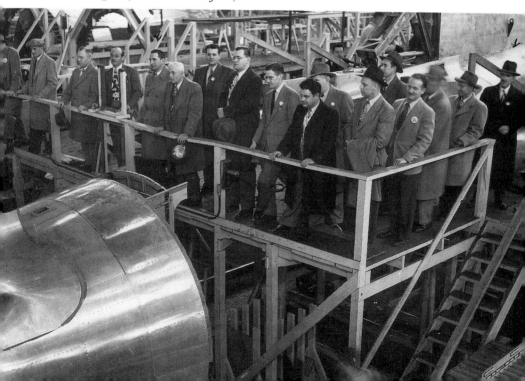

Above, author sightseeing at the Buddhist Temple of the Thousand Lanterns, Kyoto, Japan in 1958. Below, author dressed up as Santa Claus at a U.S. Embassy Christmas party in Tokyo. (*From author's files*)

CHAPTER 13

The Amelia Earhart Story, Part 1: The Web of Mystery

OVER A HALF century ago, on July 3, 1937, Pacific Western Hemisphere time, one of the great tragedies in aviation history occurred when Amelia Earhart and Fred Noonan disappeared somewhere in the Pacific while attempting to be the first to circumnavigate the globe at the equator.

The first leg of the flight, from east to west, was successful. The plane left San Francisco and landed in Honolulu. On the second leg, the flight was aborted after the plane ground-looped on takeoff from Luke Field in Honolulu. The plane was shipped back to the United States for repairs. On the second attempt, this time flying west to east, the plane flew to Miami, where Pam Am was asked to reevaluate the airworthiness of the aircraft. I was put in charge of the project.

It wasn't my first contact with Amelia Earhart. In 1928, when I was twenty-one, I was introduced to her when William P. MacCracken, under secretary of commerce for air, invited me to accompany him to welcome Wilmer Struts, the pilot, Louis Gordon, the mechanic, and Amelia Earhart, the aviator. They had just landed in the United States after crossing the Atlantic Ocean in a Fokker monoplane. It was spellbinding to meet the great "Lady Lindy," who, at age thirty-one, had electrified the world. Besides her courage, she was beautiful— slim, with a boyish, windblown haircut and an endearing smile. Like all the young men in America, I was in love with this flying daredevil.

Earhart set many records, won numerous trophies, and was given the Distinguished Flying Cross by the U.S. government, while the *National Geographic* gave her its highest gold medal.

Fred Noonan, her navigator, was a man with a smooth personality whom I met in 1931 at Pan Am's Dinner Key operations building. When I was starting pilot training, I was assigned to Fred Noonan, who was then Pan Am's instructor in celestial navigation. Because of my difficult name, he called me "Dutch." From him, I learned to handle the sextant and octant with great ease. He once told me, "I am not a pilot, but I can always tell you where we are and where we're heading." He often told me stories of how he learned navigation on ships. We had remained good friends even after he left the company.

Ninety percent of what I have to relate on the Earhart/Noonan mystery is based on fact, the other 10 percent is based on logic, leading to obvious conclusions. The story breaks down into two parts. The first part consists of the mysterious happenings in the Pacific over a period of several years before World War II; this became a shroud of intrigue that cloaked their disappearance far from the eyes and ears of the American public.

The second part takes place later, fifteen years after World War II, when I spent seven years in Japan as an emissary of the U.S. government to help set up Japan's civil aviation industry. During that time, I had learned to speak, read, and write Japanese fluently and made many friends there. One day, a Japanese official revealed to me, in confidence, the missing link—Japan's role in the mysterious disappearance of Amelia Earhart and Fred Noonan.

To understand the Earhart/Noonan story, it is necessary to fully comprehend the background and behind-the-scenes struggles between the United States and Japan for strategic military bases in the Pacific.

By 1935, almost everybody in the world knew a global war was imminent. Within a two-year period, the Nazis had assassinated the Austrian chancellor Engelbert Dollfuss; in a plebiscite, the German people had overwhelmingly voted for Hitler as *Führer*. The Nazis then repudiated the Versailles Treaty and began to build a massive army, navy, and air force.

Though Winston Churchill was warning the British Parliament

about the menace of German air power at that time, few in Great Britain were listening. The world was still in a deep Depression. Dramatically, in 1936, Germany annexed the Rhineland. In Asia, Japan was making such deep incursions into Chinese territory that Chiang Kai-shek was obliged to declare war on Japan despite fighting a revolution within his own borders. At the time, Europe and the United States were more apprehensive of Stalin and Communism than of Hitler and Nazism.

The Spanish Civil War began in July 1936. Soon Germany and Italy came to the aid of General Franco and the Spanish rebels. Germany supplied Franco with troops, massive supplies of munitions, plus military expertise and German pilots to fly their Stukas to dive-bomb and terrorize the civilian population.

Despite the Franklin D. Roosevelt presidency, Americans were mostly isolationist and generally wanted no part of foreign entanglements. The majority of the people, including most politicians, figured the coming war would be a million miles away, with the United States protected by the Atlantic and Pacific oceans.

In retrospect, America was in the war and didn't know it. Germany had been sending secret agents to America to foment trouble and fund pro-German political groups and religious leaders who favored Hitler's Germany. Meantime, the Japanese were stockpiling supplies and potential war material purchased in America; for several years before World War II, Japanese ships were lined up outside the port of Seattle waiting to load scrap metal.

It even took a long time for U.S. officials to comprehend that the Japanese would and did commit acts of sabotage in the United States while both countries remained at peace. Meanwhile, the FBI was uncovering evidence of Japanese sabotage, as was U.S. naval intelligence. These reports were flowing back to Washington. Externally, the government seemed to have its hands tied, while internally, the Navy had long concluded that war was inevitable and there was a growing need for military bases in the Pacific to counter Japan's hostile saber-rattling.

Action had to be taken swiftly, but in such a way so as not to offend Japan, with its powerful naval force. The Navy's conclusion was to "assist in the development of Civilian air routes and bases in the Pacific which in war time could be converted to military bases."

Concurrently, Pan Am was pressing the government for rights to islands in the Pacific to be used as refueling stops for trans-Pacific travel. The main problem was Juan Trippe himself. Assistant Secretary of State Adolf Berle, who disliked Trippe because of his manner and bullying tactics, said, "I do not trust Pan Am."

Secretary of the Interior Harold Ickes said, "Trippe is unscrupulous."

President Roosevelt was blunter still when he said, "Juan Trippe is the most fascinating Yale gangster I ever met."

The animosity between the President and the head of Pan Am was growing. Trippe was already suspected of collusion in getting mail subsidies from the U.S. Post Office, and was under investigation by Senator Hugo Black's committee. Postmaster General James A. Farley and the Black committee were thwarted in their investigation when a postal employee suspiciously set fire to twenty-four file drawers of mail contracts suspected of being tainted.

The postmaster summarily canceled all mail contracts—except for Pan Am, which received only a slap on the wrist and a reduction of 10 percent of its mail subsidy. Why? The answer was simple. A practical politician, Roosevelt was shrewd enough to realize that Pan Am might one day be a valuable asset in the Pacific.

The crux of the problem was that after World War I started, the Japanese Imperial Navy took over the Caroline Islands, the Marianas, and the Marshall group (formerly controlled by Germany), and laid "claim" to them. Known as Micronesia, these were islands in the western Pacific that were east of the Philippines and north of Melanasia. However, at World War I's end, the League of Nations refused to recognize Japan's claim, and instead gave it a mandate to set up responsible governments on the islands with no military buildup.

But the Japanese had another scenario. In retrospect, this was its first step toward a war with the United States. Japan refused to allow visitors to these islands. The frustrating part for the United States was that it had not joined the League of Nations and had no forum to challenge Japan's conduct in the Pacific.

But rumors and U.S. Navy intelligence sources persisted that Japan was building extensive military bases on these islands. There was no legitimate way the United States could confirm or deny this information. Courtesy visits by foreign naval ships were denied. By 1923, it was the Navy and Marines who decided that these islands and military installations posed a threat to U.S. security.

In an attempt to confirm the rumors, Marine Lieutenant Colonel Earl "Pete" Ellis was asked to visit the Marshall and Caroline islands posing as a German trader. He did, and what he found were heavily fortified islands. It confirmed an earlier report he had written predicting that Japan was preparing to attack the United States and would strike first at Pearl Harbor using aircraft carriers.

Unfortunately, Colonel Ellis was fatally poisoned on Koror in the western Caroline Islands. His warning was the first. The second warning came from General Billy Mitchell, who in 1923 tried to warn his superiors that enemy planes, flying off aircraft carriers, could destroy U.S. warships. He added that the next war would be in the Pacific, with the Japanese mounting a surprise attack on Pearl Harbor on a Sunday morning. Mitchell was court-martialed and his report remained classified for almost four decades.

By the early thirties, when the League of Nations finally got around to asking Japan why it would not allow visitors or inspectors to the mandated islands, Japan withdrew from the League. At that time, no member of the League was strong enough to challenge the might of Japan.

But there were other islands in the Pacific, and so a political chess game was started. At stake was the security of the United States. How could a militarily weak America "occupy and fortify" the surrounding islands without triggering a war with a highly militarized Japan? The United States, still in a deep Depression, was in no position physically, politically, or psychologically to go to war over a few coral reefs, let alone wage a war thousands of miles from its borders. Thus, another plan was needed, one that would arouse less concern from the Japanese than if the American military occupied the islands.

Roosevelt received a confidential report from the secretary of the navy that Pan Am had better aircraft and was better equipped than the U.S. Navy for aerial exploration with its weather forecasting and advanced aerial technology. And Pan Am had been clamoring to set up a commercial air route with island stops along the way to the Philippines and China. It was the right request at the right time. Pan Am was given five-year, renewable leases to build seaplane bases on Wake Island, Sand Island, Kingman Reef, and Johnston Atoll, all under the watchful eye of the Navy.

Wake Island was halfway between Midway and Guam. Originally explored by Americans in 1840 and claimed by the United States in

1899, it had been charted by the Navy in 1923 but was currently deserted. Pan Am suddenly had refueling stops at Guam, Wake, and Midway.

Enter the Pan Am Clippers. Japan was very much aware of what was taking place, but instead of making formal protests to the U.S. government, Japanese naval officers suddenly "aired" their protests in the Japanese press about Pan Am's routes in the Pacific: "This is an incursion into our sphere of influence; commercial airline seaports are easily convertible to Navy air bases."

Then the agitation moved from mere words to action as the confrontation heated up to a different level when it was announced that Captain Edwin Musick in a Clipper would make the first commercial flight to the Philippines on November 22, 1935. Just as the United States was furious at Japan's takeover of the mandated islands, Japan was furious at the United States and seething at Pan Am's commercial routes over what it considered "its" domain.

Japan then took some serious and dangerous steps to try to stop Pan Am before Musick's inaugural flight. A China Clipper, on a test flight off Alameda, California, on January 5, 1935, with Captain Sullivan at the helm, met with a serious accident. The plane was picking up speed in the water during a takeoff when a horrendous scraping noise was heard. The captain aborted the takeoff. On inspection, ten long, deep slices were discovered under the hull. An investigation revealed that the plane had run over a large concrete block that was porcupined with metal spikes and lay submerged just beneath the surface of the water. Luckily, the plane was saved and no one was hurt.

While it was not classified as sabotage at the time, there was no other explanation. How could this heavy, massive object find its way into a cleared channel in the exact path of the Clipper? Further investigation in the lagoon located other, similar obstacles directly along the flight path.

A year earlier, in 1934, the Japanese aircraft designer Kawanishi was working on a new seaplane, and along with top Japanese naval officers, was very much interested in Pan Am's S-42. The Japanese embassy in Washington, through the State Department, arranged for a courtesy visit by Japanese naval officers and engineers to the Sikorsky plant in Connecticut. When informed, the Navy quietly ordered that the plant not show the new planes to the visitors.

A year later, when the Japanese launched their new seaplane known as "Mavis," it proved to be a slightly larger, mirror copy of the S-42, from three-blade propellers to twin tail fins. U.S. intelligence officers learned that some parts of the design of the S-42 had become public knowledge through articles in aviation magazines, but many crucial top secret sections could have been obtained only through theft of American design plans by espionage.

Another mysterious happening took place when the FBI captured two Japanese agents who had sneaked onto a Clipper before a Pacific flight and were trying to change the calibration of an advanced direction finder developed by the radio genius Leuteritz. It was an attempt to have the plane lose its way and crash in an effort to discourage Pan Am flights in the Pacific.

The final straw was the mysterious disappearance of the Hawaii Clipper on July 29, 1938. When weekly flights from San Francisco to Hawaii, Guam, Manila, Midway, and China were becoming routine, the Hawaii Clipper left Guam in good weather. It unexpectedly vanished without leaving a trace.

A massive sea hunt took place and an oil slick and bits of wreckage were found, but they proved not to be part of the missing Clipper. If the aircraft had crashed, some evidence would have remained on the water. One theory stated that a Japanese kamikaze officer sneaked aboard and blew himself up with the plane; the most persistent theory was that two Japanese naval officers had stowed away on the plane, and hijacked it to a base several hundred miles away. The reasons for this scenario were more compelling: (1) Japanese naval forces had no amphibious plane of the caliber of the Clipper; (2) a Chinese man, after helping raise millions in the United States, was carrying an estimated $3 million in relief funds to Chiang Kai-shek; and (3) there was no way the Clipper, with its highly experienced crew, including a radio operator, would not have radioed if it had encountered trouble. Only a hijacking would have prevented this.

The FBI and other investigators refused to accept that a plane with the safety record of the Hawaii Clipper—which had just flown over five thousand miles, was well maintained by the Pan Am staff, and in close contact with Guam and other radio stations—could simply disappear.

There were, of course, other incidents, such as the subsequent emergence of the Japanese seaplane "Emily," which turned out to be an almost mirror copy of the Boeing China Clipper—with exact duplication of the Pratt & Whitney engines.

Against this festering Asian backdrop in 1936, enter Amelia Earhart, probably the most famous woman in the world. She was the holder of numerous flying records, from being the first lady to cross the Atlantic solo, to altitude records in a helicopter. Now, Amelia Earhart wanted to be the first person (male or female) to circumnavigate the globe.

George Putnam, Amelia Earhart's new husband, was a publicity hound and word soon appeared in the newspapers of her intentions. Her fame increased even further, and soon she could not fulfill all the requests for personal appearances. When Purdue University offered her a staff job as visiting counselor to women at the university in Lafayette, Indiana, she accepted. She was one of the first feminists to spearhead women's rights.

Earhart was so successful as a lecturer to women's groups on campus that the university trustees voted to offer her a grant of $50,000 toward a new plane to fly around the world. (It was later speculated that the U.S. government may have been behind the grant.) An excited Amelia accepted and immediately ordered the most advanced nonmilitary aircraft of its day, a twin-engine Lockheed Electra 10-E. Her first request was to have the ten passenger seats replaced with gas tanks, which, along with the wing tanks, gave the plane a range of forty-five hundred miles.

In July 1936, she officially took possession of the aircraft and never had second thoughts about flying around the world. Her plan soon went into effect. Putnam was asked to make arrangements with Standard Oil and Pratt & Whitney to store fuel and spare engine parts at various stops worldwide. The U.S. Navy eagerly offered to install a landing field at Howland, a small island in the Pacific just southeast of the mandated Marshall Islands.

She hired Paul Mantz, a brilliant aviator and movie stunt pilot, to be her technical adviser. For her navigator, she selected a man considered to be among the finest navigators in the world, Commander Fred Noonan, Pan Am's former top navigator who pioneered the early Clipper flights to the Philippines, Guam, Midway, and Hong Kong. In his forties, Fred had only recently been married, but he had his wife's blessing to make the historic trip.

When plans were complete, permission for the flight was granted by the U.S. Coast Guard, as well as authorizations from individual nations to land in Australia, New Zealand, and other countries along her route. She also agreed to take along Paul Mantz as co-pilot on the first leg of the flight from Oakland to Honolulu as part of the shakedown flight (this was merely a favor because Mantz's fiancée was on vacation there).

The plane took off on March 17, 1937, and landed fifteen hours, fifty-two minutes later at Wheeler Field in Honolulu. The crew rested for three days, and at Mantz's suggestion the plane was moved to Luke Field because of its longer runway. Mantz remained behind when Amelia and Fred prepared for takeoff to Howland Island on March 20. But the plane was overloaded and the runway was not long enough. When she realized the plane would not lift off the ground, takeoff was aborted. The Lockheed ground-looped and the undercarriage collapsed, damaging one wing and rupturing a wing tank. But cool-headed Amelia had cut the switches, which ended the danger of explosion. No one was hurt.

By coincidence, Captain Lodeseen and I, flying the China Clipper on a flight from Manila to Honolulu, arrived shortly after the accident. We checked into the Hawaiian Hotel, where we bumped into Fred Noonan. Over a beer, he told us about the crash, then, explaining that he had to return to the field, he suggested we join him. It had started to rain and it was pitch-black as we drove back with him. Then we entered the hangar to look at the shattered Electra.

The wheels were sheared off, and the undercarriage had suffered considerable damage. Both propellers were bent out of shape. The right wing was crumpled and the right engine mount was bent and twisted. Not only was there a crack in the wing gas tank, but the cabin gas tank had sprung a leak. All the equipment was in a pile on the floor of the hangar. I inspected some of the advanced radio and direction-finding equipment, which I knew came from a military source.

As I took stock, I questioned why there was no life raft among the equipment. The reason was that the Lockheed's past history indicated that this aircraft, with its normal gross load of 12,500 pounds, could not stay afloat longer than ten minutes. The Earhart plane carried a load of 16,500 pounds.

Aviation experts around the world expressed opinions of what had to be done to the Lockheed to prevent another aborted takeoff. I had some thoughts as well, but didn't get to voice them at that time. We returned to Honolulu and next day continued on our flight to San

Francisco. The broken bird was subsequently shipped to Lockheed for repairs at Burbank, California.

Everyone offered advice, but few authorities agreed on the cause of the accident or how to prevent it from happening again, which only agitated Amelia Earhart. Her aviation expert, Paul Mantz, maintained that the plane was overweight with a full load of fuel and could not pick up enough flying speed for takeoff. He could not advise her on how to correct the problem.

Amelia also consulted with Navy experts, and they recommended that the round-the-world flight should be in the reverse direction— from west to east. This was not really a "solution" to her problem, but it was broadly hinted later that the Navy was secretly involved with her flight.

Amelia made the decision to continue with Fred Noonan as her navigator despite her awareness that he had been fired from Pan Am for excessive drinking. George Putnam wanted to get rid of Noonan, but Amelia overruled him and insisted he stay. With only two people on the flight, Putnam was worried that Noonan could steal Amelia's thunder if he exploited the trip with a book and public appearances. Putnam then agreed to let Noonan continue, but only after he signed away his book and publicity rights. It was Earhart's flight, period.

Her second attempt started in Oakland on May 20, and after stops at Tucson and New Orleans, the plane finally landed in Miami on May 23. Juan Trippe had offered my services to help Amelia with her aircraft, so once again, I was pulled off a scheduled flight and assigned to assist Amelia Earhart in any way I could. I was certified by the Civil Aeronautics Board (CAB) to sign off an aircraft as airworthy after any changes or modifications.

When I met with her in Miami, she was arrogant and complained bitterly about the advice she received from all the so-called experts. I was in a bad mood myself, as I was losing flying time toward my captain's wings. Our meeting was not exactly pleasant. She was brusque and ill mannered. She questioned me and I answered her about my background and experience. Then she said, "Have you ever helped anyone else on a major flight?"

"Yes," I said.

"Who?"

"Well, I worked with Lindbergh on converting his land plane to a seaplane. I helped Laura Ingalls—"

"Laura Ingalls?" she said with disdain. Laura was another lady aviator with many flying records to her credit, including doing more loops and more barrel rolls than any other pilot, man or woman. These two women were in fierce competition.

"Yes, preparing her for her record-breaking trip around South America. I recommended more-powerful engines and made other adjustments to increase her speed by about eight miles an hour."

"Is that it?"

"No. I helped Howard Hughes prepare his plane for the Miami and Opa-Locka race. His plane simply was not fast enough. By changing the aerodynamics and making other corrections to increase the speed of his plane, he won the race."

"All right. My sinuses are bothering me, so let's start tomorrow morning at 9:00 A.M. sharp."

Next morning, she appeared more amiable. She had called Howard Hughes (who promptly notified me of the conversation and was very complimentary). We went on to inspect the plane, and I made copious notes, as I also remembered what I had seen of the plane in Honolulu. The following were my recommendations:

1. Because the plane must carry a gross weight of 16,500 pounds, each of her present engines was not powerful enough to keep the plane aloft if one engine failed. I recommended Pratt & Whitney's 550, HP SIHI, with new carburetors and heat doors for more power. Pan Am had just received delivery of several such engines, which were still packed in Cosmoline. She could buy two from Trippe.
2. Complete inspection of the fuel tank plumbing.
3. New direction gyros.
4. Strengthening of engine mounts and fire shields.
5. The installation of a trailing antenna for better radio reception and transmission.

I told Amelia how much this would cost, plus the weight of each part for her weight and balance record.

Her problem was money. Despite contributions and sponsors, she had been obliged to hock her house and everything she owned for this flight. Now she was faced with new modifications. Putnam was also strapped, though he was trying to line up more sponsors. The government's official contribution was to give her some very costly radio and direction-finding equipment. She could not afford all the extras I recommended.

That evening, she made several calls and was able to raise additional funds, although not enough. She told me she was still $2,000 short. At that point, I personally pledged the final amount to her.

The new, two-pitch propellers were flown in from Hamilton Standard; the Pratt & Whitney Wasp major engines, while new, had not yet been classified as secret by the U.S. government, or if they were, she was given permission to have them installed. For more power, these engines were built to use 100-octane aviation fuel for takeoff, and could switch to 80-octane for cruising.

Greg Askew of Pratt & Whitney supervised the installation of the engines and adjusted them to develop new takeoff procedures at 1,900 rpm, using twenty-eight inches of mercury. It would permit Amelia to lift off with sufficient power from a short runway. The 100-octane fuel was carried in a special tank to be used only for takeoff and climbing. This would have to be done at full throttle.

Everything was installed around the clock and tested, so I got little sleep during the reconditioning. I also insisted on rubber pads underneath the cabin fuel tanks to prevent crushing on the bottom in case of another ground loop. Amelia hovered over us while the work was being done, and I could see that she was more and more impressed when we completed the job efficiently. The test flight showed a remarkable improvement in the power, performance, and range of the Lockheed.

On the morning after the work was completed, she asked me to come over for a final inspection and last-minute comments. Again, we went over the plane in minute detail. I then made a final suggestion, the same one that had helped Howard Hughes and Laura Ingalls increase their speed: apply a thin coat of clear lacquer over the plane and polish it to a mirror finish. This would cut down wind resistance. She agreed. On the second test flight, the plane performed beautifully with an increase in speed of 8 miles per hour.

Amelia used voice communication only and I felt the new trailing aerial would help despite the fact that voice was good only for short range and was affected by static. There is some confusion about this; it was later rumored that because of weight, she had the trailing antenna removed in Miami. This wasn't true, I checked it myself. Another unsubstantiated statement held that the antenna broke off when it wasn't reeled in before landing at Lae.

The reconfigured Lockheed was now a flying laboratory containing the most advanced aircraft technology in the world. Amelia's military equipment and the construction of a landing field at Howland Island, and the U.S. warships in the Pacific to "oversee" the trip, cost the U.S. government $5 million. In 1992 currency, this is equivalent to $100 million. Obviously, America had a major stake in this historic flight around the world. Before they took off, Amelia gave me a hug and a big kiss and thanked me for my help. Although we had met only a few times, she considered me a friend.

The flight proceeded smoothly to Puerto Rico, Brazil, Africa, the Sudan, Ethiopia, India, and Burma. En route to Singapore, Amelia was forced to return to Burma because of a monsoon. On her next attempt to Singapore, she battled a fierce storm. The plane later went on to the Dutch East Indies, but engine and navigational difficulties required repairs and adjustments. This was handled by an American engineer named Furman.

The flight continued on to Darwin, Australia, for a two-day stop, then went on to Lae in New Guinea. The next leg was 2,550 miles away to the new U.S.-built airport at Howland. It was to be a flight completely over water. Helping Earhart and Noonan would be some U.S. naval warships: the USS *Swan* was stationed between Howland and Honolulu; the USS *Ontario* would patrol the water between Lae and Howland, while stationed at Howland was the Coast Guard cutter the USS *Itasca*. These ships would be prepared to receive and send Amelia radio signals as well as homing signals.

On July 2, Amelia Earhart and Fred Noonan took off from Lae, heading for Howland. Near their destination, the plane mysteriously lost contact with its Navy watchdogs and vanished. For the next thirty days, the most massive sea search in history took place. U.S. warships, Navy aircraft from carriers and other Navy and civilian vessels combed approximately three million square miles of the Pacific but could find no trace. The search cost the government an additional $4 million, the equivalent of $80 million today.

President Roosevelt formally asked the Japanese government for help. Though it agreed, no Japanese ship ever left port to participate in the search, while two naval vessels at sea made a half-heart attempt.

Speculation was rampant, and everyone had a theory from Fred

Noonan's drinking to a raging storm. I discount the drinking. Drunk or sober, he was the best navigator I ever met. He had already proved his brilliance by guiding the plane around the world along the equator without a problem. The flight was shy of completing the circumnavigation of the globe by seven thousand miles.

It was a tragic loss that haunted me for years. I often wondered if Japan had a role in the Lockheed's disappearance. It would be years before I uncovered the answer in a most unusual and surprising manner.

CHAPTER 14

Adventures on Devil's Island

FRENCH GUIANA is a small country of thirty-two thousand square miles, situated on the northeast corner of South America bordering the Atlantic Ocean on the north and sitting in a pocket on Brazil. While its forests are valuable to France, placer gold mining and shrimping, along with timber products and bauxite (a principal source of aluminum), make it a valuable French colony.

The most horrifying aspect of French Guiana was the notorious Devil's Island, *Île du Diable*. This three-island group, twelve miles off the northwest coast of French Guiana, was created as a place to isolate France's political prisoners. Its most famous occupant was Captain Alfred Dreyfus, a French military officer who was found guilty of treason on trumped-up charges in 1894. This so outraged the French people against the military that it became the most controversial trial in French history. The famed author Émile Zola denounced the verdict with a pamphlet published in 1898 entitled *J'Accuse*. An embroiled France was divided into two camps, one for and one against the verdict.

Dreyfus was brought back from Devil's Island for a second trial and he was declared guilty again, but the uproar was so great that Dreyfus was pardoned. However, with time, new evidence of Dreyfus's innocence surfaced, and he was completely exonerated in 1906.

Accounts of the Dreyfus Affair were read with avid interest around the world, and Devil's Island, where Dreyfus languished for years under outrageous conditions, became the most infamous penal colony in the world.

In the late 1930s, French Guiana became particularly important to the United States, which operated its small commercial airfield. The drumbeats of war were echoing in Europe, and it was time to set in motion American defenses. The decision of the U.S. government was to build a runway sufficiently long to accommodate military aircraft. It would be funded through the National Defense Reconstruction Program.

Pan Am, which had a mail contract with French Guiana, was called on to front the operation. The person who was required to do the work for Pan Am had to be an aeronautical engineer and be able to speak French. Enter French-speaking yours truly. I arrived at the capital, Cayenne, at that time a depressing tropical city. After a meeting with the governor of French Guiana, he directed me to the office where I could fill out forms and get my permits.

With the paperwork done, he said, "Would you like to make a trip to Devil's Island?"

"Yes, certainly," I replied, remembering the Dreyfus Affair from my history books. "It will have to wait about three weeks until I review the situation at the airfield and make a list of supplies."

In those three weeks, we staked out a new runway, one that would run from east to west because of the prevailing winds. Then I drew up plans for the facilities, including the tower, and transformed them into blueprints for the construction crew. Finally, when the supplies and the construction supervisors arrived, I told the governor I was ready to make the trip.

Experience taught me never to go anywhere unprepared, so I checked into conditions on Devil's Island. The scuttlebutt was impossible to believe. Most of these men were not criminals in the usual sense, but even anarchists deserve humane treatment. I decided to be a morale booster as a good Christian. There were 390 inmates on the island, so I ordered sufficient packages of cigarettes, wooden matches, and hard candy to give to these men.

The only transportation to Devil's Island was by a single steamer, a rickety affair over 50 years old, the same one that transported Dreyfus. As it huffed and puffed its way, twenty-foot sharks swam around the boat, either in anticipation of someone falling in or for garbage usually dumped into the ocean by ships from the penal colony. Another of the ship's chores was to dump into the ocean prisoners who died or were killed. The sharks never complained that there was no such thing as a free lunch.

Though twelve miles off the coast of French Guiana, the islands were forty-five miles from Cayenne. We reached the island that housed the administration building, hospital, and laundry. At the last minute, before departing Cayenne, I had added baskets of fresh fruit, so I took along four Pan Am employees to carry the gifts. We gave a handful of gifts to those supervisors in charge and then asked the guards to open the cells where the prisoners were held.

The prisoners were located on another island, so we boarded the ship for the short trip. I was asked to add another person to our retinue, a sort of guide (spy)/island public relations person. The solitary confinement cells were small, about six feet square, so I asked the guide to open the cells to enable us to talk with the prisoners. The cells had heavy doors and I noted that some cells were so small that prisoners were forced to crouch in a sitting position. The only ventilation and light came from a small opening.

I spoke to them in French, giving them presents and listening to unbelievable stories. The slightest infraction was treated harshly by the guards, as were requests for medical treatment. Human rights were totally ignored and the men were treated like animals. A number of years ago, three prisoners escaped from Devil's Island, and one, Henri Charriere, wrote a book called *Papillon* about conditions there. It was no exaggeration.

I wanted to make sure the cigarettes, candy, and fruit went directly to the prisoners and were not siphoned off by the guards or the administrators. I insisted on handing them out personally. The stench was unbelievable. The men, unshaven, hadn't washed in months. All were scarecrow-skinny, many with uncared-for rashes and animal bites. Their clothes ranged anywhere from shabby to rags.

It was heartbreaking to hear that no one had ever come by and given them even the smallest gift. The hospital was used mostly to care for the paid workers. At each cell, the guard would pound on the door with a club and the prisoners, thinking it might be mealtime, did not bother to answer.

"You have a visitor," the guard would say. The prisoners then responded and were amazed that the visitor could speak to them in their own language. It took all day and most of the night to complete the tour. Since poor weather had begun to set in, we remained overnight. Our group slept in the hospital.

The next day, I was shown the kitchen and the laundry. As we looked out at the rocky shoals, the dorsal fins of large sharks were visible, casually swimming around, waiting for their daily garbage.

"What happens after prisoners serve their time?" I asked the guide. The answer was they were given white uniforms with horizontal stripes to identify them and they were called *libres* (free ones). However, though they were free, they were restricted to French Guiana and had to forage for themselves in the jungle to survive. Though these men had paid a heavy price to society, they were no longer welcome in France.

After returning to Cayenne, I could neither eat nor sleep for several days. This was a time capsule of the Middle Ages—men whom time forgot. But I still had a job to do, and I went searching for a site that was high enough and firm enough to build a navigation tower on. Finally selecting the right place, I put hatch marks in the trees that had to be cut down. Suddenly, I was surrounded by four *libres*, who seemed to have risen out of the ground. They were brandishing homemade knives.

One of them shouted, *"Arrêtez! Donnez-moi vôtre l'argent!"*

"Je n'ai pas l'argent français." So I emptied my pockets to prove I had no money. In French, I said softly, "Put the knife down. Let's talk." Surprisingly, they sat down.

"What do you need money for?"

They told me the money was to buy drugs for the pain from which they all suffered. They showed me their ravaged bodies.

"Meet me here tomorrow and I will bring my medicine for pain and headaches, which we can share." This surprised them very much, but they seemed to take me at my word. The next day, I did return with quinine and aspirin and other pain relievers. I also brought cigarettes and candy for them. They didn't know how to express their gratitude. I told them I would return again soon and share more medication with them.

Returning to the construction site by a new route, I chanced upon a little hut with no doors but with a post near the entrance. I knocked on the post and a little old lady emerged. She was shabbily dressed. *"Bonjour, madame, comment allez-vous?"*

She stared at me and then walked away. Several times a week, as I passed by, I knocked on the post. She would emerge and we would look at each other and say nothing. She was not unpleasant, probably just frightened of this tall, young stranger. One day, she invited me in to share her meager supply of homemade wine. Then she talked. She was a Frenchwoman whose husband had been sent to Devil's Island. She followed him there and waited until he was free. When he became a *libre* and could not return to France, he built the shack where they had lived together until he died. Now she was cared for and kept in food by the other *libres*. I promised myself I would do something nice for her.

We made progress with the airport as more technical crews started arriving with equipment. The ground at the airport was made up mostly of bauxite, an impure mixture of earthy hydrous aluminum oxides and hydroxides, the principal ore of aluminum. It packs very hard and makes a beautiful base on which to build a concrete runway. Then the work started in earnest to adhere to our schedule.

On one occasion when I had to visit the governor, we discussed the conditions of the prisoners and the plight of the *libres*. He gave the usual Gallic shrug, sympathized with the situation, but he was merely an administrator. The strict guidelines were set down by the government. He told me a prisoner, René Levant, was to be executed in five weeks. He wondered if I would like to talk to him. I agreed.

René, a captain in the French Army, had come home early one day and found his wife making love with another man. He killed them both with his dagger. It turned out his wife's lover was a French general. Instead of being freed for a crime of passion, he was found guilty of "treason" and sent to Devil's Island. Now he was scheduled to be guillotined.

The French Revolution had given birth to *Liberté, Égaliteé*, and *Fraternité*, but some had a lot more equality than others. *Vive la France!*

"René, what can I do for you?" I asked the wretched man.

"If I am going to be executed, then I would like to die in my captain's uniform."

"Where is it?"

"With my mother in Marseilles, France."

I told him that I was scheduled to fly to France to get additional permits signed for the airport. "I will try my best to grant your wish." He wrote down his mother's address.

"Thank you," he said. "Now I have one last wish. I would like you to be with me when I am executed."

It was not exactly a prospect to look forward to. I had made a gesture of goodwill to a man without friends. I had no choice but to accept. On impulse, I asked for his measurements just in case his mother didn't have his old uniform.

The following week, I had occasion to return to Miami. I called all my doctor and dentist friends asking for all the spare medications and sample drugs they could spare for the *libres*. Then I bought two cotton housedresses at Sears for the little old *libre* widow. Following another one of my inspirations, I hunted down a secondhand crank phonograph and some French records. The new radios and phonographs ran on electricity and there was none where she lived; the gramophone would ease some of her loneliness.

By now, the runway and the flat-rolled taxi strips were set. A large, four-engine aircraft would have no trouble landing here. It was several days after my return that I was scheduled to go to France. We flew by seaplane to Natal, Dakar, Senegal; Morocco, Spain, and then Paris. The government officials stayed at the American embassy while the crew and the rest of us stayed at Orly Airport.

On the weekend I went to visit René's mother in Marseilles. She requested I take some pictures of her son and send them to her. As for the uniform, alas, she did not have it, as the first wife had claimed it; she worked in a sailor's dive called Le Rat Mort (The Dead Rat).

I went there and found the wife to be a buxom blonde. When I explained my mission, she spit on the floor. "I don't want to talk about that SOB." I returned to Paris.

When I asked U.S. ambassador Walter E. Edge for help, he said, "Henri, you just ran into one of the most difficult things in life. For some reason, no French citizen wants to do anything for the convicts on Devil's Island. They've been sent there for treason or other horrible crimes and the French people expect them to suffer. But let me talk to my people and see if we can help."

The next morning, I received a message from the ambassador to meet with General DuPont at French Military Headquarters. The general and several staff officers met with me and we discussed the anticipation of war with Germany and they asked about the progress of the airport on French Guiana. I also told them about the conditions on Devil's Island, but what surprised them most was why I was allowed to give cigarettes and candy to the prisoners. Then came the big question. What favor had I come to request?

I told him I needed a captain's uniform for René Levant, who was about to be executed. He and his staff were well aware that he had killed his wife and her lover, a fellow French general. They didn't laugh, as the French view romance differently from anywhere else in the world. To them, love is a serious matter.

After a lot of verbal circling and getting nowhere and figuring I had nothing better to do, I asked why they didn't shut down the hellhole called Devil's Island? There was no answer, only some turning away of their eyes. Finally, the general said, "I am not permitted to do anything for a criminal. However, I will see what I can do. Perhaps I will take it up with the government." As I departed, I handed his aide René Levant's measurements.

To my surprise, the next morning I received a package containing a uniform, delivered by a French sergeant who saluted me. Inside was a note saying the uniform was *not* from General DuPont but from some of Levant's fellow officers. I had the strange feeling that each of these men, for just one moment, had put himself in Captain Levant's shoes and said, "There but for the grace of God go I."

When the airport business was concluded, we flew back to French Guiana and landed on "my" airfield, which was not quite finished. It was coming along splendidly. The next day I took the uniform to Devil's Island along with my camera. It fit him well, and on his chest were the correct number of campaign ribbons he had earned during his career. I took four rolls of film to send back to his mother. The execution was two days away.

He notified the governor that he didn't want a priest to give him last rites, but I insisted that I needed one if I was to watch his execution. He relented.

On the fateful day, in front of the guillotine, I gave him a hug and a kiss on each cheek in the French tradition. He hugged me back fiercely and said but one word, *"Merci!"*

He walked over to the guillotine, knelt down, and placed his head on the block—and "zoop" the blade came down. In an instant, he had gone from being a friend to a spirit that would haunt me forever. It was the most devastating sight I had ever witnessed.

With disgust, I watched the workers remove the captain's uniform and throw the naked body and head to the sharks. I was sick, so I returned to my quarters in the hospital a very disillusioned human being. A message awaited me to fly to Miami the next day. At dawn, after a sleepless night, I packed the uniform to mail back to his friends, then walked to the airfield to pick up my flight.

In Miami, I was quizzed by military-looking "civilian" officials on the progress of the airport and navigational equipment. Satisfied with our progress, I was given a twin-engine Lockheed airplane for official use in French Guiana. Flying always calmed me down, so I was grateful for the opportunity to get behind a wheel.

The one thing I never forgot to do in Miami was to scrounge medication for my *libres*. My mother got the family to help me, but she couldn't resist saying, "Poor, soft-hearted, Henri." I could not be immune to man's inhumanity to man.

The navigation tower was making wonderful progress with the new beacons, which a pilot could home in on. With airfield matters well in hand, I took a few days off to visit my *libres* and drop off the medication. Since the execution, I looked at these men differently, not as a group, but as individuals, free men who lived like jungle animals, restricted to the forest to try to survive. That very afternoon, an idea flashed through my mind. Somehow, I must find a way to help those poor souls. Before I left French Guiana, I promised them, we would have to have a picnic. As the time was drawing near, we settled on a date.

The place we agreed to meet was several miles from Cayenne, a long, flat, hard beach that could serve as a runway. It was a simple matter to land there in the Lockheed, where I was met by thirty-nine *libres* plus the old lady wearing her Sears party dress—one of the cotton frocks I had picked up for her. From the plane, they carried out the roast chickens, the dumplings, potatoes, fresh loaves of French bread, and wine. It was a wondrous sight to behold. Through it all, they told me the stories of their lives as the gramophone played music and my mind kept coming back to the problem of how to help them.

When it was dark, some of the men took me on a sightseeing canoe ride up the Cayenne River. I picked up the big emergency flashlight from the plane and got into the long dugout. When the flashlight was turned on, I was facing great, big crocodiles. That was frightening. They also showed me an unusual sight, walking catfish. These fish roamed over the land and returned to the water. The *libres* had no shortage of fish to eat.

When we arrived at our "secret" destination, they showed me where they dug into the mountain for gold. Setting up a hibachi, they melted the ore. As gold melted first, it dropped down as nuggets the size of peanuts. From this high-grade gold they made beautiful jewelry like filigreed butterflies and bees and other shapes. They gave me several presents to take with me.

Suddenly, I had an unexpected confrontation with the *libres*. Before they returned me to my plane, they demanded reassurance that the navigation tower was not there to detect or track them down. I explained as simply as I could the purpose of the tower, but I don't know if they ever accepted it.

When they calmed down, I asked them where they would go if they could leave French Guiana. "Trinidad. It is the only country that would accept us." They had often thought of leaving, but they had no means to do so. Of the thirty-nine in this group, only twenty were healthy enough to travel. The rest knew they were too ill.

When I had occasion to see the governor on business, he made me a present of four guillotined heads that had been shrunk and mounted on a board. Underneath, in big letters, it said, "For Dr. Henri Keyzer-André." It was a sinister reminder of the island.

In time, we completed the airport but I asked the *libres* to have faith as I promised to help them and, from time to time, visit them. I did, at least once a year. It wasn't until after the war when the big DC-4s were flying through Cayenne that I visited the city on an inspection trip. I made a deal with the chief mechanic at the airport. In exchange for a new Ford station wagon, which he would receive immediately, arrangements would be made to bring in one *libre* at a time to the airport, dress him in a white mechanic's coverall, then hide him in the baggage compartment of a plane headed for Trinidad. When all twenty were out, I promised the chief mechanic in Trinidad that he, his wife, and daughter would get a two weeks' vacation in Hawaii on me. Both ends were covered.

It took eighteen months before I was informed that all twenty *libres* had arrived in Trinidad safely. No one was aware that I had also made arrangements for some church people (who must remain nameless) to help these men get resettled when they got there. Years later, I was advised by a church member that all of them were married, working, and living happy lives. It gave me an all-time high. Legally, it may have been against the law, but morally, I knew I had done the right thing.

Not long afterward, the French government closed down Devil's Island.

CHAPTER 15

Pan Am Goes to War

JAPAN WAS NOT the only country trying to penetrate America's zone of defense. Germany was foreshadowing its intentions as well. With some devious moves such as using bogus names, Germany was setting up commercial airlines and airports all over South America with connecting links to Germany. In retrospect, Japan wanted to conquer Asia and the Pacific, and the United States stood in its way; Germans had long-range plans to invade North America through its underbelly, South America. The only group of people who seemed to be waving the American flag on both fronts was Pan Am.

It should be remembered that prior to World War II, the United States had no all-purpose intelligence-gathering service other than the very able Office of Naval Intelligence (ONI), and on a less grand scale, the Army intelligence officers attached to embassies around the world. The FBI was limited to investigations of federal crimes and espionage strictly within the borders of the United States.

It wasn't until September 1, 1939, when Germany invaded Poland and, in turn, Great Britain and France declared war on Germany, that World War II did break out in Europe. The Roosevelt Brain Trust realized that the United States desperately needed sources of accurate information. This could be accomplished only with a broad intelligence service of its own—and rapidly. To head it up, the President selected attorney William Donovan.

Churchill immediately offered the services of the finest intelligence expert in Britain, William Stephenson, later known by the code name

"Intrepid." The two men helped create the Office of Strategic Services (OSS), which was headquartered in Rockefeller Center in Manhattan. After the war, the OSS was converted by President Truman into the CIA.

Donovan was making so many Clipper-ship trips to the United Kingdom and Europe that reporters who tracked him jokingly referred to his "fifty-trip Clipper ticket."

Back in 1936–37, Juan Trippe was feeling like a walnut caught in a nutcracker with the sabotage in the Pacific on one side and the Germans' competition in South America on the other. It spurred him into building a bigger and better seaplane, the "Super Clipper."

Upon returning to New York from Martin Clipper tests on the West Coast, Trippe assigned me to the Boeing factory in Seattle. I was beginning to feel like a yo-yo. A great concern was that I had very little social life. I didn't stay long enough in one place to meet many girls and I was getting lonely. Male company is good up to a point, but I wasn't getting any younger. My move to Boeing in 1936 made me realize that in one year I would be thirty years old. In addition, I wasn't accumulating enough flying time to make captain. The only good part was that I was saving money and living off a generous expense allowance.

Boeing had just won the Trippe contract to build six Boeing 314s in eighteen months for a price of $550,700 each. Boeing, builder of the B-15 bomber for the U.S. Army Air Corps, calculated that it could adapt the bomber's design, with its large wings and powerful new engines, to a huge flying boat. The planes were scheduled to be completed by December 1937. Unfortunately, the first plane was not acceptable until March 1939 because everything that could go wrong did.

I remained at Boeing for seventeen months, as Boeing engineers and designers had to receive on-the-job training from Pan Am engineers and pilots with seaplane experience. However, when the B-314 was finally completed, it turned out to be one of the finest aircraft in history, as well as the most luxurious.

It could carry thirty-five passengers on transatlantic hops and seventy-four passengers on shorter hauls. Its takeoff weight was over forty-two tons and it was powered with four 1,550-horsepower Wright Cyclone engines.

The B-314 had a range of 4,275 miles, but despite a ceiling of twenty-four thousand feet, prewar planes were not yet pressurized, so it dared not fly above twelve thousand feet because of lack of oxygen. Cabins were luxurious and the plane boasted a honeymoon suite. Passengers were babied by French chefs, and air stewards served gourmet foods on fine china along with the finest wines and champagnes. It quickly became the most popular commercial airliner in the world.

On June 28, 1939, Pan Am inaugurated its transatlantic service via a northern route through Gander, Newfoundland, to Great Britain, France, and Portugal even as the war clouds loomed in Europe. Returning prewar flights were crowded with fleeing refugees from all European countries. At the start of World War II, Pan Am was obliged to terminate its overseas Clipper flights to Great Britain and France. From then until 1942, all Atlantic crossings followed the southern route to Lisbon, Portugal, with the exception of one trip to Foynes, Ireland, on September 30, 1939.

My trip to Foynes started in Baltimore, then on to Port Washington, New York, New Brunswick in Canada, and then to Gander. From there, we flew directly to Foynes. We came back via Southampton, Le Havre, and Lisbon.

The demand for passage from Europe to the United States was so great that Pan Am had to create a priority method of selecting its passengers and a single flight might carry as much as a 13,620 pounds. It was ironic that Roosevelt selected a flight on a B-314 Clipper when he flew to Casablanca.

The war made me an important asset to Pan Am. Besides assisting in the development of the B-314 and knowing the plane, I was fluent in many languages. The combination put me in demand as a co-pilot. I was logging flight time at an increasing rate. Pan Am's weekly European schedule doubled to twice weekly and then to three times a week.

I felt it my duty to fight in the war, so I impulsively joined the Marines, listing Pan Am as my employer. I was quickly yanked out. It seems that flying into the war zone was considered a higher priority. And it was, because we had more to worry about than warplanes and antiaircraft fire (both hostile and friendly).

That winter, possibly the worst storms in the history of the Atlantic occurred between November 1939 and March 1940. In November alone, we had to delay five of the eleven scheduled trips for two or more days because of the weather. The weather caused severe surface icing and delayed flights. Pan Am had to move its base from Port Washington to points farther south. In the next few months, 60 percent of the eighty-seven scheduled flights were delayed from one day to two weeks because of inclement weather.

When Bermuda, part of the British Empire, became an important part of the antisubmarine war—its port was used by British and Canadian warships and its airport was where the RAF and the RCAF flew regular sub patrols—Pan Am moved again to the Marine Terminal at the new La Guardia Airport in New York. Despite weather delays, in 1940, the airline carried 30 percent of all transatlantic mail—some 250,000 pounds eastbound and 200,000 westbound.

Again because I was fluent in French and Portuguese, Juan Trippe singled me out for another special job. This time, it was felt that the North Atlantic storms were too difficult to overcome, and a South Atlantic route other than Lisbon might improve our performance. As a special representative of Pan Am, I was empowered to scout West Africa in the vicinity of Dakar to try to locate a suitable landing site for a Clipper with a facility capable of servicing and maintaining the huge seaplane. Before leaving, I consulted naval and State Department experts regarding U.S. relations with countries on Africa's west coast. It was a lesson I had learned on my trip through Russia.

I went by ship to Bissau in Portuguese Guinea, just below Dakar, Senegal. By air, on a Great Circle route, this was nearly 3,334 miles, almost the same distance to Gibraltar, though it may appear longer on a flat map (Mercator projection). On arrival, I contacted the Bissau officials, explained my mission, and asked for their cooperation. There was little interest until I pointed out the economic benefits to the country from such an installation. It didn't take long to get a unanimous decision in our favor.

Bissau assigned some experts to work with me and we pored over maps and selected several sites for scouting purposes. By far the best location was Balama, a town of four hundred inhabitants, situated near a river. With an average of seventy-five inches of rain a year, it would make an ideal site for year-round flying. The country was mostly lowlands and swamps inhabited by crocodiles, water buffalo, leopards, monkeys, and a variety of snakes. The chief vegetation was cotton trees and palm trees, but the crops were fruit trees, guava, mango, bananas, and oranges.

Testing the river, we found the depth to be sufficient to land our
Clippers. I had no difficulty speaking with the locals, though their
Portuguese and mine were somewhat different. Everyone was willing
to go to work at once. I negotiated the arrangements for landing rights
and set about surveying the area to map out the territory we would
require for landing, refueling, and maintenance facilities with an airport building and a staff house for crew and passengers. This was a
natural safe harbor in case of bad weather, and the natives were
extremely helpful.

After a few weeks, the locals organized a safari for me that would
include some hunting, and though I was not much on killing animals, I
agreed to go. It was then I learned that the area was infested with a
species of leopard considered more dangerous than lions and far more
ferocious. A charging leopard always leaps for a man's head or throat,
fastening its teeth on the neck and tearing him down. The leopard did
not just kill for food, it killed for pleasure. On this safari, our tracker
spotted a large leopard and our guide killed it. It was mean when it was
alive and it looked just as dangerous stretched out on the ground dead.

I continued my work and calculated everything required to get
started, then wired a report to Juan Trippe requesting a detailed
laundry list of supplies. I negotiated for the purchase of enough land to
build a base, with additional room to grow. Meanwhile, I was taken on
another safari to the small town of Buba about thirty-seven miles away.
On this outing, a huge leopard attacked a buffalo in front of us. With
alacrity, several guns in our party shot both animals. The natives
carved up the buffalo and brought along the meat to Buba. To my
amazement, we found a group of white people there. The town was
expecting us and had arranged a celebration, so we donated our meat
to the cooks.

The feast was slated to begin between 6:30 and 7:00 P.M., and
everyone came dressed in light tropical clothing. I wore short white
pants, white socks, and a Tagalog shirt I had picked up in the Philippines. In the gloom, you could see little bats flying around snapping up
insects. Other than that, the air was still and pure. At dinner, I was
surprised to be seated next to a beautiful blonde girl I hadn't seen
before. She had a pinup, movie star's type of body, and she was
extremely bright.

Her name was Krystina Van Pettersen an anthropologist who had been born in Norway. She was thrilled that I could converse with her in her native language, and we laughed because the natives were looking at us, two blonds in their midst. She told me about her research on the various tribes who spoke Balante, Fulani, Crouoo, and Mandingo, besides Portuguese, and wanted to know if I'd be interested in joining their expedition and help record the native beliefs; their religions were Islam, Roman Catholicism, and a strong belief in the star Sirius. I told her about the work I was doing and said I would be tied up for weeks, perhaps months, building the Pan Am base and communications center.

By night's end, I knew I was falling in love with Krystina. Instead of my going with her, I convinced her and her group to accompany us on safari for the next few days. They did, and we enjoyed their company before they left to make their way to, what is now, the Upper Volta in the Mali Republic, to study the Dogon tribe. By the time the group took leave of us, Krys and I already professed our love for each other. We arranged to meet in London, where her father, a pioneer radar scientist, worked on secret projects with the British military forces.

By the time we returned to base, we found our supply ship had arrived, along with Pan Am construction crews. Like old pros, and with the help of the locals and the Portuguese government, we completed the base in one month, several weeks ahead of schedule. I took the first ship home to announce the southern route was now open for business.

When I reported to Trippe, he grunted, "Fine, now go back to flying status, we're short of pilots." I never got a thank-you. It was nothing new, but it still rankled. At headquarters, everything was in chaos. Hundreds of thousands of refugees from all over Europe were waiting at the Tagus River near Lisbon. There was an onslaught of letters, telegrams, and phone calls pleading for transportation. Portugal was neutral, but it was a small country and it was being overwhelmed. The demand for seats on the Clippers to America was astronomical.

I had finally made captain but flew two more trips as co-pilot before I knew about it. The airport at the Tagus River consisted of a small, fifty-year-old shack with a pier that extended into the bay. It was called "Cabo Rivo." Day and night, crowds gathered out there, but it was more eerie at night. There were clusters of people lit up by pole lanterns standing silently and waiting. It was like a city of lost souls, each one wrenched out of his or her homeland, waiting for some nameless, faceless clerk to decide if it was their turn to get on a flight and survive.

Inside our little building were the customs officials of the Garda Fiscal. Pushing, shoving people crammed the counter. Other officials present were diplomats from the U.S. embassy, the Portuguese secret police, British marshals, diplomats, military officers of various countries, couriers, and members of royalty displaced by the war. No doubt there were also enemy spies among them.

The captains, including me, broke the rules, as we took more people on board than safety regulations allowed. So people sat strapped to toilet seats flying across the Atlantic, or hunkered down in closets, or sat in the aisles for fourteen hours. As captains and concerned human beings, we could do no less.

I was proud of being a captain of a super Clipper and I had two stars on my wings signifying my rank. Not long afterward, I would have three stars, master ocean pilot. Despite my rank, I was a softie, because I found it heart-wrenching to taxi along the bay watching adults who couldn't get on a flight crying like babies.

Taxiing along the Tagus River, with Lisbon to starboard, we'd pass ships anchored on the river. Some with American crews would blink us a safe voyage in Morse code. The radio man would bring me an Aldis lamp to acknowledge the good wishes.

The navigator would then chart a course from the Cabo do Rochoa lighthouse at the mouth of the river and flick on our navigation lights to make certain everything was working. The plane was now transformed into a ghost, hugging the surface of the sea, the radio silenced so that no hostile, or potentially hostile, warship or plane knew who or where we were. We flew west step by step, like a blind man tapping his way forward.

It's one thing to be second in command and let the captain take all the responsibility. It's different when one is captain and in charge. Friends call you "sir" and you're often called "the old man." Indeed, I was an old man of thirty-four. Each return trip to the United States seemed more difficult. There were people I knew casually from Holland and other countries who were now desperate in their efforts to fly with me, but the order of priorities was set by the company. If the rules were not adhered to, it would have created chaos and we'd have been swamped. It was most difficult when I met close friends of my family along with their children.

We treated the passengers as royally as we could, and each trip made me feel like a guardian angel. I never forgot to say my prayers at night to thank God for another safe voyage and hope for an end to the raging war.

No two flights across the Atlantic were the same. On one special trip, supposedly a mail flight, I had on board the king of Greece, the movie star Ilona Massey, and Don Carlos, now the king of Spain, along with various ambassadors and State Department officials. I was given secret instructions to make a stop on the coast of Africa for a special pickup. I didn't learn until years later that it was material for the first atomic bomb.

Krystina was always on my mind, and I had a small black-and-white snapshot of her in the flight cabin. On my return to New York, my first stop was to check if any mail had arrived. But for months I didn't hear from her. There was one lapse when I didn't get a letter from her for three months. When the letter finally arrived, she wrote about her difficulty getting back to England and how overjoyed her family was about our official engagement. She desperately wanted me to meet her family and to make our wedding arrangements. She was twenty-five and I had just turned thirty-four.

Getting time off from my job proved to be difficult. There was a shortage of captains and crews. The Lisbon flights were crisscrossing three times a week, and no one seemed to care that we were tired, least of all the crews themselves. But I needed this time off. Trippe finally agreed to let me have a few days in England if I flew as a member of a special flight to Liverpool. Trippe handed me a letter to John M. Winant, the new U.S. ambassador to the Court of St. James's. "Do not wait for an answer," he said, "but give them a message from me." The message was that Pan Am would stand by to serve England in the event she was invaded.

On the way, we stopped at Horta in the Azores to allow a storm to abate, then we flew to Liverpool. Important as my message to the ambassador was, I had an important message of my own. I was going to Coventry to see my girl. When Ambassador Winant got wind of my rendezvous, he lent me an embassy car and coupons for gas.

With a pounding heart, I searched the streets until I found the address. It was a lovely, modest house with a typical English garden decked out with a display of beautiful flowers. As I went to the gate, everyone came out of the house to greet me and Krystina flew down the path and jumped into my arms. The others turned out to be the friends who were to be bridesmaids. The only dark cloud was her father, who had a stern look. I thought he might be somewhat difficult to persuade.

But Mr. Pettersen turned out to be a fine gentleman and he gave us his blessings. He never confided in me about his work, but I had learned from my own sources of his contribution to early radar. Her parents gave us an engagement party the next day, and I met numerous friends and neighbors. As a surprise, I gave Krys a small box from Tiffany, a two-carat diamond ring. We chose June 18 of the following year as our wedding day, to coincide with her birthday. There were many arrangements to be made, which she insisted on doing herself despite the task of finishing her book on Africa.

Making plans in wartime is always risky, as I didn't know where I'd be stationed. It could be anywhere from New York to Miami, Africa, or South America—but wherever Pan Am sent me, that would be home. My leave was over much too soon and I returned to New York and my flying duties.

For the Allies, the war, instead of taking a turn for the better, took a turn for the worse. Germany invaded Denmark and Norway. Soon most of Europe, including France, fell before Hitler's *Blitzkrieg*. British and Allied forces retreated to England from Dunkirk. I was very worried about Krystina and her family as the war became personal.

The disaster of the fall of France made Lisbon a singularly valuable listening post. Its radio station was the only one in Europe not in Axis hands. The Pan Am crews picked up odd bits of information from their counterparts in neutral Portugal. These were passed on to Juan Trippe, who in turn passed them on to the War Department. It helped take some of the tarnish off his image.

It seemed like a treadmill; take off from Long Island and land in the Azores fifteen hours later. Spend the night on land and take off the following morning, only to land along the flare paths of the Tagus River in Lisbon seven hours later.

Wherever I was, I wrote to Krystina often, but her letters to me arrived only at my New York address. As London was being bombed regularly, her letters were sporadic. Often, I received nothing for weeks, then I got a bundle all at once. To show me the progress she was making, she sent me part of her book on the native myths of Sirius creation.

Telephoning London was out of the question, so our only contact was letters. There were no more Pan Am planes heading for Great Britain for me to hitch a ride on. Suddenly, I was yanked out of the flying schedule and told to report to Juan Trippe. I was afraid it was bad news, but it wasn't.

"Because everything is in such a mess, I'm making you the Pan Am superintendent of Latin America. It's going to take a lot of expertise to straighten out the mess."

It was delightful to think I would now have a permanent address somewhere. I dashed off a long letter to Krystina, then flew down to Miami to visit with my family and to coordinate the details for the Latin American Division. Trinidad was where I would set up my headquarters.

It didn't take me long to find a house. It was called Bagshott, and was completely furnished and fully staffed. The house even came complete with a dog, a German shepherd called Rex, who immediately jumped on me and began to lick my face. I wrote Krystina the longest letter full of the minutest details.

I plunged myself into the work and quickly uncovered the problems. Most stations had been set up for seaplane landings, with the South American destinations getting the older planes. In addition, new land planes were now coming into existence and there was a great need to start building airfields because land planes were faster and could carry large loads. The era of the seaplane was winding down.

In addition, each of the managers before me had set up a different set of procedures so it was a mess of conflicting entanglements. It was chaos, mostly because little attention was being paid to South America. It would require heavy negotiating with foreign governments to set matters right, develop new airfields, and acquire landing rights.

It seemed as though I was working around the clock, and at last I got things going, mostly because I began replacing personnel. I was learning lessons on how to toughen up. If only my mother could see me now. Each report I turned in to headquarters seemed to show improvements in the division, and Pan Am granted me almost everything I wanted.

One day I received a letter from André Priester. England had been suffering severe bombings during massive German air raids. He knew of my engagement to Krystina and suggested that perhaps I might wish to take a brief holiday. He would arrange for me to hitchhike to England on a KLM DC-3 airliner now being operated by BOAC, as Holland had been overrun. I grabbed at the opportunity.

We landed in the rain and it rained all the way to Coventry. But I was in for a greater shock. Most of the city had been devastated. When I arrived at her neighborhood, I was too stunned to speak. The houses had been turned into rubble. All that was left of Krystina's house was a tiny rose—the drops of water from the petals seemed like tears.

The air raid warden told me that the Pettersen family, along with most of their neighbors on the block, had been wiped out. For the second time, my beloved had been taken from me under tragic circumstances. I fell to my knees and prayed, trying to find solace in God. Then all that was left were tears.

CHAPTER 16

I Adopt Three War Orphans, Then Seek a Wife

I REALIZED that I was not the only one to suffer a loss because of the war, but that didn't help the ache in my heart. Ambassador Winant and his staff were extremely compassionate trying to give me hope by checking records and contacting the Pettersens' friends in Norway on the off chance they were still alive. Even the Norwegian ambassador offered his staff to help in the search. But it was to no avail. I finally left for Lisbon on a DC-3, and from there I co-captained a Clipper back to New York.

Priester extended his sympathy, but Juan Trippe said nothing other than to tell me to get my ass back to South America lickety-split and straighten out the Pan Am problems there. Returning to my house, Bagshott, in Port-of-Spain, Trinidad, was difficult for me, the house that was to be Krystina's. Though she had never been there, I could feel her presence. She was always on my mind. Even my dog, Rex, sensed my loss as he accompanied me on long, lonely walks around the hills.

Before long, I plunged back into my work and slowly began to make headway. Unknown to me until later was the fact that the U.S. government had finally gotten around to taking a long, hard look at South America. Trippe, through various friends and henchmen, made the government aware of the South American problem with its large German and Italian populations and Nazi and Fascist leanings in Brazil. Then there was the German airline, Lufthansa, and its ties to

151

other local airlines that formed a link between South America and Germany. As it had in the Pacific, the United States needed all the help it could get to create military air bases in South America quickly, particularly if America was ever plunged into the war and had to prepare its defenses.

President Roosevelt agreed, and he and his cabinet decided to make use of the Reconstruction Finance Corporation (RFC), an agency created during the Depression, and apply it to the war effort. An $8 million emergency fund was allocated to an RFC subsidiary to establish the American Republics Aviation Division.

William Burden, an aviation specialist, headed the program. He was aided by investment broker William D. Harding and attorney Allen Dulles. Trippe offered the government help, as he had people who possessed expertise in aviation, engineering, and languages. And so I became involved in the South American problem.

Around this time, because of the necessities of war, land planes were making rapid advances as more and more people and priceless cargoes had to be flown swiftly over long distances. These planes were far more efficient, and it was becoming increasingly obvious that commercial amphibious planes would soon be extinct. The pressure of time made it impossible to negotiate treaties with all the South American countries for the construction of military air bases. Using subterfuge, Pan Am and the U.S. government became allies once more. Secretary of War Stimson asked Pan Am to build landing fields and communication centers all over Latin America under the cloak of commercial activity. Trippe agreed—however, on his own, he went one step further when he bought into Sociedad Colombo Alemano de Transportes Aereos or SCADTA, a Colombian airline using German planes and employing mostly German personnel.

Then two important decisions were made: (1) the government asked the Rockefeller family, at that time majority stockholders of Esso Oil (now called Exxon), to stop selling fuel to the Axis-controlled airlines in South America (particularly Germany's Lufthansa, and Italy's Aereo Transcontinentale), as a matter of national defense; and (2) Burden was successful in diverting two dozen C-47s, the military version of the DC-3 planes, to expand Pan Am's South America air routes.

All German nationals in SCADTA were to be fired. Trippe did this very reluctantly, although the reason didn't come out until much later. Trippe, who bragged continually about his super-patriotism, was not averse to "forgetting" to obey his government's orders. He refused to fire Erwin Balluder, manager of the Pan Am Western Division, whom U.S. Naval intelligence classified as pro-Nazi despite his having become a U.S. citizen in 1935. Balluder and another alleged pro-Nazi, the Austrian Von Bauer, head of SCADTA, were close friends of Trippe's and he tried to retain them.

Trippe, never one to lose sight of potential financial gain, eventually presented the government with a bill for over $1 million severance pay for SCADTA employees. It wasn't until the United States declared war on Germany that all German employees were finally cut loose.

While all this was going on, I continued my investigation by flying around South America and talking with Latin American travelers. I learned that Pan Am service had deteriorated. Because seaplanes flew mostly in daylight, so they could land on water, there were constant weather delays. As the demand for seats increased, passengers complained they were being packed into planes like cattle. The relationship between the airline and South American governments was poor and the American ambassador reported that Pan Am personnel, mostly local citizenry, were arrogant, rude, and unfriendly compared with other airlines' employees. An overhaul was imperative.

With the DC-3s about to come on line, I also had to study the aircraft. But it was an easy plane to fly, and it didn't take long for me to go through pilot training and get checked out. All in all, I was soon working around the clock, putting in twenty-six-hour days.

Priority one was to set up and build airports in Cuba, Mexico, and Brazil, although once Lufthansa left that country, we had its ready-made airfield. And, of course, SCADTA gave us access to Colombia and other Latin American countries. Mexico was no problem.

Before I was sent to South America, Erwin Balluder was the man in charge. One of his jobs was to prepare manuals on how to service and maintain the DC-3s. These were extremely difficult to read, as few people had the education to understand them, so it required twenty-five people to service one DC-3. I had seen enough, so I flew back to New York to make my report and recommendations.

Before Trippe and all the vice presidents, I spelled out the atrocious conditions existing in South America, which had already cost Pan Am $500,000. Besides the problems already mentioned, there was no refrigeration available, so farm-fresh agricultural products, which required immediate transportation, were rotting on the airfields. In addition, the arrival/departure times were a disaster, and countries complained that sending mail on a regular schedule by Pan Am was impossible. They were threatening to cancel our contracts.

To add insult to injury, I pointed out that the barges used to meet seaplanes were not kept properly and were leaking or falling apart. The list went on and on for several hours. When I finally stopped, I looked around the room, expecting some sort of acknowledgment from Trippe or the executives. Instead, everyone was mad as hell. It seems that what I had pointed out was the poor job these very vice presidents were doing. The meeting ended with the VPs condemning every item in the report. The final cut of all was the comment, "You are trying to ruin the reputation of all the people in the company."

Juan Trippe had the last word. With a voice dripping with sarcasm, he said, "Since you have so many recommendations to make, Henri, don't you think you had better get back down the line and get some of those things straightened out? You don't like the system after we spent all that money, well, goddammit, you have six weeks to improve what we did. Otherwise, you're fired."

First I was dumbfounded, then I was furious. I had been asked to do a job, and when I had done it, I was condemned for doing it and told I was wrong. *Then* Trippe practically admitted I was right by telling me to fix everything in six weeks or I'd lose my job. I was ready to quit in disgust.

Juan Trippe had sent me out on difficult assignments before and had never said "Thank you." He was treating me as if I were his lackey, and I resented the fat-assed executives in New York who never did their jobs properly and continually looked for scapegoats. To calm down, I went to the nearby Episcopalian church and prayed for help, remembering all the while what my mother had warned me about people. Maybe Trippe didn't care, but there was still a war going on and I felt I had a contribution to make.

That evening, I had a dinner appointment with the Gardners—good friends in New York—so I delayed my flight south until the next morning. Lucky for me that I did. The Gardners had a nine-month-old baby playing in a crib in the living room, and as I was a sucker for kids, I watched her with fascination. She was perpetual motion. Suddenly she picked up a toy with colored beads and I was instantly inspired. The mechanics and helpers couldn't read the technical manuals—in fact, they could barely read—but they *could* see color differences.

The next day, I called Trippe and asked for his cooperation in overhauling the maintenance shops along with all the operations.

"Yes, you have my authority for whatever you need to straighten out the mess—everybody will work with you, but you still have only six weeks. Now get the hell down there and get to work."

This time, I smiled. He knew I had done my job, but I realized he couldn't embarrass all his cronies in front of a pipsqueak engineer. I went to my family's home in Miami, and for two days thought out everything on paper.

Getting started was the most difficult part. I had to convince the Miami overhaul base to paint different colors the size of half a square on the planes exactly where servicing equipment had to be attached. The other matching half of the square was to be painted on the equipment. When placed together correctly they formed a one-color, ten-inch square.

The next problem was to design a small cabinet, about six feet by six feet by one foot, to house all the spare parts needed to service a plane. These would be hung on doors, and each morning the chief mechanic or his assistant could check each cabinet and refill the missing parts. If you knew what each airplane needed, short of a major overhaul, a large inventory was not required.

But the course of true repairs never goes smoothly. Many bases had tossed their "mysterious" spare parts aside, so we had difficulty finding them. Those who resisted were fired and others hired. I found that the ambitious young people in the company caught on quickly and performed with pride and efficiency.

In the end, it took seven colors for seven people to service a DC-3. People recognized their equipment by color, and we even painted spots on the ramp where each one stood in his individual color to service his part of the plane. My spending money annoyed Trippe. I had new barges built and taught the marine personnel how to bring the seaplanes to the barges with finesse.

Half the people in South America working for Pan Am didn't know who I was. Those who knew couldn't pronounce my name. For the time being, my name became Mr. André and tension eased up a bit. Changes are difficult to instill, and they were taking time. The value of money in each country fluctuated, so I arranged for Pan Am to make sure workers were equally compensated.

If I had to blame one person for the mess, it would be Balluder.

Either he sabotaged Pan Am deliberately, or he didn't know what he was doing but kept on doing it anyway. I had the worst time trying to make my changes in San Juan, Puerto Rico, and again I could see the clumsy hand of Balluder.

Finally, it all came together. I delegated authority to station managers and chief mechanics who understood exactly what had to be done. It was up to them to keep it running smoothly. As the problems began to resolve themselves into routine, I knew we now had an efficient operation. It took longer than six weeks, but there wasn't a peep from Trippe and I wasn't fired.

Easing off from my heavy schedule, I spent more time in Trinidad and was able to enjoy my beautiful home. Despite the loneliness, it helped ease the pain of losing Krystina. But once I was comfortably settled, a new problem confronted me. The mothers in the local social circles in this island country were hard at work getting their daughters to meet eligible bachelors, and I was a bachelor. There was a deluge of invitations to country clubs and parties. What I had ignored before was suddenly appealing. I was approaching forty and still unmarried. Not only had the local mothers designated me as a target, my own mother was giving me the business.

I always kept in shape and maintained my weight at 175 pounds. I walked, biked, swam, studied judo, and played tennis at a nearby country club. The women members were real Latin beauties and all from nice families. They had come over from Argentina to work in the USO. But I was astute enough to notice that those Pan Am men who had come down to work and married some of these girls had problems after they returned home. Their wives didn't know how to run a house because they all grew up surrounded by servants. They didn't have to wash their clothes, prepare a meal, make a bed, or even do the shopping. A Latin American wife from an upper-class family, couldn't seem to operate without a servant. The underlying problem was that native servants were paid very low wages.

Often a Latin wife would start inviting mothers, brothers, uncles and aunts—a whole colony of relatives anxious to see how the new husband catered to their precious daughter. Even when I moved around, to Rio de Janeiro, Montevideo, and Buenos Aires, the so-called aristocratic *señoritas* were like barracudas out to devour you. So emotional needs took second place to the necessities of war. When I told one marriage-minded *señorita* that I was incapable of fathering children, she told all her friends. Soon I was besieged by a different type of young women, those who were more interested in a less permanent romance.

As new procedures began to function well in Rio de Janeiro, Montevideo, and Buenos Aires, I still didn't hear a single comment—good *or* bad—from the head office. My salary checks continued to arrive, so I knew I was still employed. It was like working in a vacuum. I felt it was time for me to take a few days off and visit Bill MacCracken. Though he was now a lobbyist for the American Optometric Association, he still had strong ties to Juan Trippe and the aviation industry.

Wartime Washington could only be compared to a beehive overloaded with worker bees. There were no empty hotel rooms, so I stayed with the MacCrackens. I wasn't there a half hour before Juan Trippe called me and asked me to take the train to New York at once. So much for my three-day vacation.

Trippe tossed me a new assignment. "I want you to fly to Liberia and meet with President Edwin Barclay. See if you can get exclusive commercial landing rights in his country. If you can, then buy enough land for an airport, hangars, and a hotel. You have carte blanche."

Though Great Britain was busy defending itself and its empire, it nevertheless complained that the United States was expanding its air routes by taking advantage of the political situation. It protested to the U.S. government that it was being swamped by American aviation. To guarantee against this, a percentage of the carrier business was supposed to be allocated to British airlines.

Once in Liberia, I learned that the country was prepared to give certain tax relief to the airline that would fly its planes under the national flag of Liberia. I contacted Juan Trippe and advised him of Liberia's plans. He wired back to check if President Barclay was ready to do the same thing with other airlines. If that were so, it became a matter for the lawyers to straighten out Liberian registry.

Trippe cabled me to fly to Sweden and see if I could set up a landing-rights deal with Swedish Airlines (SAS), so off I went. Sweden had remained neutral during world wars I and II. The country was prosperous, but the city of Stockholm was rife with intrigue as Allied and enemy agents rubbed shoulders in the cafés. I had a warm reception, but after days of negotiations and answering thousands of questions, Sweden turned down our request.

I needed a few days of relaxation, so I went sightseeing. As I walked around the city, I heard the laughter of children as I passed an orphanage. I slowed up to watch the children play. On entering the yard, a little six-year-old girl, bold as brass, ran up to me and stared. I picked her up and she put her arms around my neck and kissed me. It was love at first sight.

The matron came out and in one of my few impetuous moments, I blurted out, "Would it be possible to adopt a little girl like this one?"

She looked at my Pan Am captain's uniform and said, "Yes, sir, it certainly would be possible." With the little blonde angel clutching my hand, we walked inside the somewhat shabby house, where I filled out a series of documents. I offered a generous sum of money as a donation to the orphanage, which was gladly accepted. It would be a matter of time before my application received approval. It would also take a little time to bring her over, as I would have to wait until the fighting in Europe began to wind down.

France had been liberated when I went to visit friends at Fontainebleau. I told them about adopting a little girl whom I couldn't get out of my mind. They told me there was an orphanage nearby overflowing with war orphans. I suddenly became excited and asked to be taken over. There, I found a seven-year-old boy who asked me questions about my uniform and who kept saying, *"Vous êtes Américain, n'est pas?"* I went through the same documentary procedures for adopting this young fellow, as well, and again made a substantial contribution to the orphanage. He would be safe there until I made arrangements to have him picked up.

After making my report to Trippe in New York, I returned to Trinidad and began to make preparations for my growing family, despite the fact that I didn't have a wife. There was a new enthusiasm in me, and when I wasn't working, I was rearranging the rooms with new furniture for my two children. I even lined up a nanny/tutor for them, as my parents had done for me.

The Allies began pushing the Germans on the western front through France, Belgium, and Italy, while the Russians attacked them on the eastern front. Once again, even though the war was still on, Trippe asked me to scout Europe to see if there were any more deals I could make on behalf of Pan Am. He was never one to let an opportunity go by. He always needed an edge. He also wanted me to check around for any foreign innovations in aviation that might be of use to our company.

This time, I went to Utrecht, Holland, to inspect the Utrecht station. It was my native country, and I was curious to see how my relatives had survived the war. The Germans had bombed the hell out of the station and left practically nothing on the airfield, but the Dutch were doing a wonderful job keeping KLM operating. The people seemed eager to repair the war damage and get on with their lives.

On impulse, I went with a cousin to visit a Dutch orphanage. It was run by an elderly couple. I spoke to them in Dutch, and they livened up when I asked if I could adopt a war orphan. Just then, a five-year-old boy ran up to me and the pattern repeated itself. I picked him up and he put his arms around me. What could I do? Again, I made arrangements and, again, I made a donation to the institution.

It was only a matter of months before I would be able to arrange with Pan Am to have the three children flown to New York and then on to Trinidad. I went to Paris and there, too, the airports were devastated, but the French were also eager to get back to normalcy. I could make no Pan Am deal in France, so I returned home.

Back in New York, I was involved in numerous meetings on future planning with larger, faster land planes and global competition. I spoke to MacCracken regularly, and he kept inviting me to Washington. One day, he said; "Henri, we need you in Washington. It's extremely urgent. There's a reservation for you at the Mayflower Hotel. Bring your tux, as we're going to an important affair at the Chevy Chase Country Club in Maryland. The new ambassador to Panama is honoring the movie star Ilona Massey, but there will be people there I want you to meet." I agreed.

I took the train to Washington and checked into the hotel. At 7:30 P.M. on the dot, the MacCrackens arrived to pick me up. I tried asking what was so important about another Washington party, but both of them sidestepped the question. There were wall-to-wall people all dressed up and holding cocktails. I don't drink, so I had seltzer water and chatted with a few Pan Am executives who were there. When dinner was announced, I found myself seated next to a young, beautiful, blonde Hungarian lady with a charming accent. One of the few languages I didn't speak was Hungarian, but I vowed to rectify that quickly. We were formally introduced. Her name was Maria Rosallia Blazejosky Rado, and her father had been a general in the Hungarian army.

She had a saucy sense of humor and was soon baiting me with rapid-fire insults, a not-uncommon trait among most Hungarians. "How come an old man like you is still a bachelor? Is it true you dislike women? Who keeps you warm on a cold night? Have you ever enjoyed a real, red-blooded Magyar woman?"

I said nothing. She must have learned something of my background, so I wasn't going to let her get a rise out of me. All I did was look at her impish face and smile, so she began to splutter and wind down. When you come from a large family, as I did, this kind of bantering is child's play. She finally stopped and blushed.

She was drinking champagne when I said, "After we're married, our relationship will improve." Suddenly, she began to choke. I massaged her back gently, then she excused herself for a few minutes. Of course, by now I knew she was unmarried, and in her twenties, but she was not as sophisticated as she thought she was.

When she returned, she had lost some of her bubbliness and was more subdued. I thought I liked her better the other way. Just then, the ambassador to Panama brought over the guest of honor to our table. Ilona Massey looked at me and laughed. "Hello, Henri. Ambassador, I know this upstart. He was captain on the Clipper that took me from Lisbon to New York. Then we met again on a trip from Miami to Rio de Janeiro. When I came to look at the cockpit, he was brazen enough to ask me if I would serve food to the passengers after the steward prepared it. I said, 'I'm a movie actress, not a waitress.' And he said, 'Just think what all those people will have to talk about when they get home—how a beautiful movie star served them dinner.' And you know something, I did it."

Everyone laughed, including Maria, and soon she was back to having a good time. We danced and enjoyed our dinner. I discovered that she was a bright, intelligent young woman. I told her about my adopting three war orphans, who would be coming to live with me in Trinidad. My biggest surprise came when I discovered she was a guest of the MacCrackens. Bill had set me up.

I stayed in Washington longer than I was supposed to and got word to hurry down to Miami to start my DC-4 training at the military base at Homestead, Florida. I was free on weekends, so it was easy for me to hitch rides on planes to Washington to spend time with Maria. She realized I was a serious suitor and her attitude changed. She wanted to know the stories of the two women I had been engaged to marry and all about the children I had adopted. "They need a good mother," I said facetiously. She punched me in the ribs.

Living in Port-of-Spain appealed to her, and when I described the house, the flowers, and the weather, she was eager to see it. I said, "You'll have to marry me first." But, by now, we knew this instant romance was real and she had lost her coyness. Together, we planned an engagement party when my four weeks' training period ended. Each night, I did not forget to thank God for all the goodness that He poured on me with such abundance.

The party, taken over by the MacCrackens, turned out to be an affair with two hundred guests invited, including my family. Howard Hughes couldn't make it, but he did tell me that if I needed a ring, he could get it for me at a big discount, which was his present to me. And so I learned how the rich stayed rich—they seldom bought retail. Maria loved her ring, a two-carat diamond.

Next morning, I had to go back to work. I flew to Trinidad, as I had been ordered to take André Priester, our chief engineer, on an inspection tour of South America. This was in preparation for changing our maintenance procedures to the new DC-4s. I felt so great I think I could have flown around the continent on a cloud.

Priester was a stickler for detail and I adhered to his standards; but he didn't let anything go, from an unbuttoned coverall to grease on the floor of a hangar. Nevertheless, he was satisfied. We figured it would take six weeks of training to get the personnel ready for the new four-engine planes coming on line.

I scheduled my way through each country, working out details, and soon we were ready for the new era of commercial flying. I returned to New York with my report to Trippe, who by now knew I was preparing to get married and was in the midst of the arrangements. He made no comment on my wedding. Instead, he asked me to drop everything and go to Europe to set up more deals with European countries. This time I said, "I don't think so. It would be too callous. We have to give these people a little time to get over the war. I saw it the last time I was there. Give them a chance to get back on their feet before we talk business."

Trippe gave me the dirtiest look I had ever received. As it was the first time I had stood up to him, I'm sure he felt I was defying him. There was no doubt in my mind that he was ready to fire me. I looked him right in the eye and said nothing, but I could feel our relationship changing. There was silence for a moment, then I walked out.

There were items I wished to discuss with Trippe, but this wasn't the time. Trippe was extremely stingy with wages. Our people were not earning much money, and Pan Am was making large profits. I was afraid that once competition set in, we would be losing a lot of valuable people to more generous airlines.

The wedding took place on April 3, 1945, in Washington. As Maria was a Catholic and I an Episcopalian, we had two priests and two ministers perform the wedding ceremony. My best friend, Baron Stieno Stackelberg, was best man, Nell MacCracken was matron of honor. Ignoring our invitation to the wedding and a special invitation from his close friend MacCracken, Trippe and his wife did not come to the wedding, nor did they write an acknowledgment.

I was not going to let Trippe upset me. We had a wonderful honeymoon and then flew home to Trinidad. Maria loved the house, and a few days later, I flew her around South America on an inspection tour. I inspected, she shopped. Now I was well and truly married.

CHAPTER 17

Two Major Air Crashes

I WAS on my way back to Port-of-Spain after leaving my wife in Washington to spend some time with the MacCrackens and relatives. For me, this was to be a relaxing trip, as I was flying as a passenger on a Pan Am seaplane, a Sikorsky S-42, number NC-823. The aircraft had just returned from a trailblazing survey of the Pacific and had been refurbished as a passenger plane to operate on the South American routes.

Thus on August 7, 1944, along with 37 other passengers, I boarded the plane at Miami at the Dinner Key Base. There were scheduled stops at Antilla, Cuba, and San Juan en route to Trinidad. It was a beautiful morning, with small, puffy clouds in the sky, and I was looking forward to a comfortable flight. By the time we arrived at Antilla, the sea turned angry, with waves five feet high topped with whitecaps and a stiff breeze at about 25 knots.

The Sikorsky does not do well in rough seas, so as the pilot attempted to land, the plane bounced. The wind was blowing from the east, and the plane was coming in with too much speed for such rough seas. We finally touched, settling onto the water three miles from shore.

Then there was a whole sequence of mishaps. The Sikorsky suddenly started to water-loop, and as it spun around, it built up a large trough in front of the bow. As the trough deepened, the captain had difficulty controlling the craft, while the bow continued to dip down into the trough. Finally, the plane flipped over on its back, breaking up and beginning to sink.

First, the lights went out. The ship was in darkness when it flipped over. The violent, wrenching force that turned it upside down sent all of the passengers into shock, killing some immediately and injuring others. Several infants were killed at once as parents lost their grip and the children were hurled about. Those people who were alive, including me, were upside down, and we had difficulty unbuckling our seat belts.

I had given a lot of thought to crashing. Even though death might be imminent, I always felt it was imperative to try to help the living. Now our plane was sinking. The entrance to the Sikorsky was on top of the fuselage, but now it was down in the water. The entrance steps blocked the only exit.

Because I was deadheading back to Trinidad, I was seated in the last seat next to the steward. Both of us suffered a severe pounding on our heads when the plane bucked. Nevertheless, we managed to unbuckle our belts and fall on our hands and knees onto the overturned ceiling, now filling with water. The cockpit had broken off, and the members of the crew up front were too severely injured to help.

The only exit was blocked by the steps, so the steward and I lifted the entrance steps and I fastened them with my belt to the fuselage, freeing the exit. We went to where the "Mae West" life jackets were stored and passed them out as we unbuckled the passengers and pushed them through the exit. The frightening part was listening to the screaming and moaning of the injured, coupled with the cries of infants.

As most of the gas in the wing tanks had been used up on the flight, the empty wings acted as temporary floats and kept the plane afloat a bit longer. Then I asked the steward to stay on the outside of the fuselage while I transferred to him those passengers who were injured but alive. I had to resort to brute force to get people to leave the slowly submerging, crippled plane, and in two instances had to knock out the men who refused to leave in order to get them out of the death trap.

It was an eternity before a launch arrived from shore to pick up the survivors and the crew. There wasn't enough room, so the injured, the women, and children went in first and the rest clung to the still-floating wing. After releasing the life raft from the plane, the steward and I picked up the bodies of the dead babies and adults and placed them on the raft. A few bodies, still buckled to their seats, could not be retrieved as the plane began to sink. The steward and I undressed down to our shorts and started swimming toward shore.

Just about the time we reached the exhaustion point, fighting the waves, nausea, and seasickness, a second launch picked us up, along with the life raft containing the bodies. All the baggage was lost, together with the passports. Arriving at the Pan Am station, we were confronted with the red tape of passing through immigration and filling out forms. It seemed an eternity before the injured were taken to the local hospitals.

My first call was to the U.S. naval station at Guantánamo for help. They rushed over clothes and shoes and helped with the dead. My second call was to Miami to report the accident and order another plane to come down and take the injured crew and survivors to Miami. The infant bodies who were identified as American were put in small boxes and also taken to Miami.

When the shock wore off, I could feel the pain of all the lumps, bruises, and scrapes on my arms, hands, and legs, so I was carted off to the hospital. I called Maria and she flew in with the plane to be with me. It was only later that I would discover how hard it would be to replace my driver's license, passport, and other credentials.

As an expert witness, I had to stay for the CAB investigation and give an entire account of what happened. I made the following recommendations to the CAB:

1. An easily accessible life preserver for each passenger.
2. Further pilot training for sea landings, learning to angle across waves; no landing beyond the plane's ability.
3. Dry battery lights available in all compartments. Ample rafts for all passengers. Color code emergency equipment.
4. Locking device to secure entrance stairs for emergencies.
5. Redesign ballast water tank to help prevent looping.
6. Prepare procedures and resources at local facilities to cope with emergencies during crash conditions.
7. Set up procedures requesting help from military sources.

Pilots are trained to expect the unexpected. They are also conditioned on what to do in emergencies, the primary rule being "Save as many lives as possible." Because of this rigid training and knowing I had done everything I could, I mentally put the crash behind me and went back to work in Trinidad. One crash was not enough to make me superstitious.

Because of the vagaries of flying, what happened yesterday, except for the lessons learned, must be forgotten today—otherwise, each incident would eat into your mind and heart. The war had created shortages of everything, including pilots. Young men eager to fly and looking for adventure joined the Air Corps. Thus, it was necessary, when the occasion demanded, for me to fly a scheduled run, something my regular ground duties didn't allow as often as I would like. To me, flying was freedom and, corny as it sounds, soaring above the wind and the weather feeling almost alone in the sky was, well, heaven.

Some ex-military pilots were now entering the ranks of Pan Am. Some had been in crack-ups, or had seen too much action and were honorably discharged. Several pilots, who had brothers killed in action, were granted compassionate discharges. Whatever the reason, some had been accepted by Pan Am. Unfortunately, due to the times, they were given less than complete training and were shoved on board airlines as wheel-holders.

The planes were bigger, better, and faster than when I started out, so the new co-pilots needed more training, not less. After the DC-3, the Douglas company consulted with five major airlines on their needs and ultimately created the DC-4, a beautiful four-engine aircraft that was perfect for commercial travel. The only hitch was the government commandeered all DC-4s for military use and renamed the aircraft the C-54. Over eleven hundred of these aircraft were built.

However, the special status of Pan Am entitled it to several of the new DC-4s. Thus, on January 7, 1945, I was assigned to captain Flight 11. The ship was a DC-4, number NC-88709, a scheduled flight from New York to Rio. My co-pilot was a newcomer to Pan Am, a man in his thirties (whom I shall call Fred) who had seen combat as a bomber pilot. He had received a release from the service because two of his brothers had been killed in combat and he was the sole support of his mother.

He seemed capable enough and after takeoff, when I turned the wheel over to him, I watched him carefully. He was competent, but he didn't have the smooth efficiency airlines expect of their pilots. It was obvious he needed more experience, because I felt he was rough on the engines rather than coaxing them along, which made it difficult to synchronize them. I took over the landing of the plane at Miami and I handled the takeoff for Belem. Because I was uneasy, I decided to be extra cautious throughout the flight.

As we entered Brazilian airspace, I realized that I had been jumpy for nothing. I had given Fred the wheel and everything was running smoothly. What could possibly happen? By 1 A.M., we were passing over dense jungle lit up by the brightness of a large yellow moon. Suddenly, erratic winds began to batter the aircraft. There were no clouds, so it was hard to fathom what caused it. The only possible answer was that we were flying over mountainous terrain and had stumbled into a freak windstorm.

Without warning, the nose cones on the number-one and number-two engines blew off. The number-two propeller, attached to the cone, flew with bullet-like speed into the left wing, puncturing the gas tank. Without thinking, I automatically shut down both engines on the port side to prevent sparks from igniting the spewing fuel.

We were now flying with two engines on the right side. The manufacturer's specifications stated that this plane could fly on one engine, and we still had two. It took the two of us to trim the plane to stabilize it, but the roaring noise made it clear that the two engines were operating on takeoff power.

Over the intercom, I told the passengers, "Ladies and gentlemen. We've encountered some turbulence and there has been slight damage to the wing. There is nothing to be concerned about, everything is under control. We're heading for Galeão Airport in Rio and our ETA is one and a half hours from now."

I took the wheel and asked Fred to check on our fuel with the engineer. When he came back, the picture wasn't good. The punctured left wing tanks were empty. The two engines, carrying the load of the aircraft, were rapidly burning off the remaining fuel. Fred's face was a ghastly white as he strapped himself in.

"Everything will be all right," I told him. Whether or not I believed it was beside the point. While there is hope and you are still breathing, you keep on going.

I kept adjusting the controls, trying to find the best cruising speed—i.e., maximum speed at minimum gas consumption—while nervous passengers kept knocking on the door asking questions. They were told to buckle up. Winds kept buffeting the plane and it looked as if we wouldn't make Rio. Being the incurable optimist, I prayed, checked the map, and decided that I would make an imperceptibly gradual descent to keep our speed up while decreasing gas consumption.

Then I heard a noise I couldn't account for and began to look around the cabin. I tracked it down to Fred, whose teeth were chattering. "Get hold of yourself, son, those people back there depend on you."

I kept glancing at him sideways. Both he and the aircraft needed watching. Fortunately, I didn't have time to be frightened. I kept my eye on the right engines and checked the fuel gauges, which I couldn't trust to be accurate, and prayed to my good and true friend, God.

Without warning, Fred became hysterical. He unbuckled his safety belt, stood up wild-eyed, and, waving his arms, shouted, "We're going to crash, we're going to crash."

I instantly put the plane on automatic pilot. There was no hesitation in my movements as I unbuckled my seat belt, turned, and stood up. I was to his left and I hit him as hard as I could with my left fist. It caught him where his jawbone met his ear and he went down, pole-axed. I had never hit anyone like that in anger (except during my first crash) and I didn't know I had it in me. Buckling up the co-pilot once more, I strapped myself back in and got down to the business at hand. The young man had impeccable credentials so something else was bothering him. (I later found out he'd been shot down twice and seriously injured.)

I swear that for at least fifteen minutes the fuel gauges read empty, but as long as the DC-4 remained aloft, I was going to keep flying. Then I spotted the 125-foot statue of Christ on Corcovado, which gave me a location point to steer for Galeão Airport. The tower gave me the runway. Altitude had dropped to four thousand feet, but I was too busy to check for mountains in the region. No ifs, ands, or buts, we were going straight in accompanied by the snores of my co-pilot, Fred.

When the lights of the runway came into sight, I continued my descent, lined up the aircraft on the center line, and kept praying as fast and as hard as I could. Then one of the two engines began to stutter. I began to think of a dead-stick landing. Just as the wheels touched, only one engine was running, and it stopped as we coasted down the concrete strip. I braked the craft slowly, gently. Luckily, the hydraulic pump on the number-three engine on the right side was working. We finally stopped at the very end of the runway. I was soaking wet, but the DC-4 was intact. So were the passengers, who were hugging and kissing each other.

When everyone had disembarked, I hailed the ambulance driver and asked him to remove the co-pilot and take him to the hospital for examination of a possible broken jaw. I knew I had broken a couple of small bones in my left hand but that, too, would pass. I went to the station to report the "incident" and disqualify Fred from commercial flying for the rest of his life.

While I considered myself lucky, I still didn't flirt with superstition. Nothing had happened. There was no accident, and no one was hurt (except perhaps Fred). I could still use my left hand, so I told no one until I returned home and saw my private doctor.

It was two months after the almost-accident that I was scheduled to fly as a passenger, deadheading back to San Juan to meet the China Clipper, now pressed into service in the Atlantic. I was to take it on March 8, 1945, a scheduled flight from San Juan to Léopoldville, Belgian Congo.

The morning of the flight was a hazy day over Trinidad, with the weather so overcast that it looked gloomy, with high humidity signaling rain at any moment. This was not unusual in the tropics. The seaplane, a Sikorsky S-43, number N15066, was loaded with passengers, all anxious to get home.

Before boarding, I requested a weather sequence to see how the weather might affect my flight to Africa. Puerto Rico reported that a hurricane was brewing. I might be delayed a day. When the captain and co-pilot came aboard, they greeted me because we were all old hands and good friends. The manifest showed Flight 26 had twenty-one passengers and two crew members.

As we taxied out for takeoff, I could see the waves were rising to four feet, so it took about three miles to get lift-off. As soon as the plane was airborne, we started to experience turbulence. You could feel the plane shudder and buck, the engines groaning for power. Once through the overcast, instead of the weather improving, it took a turn for the worse.

Then the turbulence increased. First the pilot tried to gain altitude, but the air was so rough, he was obliged to lower the nose and we descended. After a few minutes, the plane began to climb. The air was turning extremely cold and the passengers were becoming restless and nervous. A couple of them were hyperventilating. Then the windows frosted over, unusual in the tropics.

With all my experience, I didn't understand what was happening outside. At the peak of the turbulence, a little towheaded boy unbuckled his belt, slipped out of his seat, and walked toward me, holding on tightly to each seat for balance. He climbed up on my lap, clung to me, and shouted, "I want to get out, I want to get out. I'm scared! I'm scared! I'm scared!"

His blue eyes were wide open, imploring me. I tried my best to calm him down by talking softly to him. When he was calm, I carried him to his seat and strapped him in. I had just returned to my seat when the turbulence turned violent. Looking out through a clear spot in the frosted window, though it was not yet visible, I saw that we were approaching Martinique through a heavy overcast.

The pilot spotted a hole in the dark clouds and he apparently was struggling to ease power off the engines. The plane went into an uneasy decline to a lower altitude and I realized we were now over Fort-de-France. As we neared the water, the plane seemed to have a mind of its own. The pilot, trying to adjust the throttles, discovered they didn't respond to power. Without heat, the gasoline, misting in the carburetors, had frozen. Both the pilot and co-pilot began to wrestle the throttles as the airplane hit a large wave and bounced into the air like a pelican.

The plane came down leaning to port, and as the left wing dipped into the water, it was like hitting a concrete wall. The wing broke off, leaving a gaping hole in the fuselage. The wind caught the right wing and the plane flipped over so that the normal entrance to the plane was now underwater instead of on top.

Both pilot and co-pilot were killed instantly. Shards of glass from the cockpit and windows flew like missiles around the cabin cutting open heads, including mine. Those passengers up front, held fast by their seat belts and hanging upside down with their heads in the water, drowned. Many who were alive were in a state of shock and could make no move to save themselves.

For me it was *déjà vu*. To see this kind of death all around gives you a terrible feeling of remorse. The helplessness made it even worse. All I had going for me was my training and my unwavering faith in God. I was not aware yet that as the plane struck the water, my mouth crashed into the bar of the seat in front of me. The impact broke off, at the gum line, three teeth on either side of the two front teeth, which missed the bar. I was in severe pain and gushing blood at the mouth. Then a loose, broken seat slammed into my leg. More blood began to pour out.

The top of my head was now in the water and it took great effort to unfasten the seat belt. I waded through the water across the aisle, where an elderly lady, seated next to her husband, was held up by her seat belt. As the plane lurched over, I freed her and tried to push her through a gaping hole at the rear of the plane. It was like trying to put a cat into a boot. With a mighty effort, I jammed her through. To this day, I don't know whether I pushed her or stomped on her with my foot to get her out. I hooked her dress to a little strut on the plane's tail. Her eyes were bugging out and were filled with terror.

Releasing her unconscious husband was no problem, though his head was cut open and bleeding. I dragged him out through the hatch, hoping there were no sharks around. I told the woman to hold onto her husband and keep his head above the water while I went back to get the emergency rubber life raft.

The raft, like the passengers, had been thrashed around and was not where it was supposed to be, but I found it and hauled it outside. I pulled the ring so it filled with air and was floating, then helped the elderly couple into the raft, tying it to the strut with a loose knot so the raft could break free if the plane sank.

Returning to the plane to search for other survivors, I saw two eyes staring at me from under a seat. With one hand, I grabbed what turned out to be a little six-month-old baby by the arms. It was coughing up water. I pinched its nose, cupped my hand over its mouth, and dove through the hatch until we hit air. The baby struggled wildly, attempting to breathe as I choked off its air passages. Trying not to hurt the child, I carefully pushed in its stomach and pumped out water until it began to cry. Its will to live was extraordinary.

I reached the strut cradling the baby and, as though by some miracle, the child grabbed the strut with a tiny hand. The rough seas had torn the life raft loose so that it was floating free. It dipped down into a trough, then rose high on a wave and was washed over to the other side of the plane with the couple in it. There was little hope that I would survive, but I desperately wanted to save the baby. There was only one chance to do so.

Waiting until the raft began to drop into a new trough, I asked God to give me strength as I tossed the baby over the fuselage toward the raft, praying with all my heart. Miraculously, He gave me the strength and guided my hand. The baby dropped into the raft like a baseball into a catcher's mitt. The lady wrapped something around the baby and comforted it in her arms.

Checking my surroundings, I saw we were about two and a half miles out as the wind began to push the raft toward shore. I wasn't sure, but I felt the tide was going out. I turned to look back at the almost submerged seaplane, now sinking rapidly, and saw a head of long hair moving in the water in the wreckage. I grabbed the hair and pulled the head out of the water, though the body was still inside the plane. It was the baby's grandmother.

Sliding down into the plane, I grabbed her from behind and began squeezing out water until she coughed. Somehow, we hit an air pocket because we were still able to breathe. I dived down and searched around until I found a kapok life preserver, which I laced onto her. But with the vest, she was too bulky to get out of the plane. I dived under her, and stomped her out with my feet through the opening until she was floating free, coughing up water and inhaling air. We had actually sunk forty feet as the wrecked plane began to settle in the water.

For an airline captain, it's a horrific sight to see a plane die. It sank below the surface soundlessly as bubbles of air escaped. The receding tide was pulling us into open water. Tension was oozing out of me as I touched my mouth and realized the extent of my injuries. Blood was also seeping out of my leg, and I knew I had cuts and scratches bleeding from a dozen places. The loss of blood exhausted me, and I was fearful that the blood from my cuts would attract sharks. I prayed that if attacked, I would be killed at once and not be chomped to death in small bites.

While the water was not cold or uncomfortable, my clothes were weighing me down. My shoes had been discarded in the plane and I had lost one sock. Holding onto the woman's Mae West with one hand, I finally got my clothes off except for my shorts. As the shore was getting farther away, I was getting weaker. The woman, luckily, was breathing regularly as she slipped in and out of consciousness.

Crazy thoughts were flashing through my mind like a kaleidoscope, and the craziest was that I hoped the shark would enjoy eating me for dinner. Mentally, I was wandering all over the place, fighting consciousness, but aware enough to put my arm through the Mae West and dovetail the fingers of both hands in a clamp as I drifted off.

When I came to, I realized I had been out for two hours and the tide had changed, pulling us toward shore. After another two hours of pain and agony, we drifted still closer to shore. By now, I was utterly spent. Then I saw a young black native girl on shore looking at us.

With all my energy, I yelled out, "Help! Help!" Then I waved my arms wildly with strength I didn't know I had. She heard me because the wind was blowing toward the shore. She pulled out a dugout canoe and came paddling toward us rapidly, slashing through the waves until she was beside us. I pushed and she pulled, but we didn't have the strength to move the old lady into the boat. There was also the danger of capsizing. In French, she told me to hold on to the woman and the side of the canoe and then she crested the waves paddling toward shore.

Soon I felt my toes dragging in the sand, so I should now be able to walk, but the ordeal had been too much for me. The tension that had kept me alive oozed out of me like air escaping a balloon. I was so spent, so tired—too tired to live—that I passed out.

When I came to, I was surrounded by more than a dozen monks, all standing around me with their heads bowed and their hands inside their wide brown sleeves. My first thought was that it must have happened, but at least I was in heaven. But when the head monk spoke to me in fractured French, I knew I was still very much alive and realized I was on a cot in a bare room. I was told later that I had been unconscious for days. They had put salves on the open wounds and bandaged my torn leg after stopping the bleeding. Apparently, the young native girl had gone to them for help.

Because they could do nothing about my missing and broken teeth, some with the nerves exposed, I could eat little except hot chicken broth. It was manna from heaven and gave me strength. My only clothing was my shorts, which the monks had washed and dried and hung over a chair beside the bed. It was then I understood that everything had been lost.

They offered me spare underwear and a monk's habit, including a cowl, and a pair of leather moccasins for my feet. One of the monks took me to the Pan Am office in a goat cart. Unbeknownst to me, while I had disappeared for four days, a Sikorsky S-42S seaplane had come from Miami with CAB investigators to look into the accident. I learned that it had been impossible to raise the plane, which had sunk in two thousand feet of water and was now a burial crypt for those who were caught inside.

The information came from a minor clerk in the office, whom I tried to question, but my swollen mouth and broken teeth made it difficult for him to understand me. He must have thought I was a mad monk. I took a piece of paper from his desk and wrote out my question: "Where is the staff?"

He said, "The staff and the investigators are on the other side of the island, you know, to see the, uh, girls and, uh, drink champagne, uh, they said something like they wanted to drink up all the champagne in Martinique."

It was the most upsetting thing I had ever heard and I should have been furious. These people were out celebrating a plane crash in which the crew and most of the passengers had been killed. I closed my eyes, feeling faint for a moment, searching my soul looking for answers. Deep down in the recesses of my mind, I understood that people rejoice in life after they've been close to death. It was like attending a wake.

My main concern was Maria and what she might have been told. I walked to the hangars and found a flight crew finishing a maintenance check on the four-engine, S-42S Sikorsky seaplane. The men saw me in the monk's attire and crossed themselves. I checked out the plane and noted that it had been serviced and the gas tanks topped. I got two men to bring out the battery cart, plugged it in, and then I shooed them away. They were too scared to deny a monk anything, but there were lots of Hail Marys. An S-42S normally needs a minimum of three people to get it into the air: the pilot, the co-pilot, and the engineer, plus a fourth when possible, the radio operator. I revved up the engines, went through the preflight checklist from memory, and sighted the wind sock. The wind couldn't have been more than 10 miles per hour. After checking the mags, I pushed the throttles forward and took off into the wind for Trinidad.

My wife had adapted quickly to life in Trinidad. Among her various activities, her favorite job was being director of the United Service Organizations (USO). This organization combined the services of the Red Cross, the Y's and community organizations religious and non-religious, which set up recreation canteens and activities for U.S. servicemen around the world.

I was so anxious to get home to see her and tell her I was alive that I was breaking every rule in the book. I was certain she had been told I was dead. My biggest problem was flying an unauthorized seaplane into U.S. airspace in wartime without proper radio identification. One of the ways to thwart enemy planes was to daily change instructions for circling the bay, so authorized planes circled to port or to starboard, depending on the code of the day. Despite the one-man crew, I arrived in Trinidad and landed without difficulty. Nobody was alert enough to check me.

When the seaplane stopped, a crew came out to hook the lines to the plane, but I took charge of the grappling hook and attached it to the bow. No one seemed disturbed about that, but as soon as they docked the S-42S, I stepped into the light in the monk's habit. The native people at the station who knew me thought I was a ghost, as the papers had already reported me killed. I walked toward them in the monk's habit and some jumped into the bay to get away from this apparition.

I hailed a taxi and directed him to the USO, told him to wait for his money (I had none), walked into Maria's office and surprised her as she was reading and weeping over telegrams of condolences from friends and relatives. All the papers had carried the story of the crash, and I was listed as killed or lost at sea. She jumped on me, tears streaming from her face as she clung to me as though we were glued together. It was troubling for me to talk, so I typed out just enough to tell her I had been hurt and that my mouth needed medical attention, but I had just flown in simply to show her I was alive. Everyone at the USO was surprised as hell, but I had to get back to the seaplane. Maria accompanied me to the dock and paid the cab to wait for her as she saw me off.

I got the crew to gas up the S-42S and unhook the lines. Then I took off, flew back to Martinique and secured the seaplane before it was listed as missing. I got the night crew to service the seaplane. No one ever knew I had flown the plane to Trinidad. I made a note to tighten security at Martinique and Trinidad.

I returned to the monastery to see my new friends, the monks, and to ask for morphine to quell the excruciating pain in my teeth. Once more they helped me. By the following day, the CAB people and the Pan Am people had returned from their sojourn into Martinique night life. They were getting set to go to Miami and despite the fact I had no passport or papers, I insisted on going with them for medical attention. I had no clothes, no money, and was still wearing the monk's habit. My mouth and face were distorted and swollen and I could hardly make myself understood.

I finally convinced the Pan Am people on the plane that I was still alive. They nearly didn't believe me, so I told them to pinch me, as the monks had when they found me. I said, "If you are good to the Lord, the Lord is good to you."

I could hear myself talking, but it sounded like, *"Iss oo ur goo do duh Word, the Word iss goo do oo."*

Writing was a better way of communicating. Because the accident was in the section I supervised, I had to make the decision of what to do about the sunken aircraft. I concurred with the Navy evaluation that since it was impossible to raise the seaplane from a depth of two thousand feet, the bodies could not be retrieved for burial.

On the flight back to Miami, I was in the radio operator's seat in the cockpit listening to the news. I heard the announcement that the United States had dropped the atom bomb on Nagasaki, Japan. At MIT, I had studied atomic energy and nuclear fission and I understood better than most the devastation it would create in Japan. The date was August 9, 1945. I had been "out of touch" for a number of days, so I didn't know that this was the second atom bomb dropped on Japan. The first had been dropped on Hiroshima three days earlier. The war would end on August 14, 1945.

The flight was uneventful and would have been pleasant except for the pain in my mouth. After we landed, both the CAB and Pan Am wanted me to write reports and answer questions. Instead, I borrowed $20, hailed a cab, and went directly to my dentist. When I entered, I told the nurse of my desperate emergency. My understanding dentist, who had also read of my death, canceled all his appointments and went to work.

It took three days of intense repairs. He had called in an anesthesiologist and a dental surgeon to work with him. They yanked out the roots, applied medication to the inflamed gums, and brought down the swelling. They worked on giving me a partial bridge until the inflammation went down. More or less normal, I then checked into the hospital for a checkup. They sutured my leg, shot me full of antitetanus serum, stitched up my cuts, and medicated the abrasions. The only thing they didn't check was the bump on my head. It seems that a hardheaded ex-Dutchman can't be hurt by a bang on the noggin.

When my gums shrank to a normal size, I got my permanent bridge a few days later. I got a new passport and credentials and I flew to San Juan, where I had arranged to meet Maria. A replacement had taken my scheduled flight to Léopoldville on the Clipper, but now I was ready to start flying again. When the Clipper returned to San Juan several days later, I reclaimed my ship, flew it to Miami, New York, then back again all the way to Léopoldville.

Maria said, "You're crazy."

By the time I returned and had some time off, an angry bunch of Pan Am and CAB investigators were waiting to ambush me. The adrenaline that had been hyping me up had eased off and I was able to settle down and give them my report and answer questions. I wrote another set of recommendations for survival in crashes, the most important of which was that seats must be in an upright position when landing or taking off in land planes or seaplanes. That recommendation is still standard today.

When I asked about the people whom I had saved, I learned that the grandmother and the little girl had returned home to Toronto, Canada. The older couple had gone back to Antigua. Some time later, Maria and I were invited to their home for their fiftieth wedding anniversary since I was a fellow survivor. They never realized the role I played in their celebration. I left it that way.

But the grandmother of the little girl found out about the rescue when her lawyer checked the reports. I refused to discuss it with her by letter or telephone. My perspective was different but not strange. I don't want people to feel obligated to me for saving their lives. Even though I hadn't flown the ill-fated plane, pilots have an obligation to bring people back safely. When we do, we consider that an integral part of our responsibility has been fulfilled.

I did remember to send a handsome donation to the monks, and I tracked down the little native girl not only to thank her but also to give her a special gift.

My report and recommendations created new rules for all airlines. All seats must be in the upright position for takeoff and landing, and the back of each seat must be well padded. I was happy to be alive, even if I was gradually becoming superstitious.

CHAPTER 18

Do Crashes Come in Threes?

FOR SOME mysterious reason, athletes are superstitious. If they wear torn socks in a winning game, they will continue wearing those same socks until they lose. Some won't shave, some will turn their caps around—and on and on.

Pilots, generally, are superstitious as well. It's difficult not to be. There is the law of averages, and while commercial flying today is safer than taking a train or driving a car, accidents happen either because of pilot error, weather conditions, or malfunctioning equipment. Of course, the matter of terrorists cannot be ruled out.

I had been flying for seventeen years before I was involved in two major crashes within seven months. True, if I had been the pilot on the second crash, I might not be alive today. But the major superstition among people who fly the planes is that accidents happen in clusters of three.

My head did not want to believe it, but you can't hide from your emotions. Nothing happened for a while, so I dismissed all superstitious thoughts. Routine work consisted of my flying the Miami, New York, San Juan, Léopoldville route with the old China Clipper. The Army had borrowed it to fly personnel back and forth to Hawaii. It was then reconditioned and returned to Pan Am.

Finally, the day arrived when my three adopted children were brought together and would be flown to New York, then on to San Juan, and, finally, to their new home in Trinidad. As I was needed on my regular run, we arranged the schedule so that I would meet the children in San Juan and spend the day with them, then they would go on to Trinidad, where Maria was eagerly waiting to welcome them.

As luck would have it, while the children were en route to America, I received an emergency call from the New York office to cancel my flight to San Juan and Léopoldville. As the company's "number-one troubleshooter," I was to proceed immediately to Martinique to check into the report that one hundred Allied military planes were not being serviced properly by civilian personnel and to take any action necessary to resolve the problem.

I was away when the plane with the children landed in New York and then continued to San Juan. There was enough daylight for the pilot to proceed, so he took off in the Clipper for Trinidad rather late in the day. The result was that the plane approached its destination in twilight. Instead of dropping flares to light up the ocean, the pilot elected to land in the gloom. As he descended, the plane hit a British boat, killing everyone on the ship. Everyone on board the plane was killed, including the crew. And my three children.

Upon being notified of the accident, I left immediately for Trinidad, agonizing over one of the most crushing moments in my life. When I arrived, there was no rescue attempt being made. Rescue operations were impossible in the dark as there were no lights and no facilities to go into the water and retrieve bodies or parts of the Clipper. If it wasn't for the compassion and understanding of my wife, I might have committed suicide.

By morning, all the tears had been wrung out of me. I was still responsible for the section, and I was charged with clearing up after the accident. I was stalking around the station like a restless tiger when Jimmy Walker came in. Jimmy was a skin diver who had taken me out several times. Impetuously, I made the decision to go down with him.

There was a buoy above the spot where the plane had sunk. Both of us went down with underwater flashlights and brought up all the bodies, including those of my three children. Three innocent faces, children who had survived a war, the loss of their families—had lost the chance to live a life of tranquillity.

The barge brought them to the dock, where they were covered up. I made arrangements with the funeral home and a furniture-maker to make coffins for all of them. Meanwhile, Pan Am had to inform the families and relatives of the deceased, notifying them that immediate burial was necessary as there were no facilities at that time to either cremate, freeze, or embalm bodies in Trinidad.

The shocking news, along with the need to convince families of immediate burial, combined to make a terrible situation. After rounds of discussions, all I was authorized to do was to make a common grave. While a bulldozer was hired to do the work, I summoned the various clergy in Trinidad to come to the common grave to recite a eulogy.

Subsequently, the plane, too, had to be buried. The law stipulated that during the war years, no parts of damaged planes could be burned or sold, as they were considered strategic materials. Though the war was technically over, the law was still the law. The Navy and other military units came up with the tools to recover the China Clipper. This was a plane that had made history, that I had flown to China, Europe, and Africa on many extraordinary flights. It now lay on the dock like so much scrap metal. I spoke with the commander, and after relating the story of the plane, he agreed we should give it a decent burial.

The wings were flattened, the bent fuselage and tail corrected, and we buried the ship with honors at Docsite, a military base in Trinidad. I bought a tombstone and had it inscribed to this gallant China Clipper, the history-making Martin M-130 plane. I had helped create it, fly it, and bury it.

And, yes, tragedies do come in threes.

Jim Haizlip, the Speed King, congratulates Amelia Earhart in a picture taken in August 1932. Standing beside Amelia is husband, George Putnam. Behind the plane, in an open collar, is the author. (*Photograph from the library of the late Herbert Rebman*)

Amelia Earhart is shown here in 1937 sitting on her famous plane, the Lockheed Electra 10-E. Its official number was NR-16020. (*Courtesy Lockheed Aircraft*)

Amelia Earhart and navigator Fred Noonan with map of the Pacific showing projected route of their last flight. (*AP/Wide World Photo*)

Last known photo of Amelia
Earhart and Fred Noonan on
either side of a gold miner
named Jacobs on Lae, New
Guinea, prior to taking off for
Howland Island. (*AP/Wide
World Photo*)

Amelia Earhart, whose daring
adventures electrified the
world. (*Courtesy Lockheed
Aircraft*)

Pan Am flew the four-engine Sikorsky S-40 to Havana and Nassau. (*Courtesy Pan Am*)

The Sikorsky S-42 trail-blazed the Pacific. Author was a passenger on one that crashed in Cuba. He survived serious injuries. (*Courtesy Pan Am*)

While christening the Boeing Clipper with a bottle of champagne, the first lady, Eleanor Roosevelt, tore a hole in the plane. (*Courtesy Pan Am*)

Douglas built the DC-4, but the military took over the planes and renamed it the C-54. During World War II, 1,100 were built. Because of its special status, Pan Am received several for commercial use. (*Courtesy Pan Am*)

The Air France Concorde started supersonic service in 1976 flying at 1,200 mph, twice the speed of sound. While being checked out on the aircraft, author performed a barrel roll. (*Courtesy Air France*)

Three of the four shrunken heads that were mounted on a board and presented to the author on Devil's Island. (*From author's files*)

The Japanese fighter plane, the Zero A6M, which copied some of the advanced technology used in Amelia Earhart's Lockheed Electra 10-E. (*Courtesy of the National Air and Space Museum, Smithsonian Institution*)

The Russian military plane, the Ilyushin IL-76 Candid jet, is capable of carrying 40 tons of freight. A similar aircraft, carrying munitions and 36 passengers and crew, crashed and exploded in Siberia. The author, the sole survivor, was severely injured. (*Courtesy U.S. Navy*)

Author, 86 years young, in front of a display of some of the honorary degrees and awards he has acquired over the years. (*Photo by Hy Steirman*)

CHAPTER 19

How Trippe Tripped Up

THE TERM "chosen instrument" is a unique phrase used by a foreign government when it refers to its country's representative airline, such as Air France for France, and KLM for Holland. Thus, each specific airline is considered an "instrument" to be used to carry its government's trade objectives abroad. When necessary, the government incorporates the airline system into defense planning.

Juan Trippe's obsession was to be the "chosen instrument" of the United States, giving him complete control over all foreign air travel to and from America. Though he always acted as if Pan Am were the chosen instrument, it never received that designation. Nevertheless, the idea was never far from Trippe's mind as he selected friends and cronies who could work their way into government policy-making levels to help Pan Am prosper as his "self-perceived" chosen instrument.

On a separate front, he lobbied hard to obtain mail contracts from the Post Office in order to subsidize his airline. His efforts, not always 100 percent honest, were successful. He also worked relentlessly to accomplish his dream—to have the finest globe-circling airline in the world. In both areas he succeeded, for as early as 1930 he publicized the fact that Pan Am was the only U.S. airline to operate overseas and represent our national interests.

Juan Trippe's ultimate goal was a Pan Am monopoly on all international flights from the United States. In connection with that, whatever whim came to mind he tested, pushed, probed, and maneuvered, using all kinds of tricks and angles. Despite our differences, I admired this man for his foresight as well as his ability to overcome adversity.

Because of my facility with languages, I was often sent out on one of his grand schemes. Occasionally, one went bust, like my adventures in Russia. Often I was sent out as a surrogate to fulfill some "verbal" deal or other, not realizing that what I was doing might be illegal. Some of these situations proved embarrassing to me, but Trippe never apologized or commented when they didn't work out. It wasn't until years later that I realized I was more at risk than Juan Trippe and I began to sense more and more that I was merely a scapegoat or, worse, a sacrificial lamb.

In the mid-1930s, Alabama's feisty senator, Hugo Black, held hearings on airline regulations, which gave Trippe conniptions. All the airlines were swimming in red ink, despite the fact that some of them had siphoned off millions prior to the market crash in 1929. The $120 million privately invested in airlines had shrunk to $35 million in value. The banks were no longer lending money to airlines and eighty companies went bankrupt. Trippe suffered the least, as he had used his Republican political influence in wangling profitable mail contracts to sustain Pan Am.

But, now, during the Democratic administration of FDR, the Post Office airmail leases were coming up for renewal and there was a near-unanimous agreement that the government had to control and supervise the airlines, just as it did the railroads.

Thus, the idea of a Federal Aviation Commission was born during the Black hearings, and its sole function was to regulate civil aeronautics. At the outset, for some reason, control over civil aviation was given to the Interstate Commerce Commission (ICC), which supervised railroads and bus lines. No mention was made of international air service. It was then that Trippe entreated the government that foreign air service was also an instrument of defense, even though his underlying concern was that domestic airlines might encroach on Pan Am's foreign routes.

To embellish and protect Trippe's position, a group of lawyers, politicians, and former high political officeholders was rounded up as a team to pitch Trippe's viewpoint. A $1 million war chest was set aside for massive phone bills, expenses, travel, entertainment, and more entertainment. A comprehensive, self-serving white paper (without attribution) was secretly prepared, and this document circulated to members of Congress, the Senate, and executive agencies. It was no secret where the document had originated.

News stories and magazine features were prepared for writers and reporters who had only to affix their names to these "authoritative," if slanted, stories. Heated arguments and a filibuster in the Senate talked the new bill to death.

In the end, the Post Office's life and death power over the airlines was passed on to the new agency, the Civil Aeronautics Authority (CAA). It established a procedure whereby an airline had to be licensed to benefit from a franchise for a specific route. It was similar to railroads' traveling over established "right-of-way" routes.

Airlines, by virtue of a grandfather clause, would continue to operate on their old routes. Each airline's right of certification depended on its rendering adequate and efficient service. At Trippe's team's insistence, the distinction between domestic and international lines was written into the bill.

Then a new wrinkle developed. Foreign countries with their "chosen instruments" insisted on negotiating with the U.S. government on Atlantic routes and landing rights. Among the countries were Great Britain, New Zealand, and Portugal. It was now obvious that Trippe was not going to throw his own wide loop overseas and make deals on his own with foreign airlines or countries. The State Department would do the trading with its foreign counterparts.

Trippe, remembering his football playing days at Yale, made an end run and demanded that Roosevelt approve overseas routes himself, as they affected national defense and FDR was commander in chief. Evidently, the President bought it. Trippe found himself a hairbreadth away from being the chosen instrument. Now U.S. domestic airlines could connect to Europe only through Pan Am. Any tampering with this would impinge on national security. Trippe played this to a fare-thee-well, despite FDR's avowal to do away with monopolistic practices.

Unexpectedly, a regulatory agency was set up to foster competition for foreign and domestic air transport. Trippe was furious. He stated that foreign airlines and steamship lines would set impossibly low rates and drive U.S. airlines out of business. When applications were requested for international air services licenses, Trippe demanded that these routes be turned down.

Mysteriously, the CAA was suddenly denied the authority to regulate international passenger fares, a sore point that would rankle the agency for the next forty years. Trippe's lobbying, plus the aid of a few political cronies, saved the day for him—almost. A five-man board was to be selected for a six-year term, with a mandate to promote an evenhanded and healthy economic climate for the airline industry.

This back and forth was like a Ping-Pong match, first one side scores a point, then the other. And as Yogi Berra was to say at a later date, "It ain't over 'til it's over."

Despite Trippe's and Priester's attachment to amphibious planes, the government was willing to encourage the airline industry by deciding that the future of aviation was in land planes, not seaplanes. While still building the Clippers, Pan Am joined TWA, American, and United in commissioning Donald Douglas to build an experimental four-engine plane, the DC-4. The government was pushing for planes to carry one hundred passengers in pressurized cabins and fly at altitudes of twenty-five thousand feet, with a range of five thousand or more miles.

In 1944, the President of the United States made a proclamation—at the International Civil Aviation Conference in Chicago—to the effect that the future development of international civil aviation could greatly create and preserve friendship and understanding among nations of the world. Thus a set of principles was proposed and tentatively agreed to by forty-eight countries (as the United States was at war, obviously its enemies did not sign at that time).

In summary, all ninety-six articles stipulated the goal was an agreement that international air transport services would be established on the basis of equality of opportunity between countries.

Juan Trippe felt that somehow he could circumvent some of these articles and get the monopoly of operating internationally out of the United States. By April 16, 1945, forty-four airlines from twenty-five countries ratified the articles in Chicago, forming a new organization, the International Air Transport Association (IATA). But this was later killed due to bickering among several nations.

Great Britain and the United States made an Anglo-American Bi-Lateral Accord, which opened the skies to power politics. The United States traded entry to U.S. airports by foreign airlines in exchange for pledges of allegiance and support from their governments. Everyone was willing to deal for competitive advantage.

The CAB had hundreds of applications for international routes. Air

Force general Hap Arnold commented that there was no law that gave American international aviation to Pan Am. But Trippe kept pushing his chosen instrument scheme. By this time, Harry Truman was President and Trippe soon found out how tough he was. When friends of Trippe approached Truman about Pan Am, they were told, in no uncertain terms, that monopoly usually ends up in price gouging and unfair policies. "Besides, why should I act to satisfy someone I dislike as much as Juan Trippe?"

Eventually, Trippe's actions proved to be an embarrassment to his board, who voted him out as chairman of Pan Am and replaced him with Jock Whitney. Not long afterward, in a power play, Trippe replaced Whitney and quickly resumed his secretive, monopolistic plans. When he called me to his office to do some more globe-trotting on his behalf, I was now more sophisticated and it was apparent that Trippe was out to circumvent the law.

I discussed Trippe's ideas with my close friend Bill MacCracken. Off the record, he told me, "You know by now how Juan Trippe operates. You know he's getting you enmeshed in his monopoly plan. I see nothing but trouble with what he's trying to do. He's got blinders on and there's no talking to him. He keeps every one of his secret schemes in his head. I recommend that you consider his plans very, very carefully and make your decisions accordingly. I cannot help you any further than that, Henri."

MacCracken was one of Trippe's advisers, so obviously he couldn't divulge anything. On the other hand, he was my friend—and wondered if I was clever enough to understand what he was telling me. I couldn't sleep that night, mulling over Trippe's plans and what Mac-Cracken had told me—and what he left unsaid.

Next day, I was closeted again with Trippe. He said, "Henri, I have a great proposition on how to sell my program to foreign air carriers. Suppose we offer foreign airlines entry into some of our domestic routes in exchange for permitting Pan Am the same privilege on some of their domestic routes? It's just like the Liberia situation. In addition, we'll let them take some Pan Am aircraft and certify them under Liberian sovereignty. Thus, these aircraft will have an interchange program with Pan American Airways. This will permit Pan Am aircraft to fly their routes as well. In addition, we offer them the opportunity to purchase rights to obtain the new Douglas DC-4s and the other aircraft when they become available, perhaps even Constellations when they're completed. This gives them the same fleet privileges—that is, lowest costs—that Pan Am has when purchasing these aircraft.

"You get over there and tell them that Pan Am is the first flag carrier in the United States for all military purposes—it's an extension of the U.S. government, the only symbol of America in the U.S. embassies. Why, we were overseas before Coca-Cola was. That's my proposition. Get over there and get those people to join us."

I took a deep breath and said, "But it's illegal. It's strictly against all the rules of aviation that were set up by the CAB and the FAA. It's absolutely against U.S. policy to monopolize routes outside the country."

"I don't give a shit what Roosevelt's lackeys signed in the Chicago, Bermuda, and Havana conventions. We'll do it my way and make history. Now, goddammit, move your ass lickity-split."

For the first time in my life, I had a pain in my stomach. Trippe's unethical behavior was getting to me. I thought I'd give it one last shot before I quit. I gathered all the letters Trippe had written to the heads of KLM, SAS, and the other airlines, and I took off on my mission.

But after months of discussions throughout Africa and Europe, I found that while most of the airlines liked the idea of getting advanced U.S. aircraft at rock-bottom prices, their legal departments were confused about the ethics as well as the legality of what Trippe proposed. Only Liberia was set to go.

When necessary, I went to the embassies for help, but I was on thin ice and could limit my requests for assistance only to matters outside international airline practices. But as their questions became pointed, it was obvious they weren't fooled. I'm sure they wondered how I was going to get away with circumventing the State Department. My last stop was Paris, but Air France didn't go for the scheme either. I was wasting my time.

As one friend in the U.S. embassy put it, "Henri, you'll never survive long enough in prison to serve out the sentence you'll get for all the illegal things you are trying to pull."

After getting word to Maria that I was coming back, I called Mac-Cracken. He told me that the State Department was extremely angry at what I was trying to do in Europe. As history proved so often, once again the messenger was being blamed for the message.

On my return, I was called to a Pan Am executive meeting to report my progress, so I had to address the very vice presidents who had given me a hard time once before.

Without pulling punches, I laid it out country by country. "I have been advised by every country but one that this is the worst case of treachery ever attempted on foreign governments. All I could sell of this proposition was the purchase of new aircraft at fleet price."

Then the critics chimed in.

"You didn't sell it right."

"You didn't do a damn thing and look at all the money you spent."

"You don't understand what we're trying to accomplish."

Hot under the collar now, I said, "To achieve what you want, you have to use unethical methods and dirty tricks while bypassing international laws. You want a monopoly and you don't care how you achieve it. Just let the chips fall where they may."

Then I was lectured to by so-called vice presidents who didn't know what they were talking about, didn't understand right from wrong, and blathered simply to show me up in front of Trippe.

Before long, they began blaming me. I was now the scapegoat, as though it was my idea to bypass U.S. and foreign sovereign aviation rules.

On the surface, Pan Am was still held in high regard by the U.S. government for its war service in the Pacific and the Atlantic and South America. So, once again, I was asked to go back with more concessions to offer the foreign airlines. Liberia still was agreeable to Trippe's deal.

I telephoned Trippe, who then asked me to purchase land for a major airport hotel and houses for personnel. I was to give a deposit on my personal account and would be reimbursed later. Imagine my chagrin when I found out that the purchase wasn't for Pan Am, but for Trippe and his vice presidents as a personal venture. The purchase was in my name.

KLM, Air France, and SAS listened politely, and again all expressed interest in the low-cost planes, but none wanted to get associated with Pan Am's scheme to flimflam international regulations.

Again, I returned to New York to make my report. They were delighted with Liberia and furious with me that the others had turned me down. Some even got downright abusive, saying I had somehow sabotaged a perfectly good deal.

Very calmly I said, "Fifty percent of this disaster is your fault and fifty percent is my fault for even working on this program. I've made an ass of myself with our government and with foreign governments and airlines by taking this crap to them. I've had a belly full of this stupidity and I won't take it anymore. I resign."

It was July 1948. Trippe asked me to stay, said that he had a deadline of October 1, 1948, to get everything in place.

"Too bad," I said and walked out of the room.

CHAPTER 20

The Last Laugh

I'VE HAD MORE than my share of coincidences. As a religious man, I believe it's the hand of God guiding me—or perhaps the things that seem to be taking place accidentally really are coincidences.

As I walked into the elevator after resigning, I bumped into a longtime friend, H. Hamilton Weber, director of the Empire State Building. He asked why I was looking glum, so I told him I had just quit Pan Am. First he said nothing, then he asked me to have lunch with him at the Stork Club. Everything was boiling up inside me and I had to spill it out to someone, so I thought, Why not Weber?

Robert Tiner, an associate of Weber's, joined us, and I told them what had just transpired. Unfortunately, I confessed it all, mentioning things I had done for Trippe, some of which I don't even want to write about.

Said Weber, "Pan Am did a lot of good things during the war, like advancing commercial aviation. It makes me sad to hear about the sorry things Trippe's involved in."

"Worst of all," I said, "I've been buying land privately for Trippe and the vice presidents and signing for it on my personal bank account. It could look like fraud. Pan Am is a public company. It could be construed as acting on inside information, as well as a case of conflict of interest. Technically, I'm the one holding the bag. Then there's the matter of circumventing international regulations, going against the policy of the United States, and undeclared ownership in foreign airlines—just a few of the things Trippe got me embroiled in."

Weber said, "I understand that numerous members of the board are a bit fed up with Trippe's obsession and behavior. Would you want to volunteer this information to the government on your own?"

"No," I said. "I'm angry, but I can't be disloyal to the company where I worked for eighteen years. Besides, I'm in enough hot water with the State Department."

We finished lunch and I had gotten it all out of my system. I felt as though I had cleansed my soul, but now I had to go home and tell Maria I was unemployed.

As the poet Cowper said, "God moves in a mysterious way." I had taken a couple of weeks off to relax with my wife and think about the future. Besides being a pilot, I had been involved in so many globe-trotting ventures that I wanted something more than just flying a plane. But other than plucking a banjo and playing the organ, what else did I know outside of flying?

At the time, Truman was running for President and most magazines and newspapers said he didn't have a chance against Thomas E. Dewey, governor of New York. Trippe had been helped enormously by the Republicans when Hoover was President, and more reluctantly by Democrat Roosevelt, who considered Trippe a necessary evil during the war. Now he had to contend with Truman.

One day, I unexpectedly got a call from the White House to have breakfast with the President. There were a dozen other people there, including Weber. Nothing was said until we were leaving and the President shook my hand. "Are you still the same honest, God-fearing man as when I last saw you in committee?"

"Yes, Mr. President."

"After the elections, let's have a talk."

The presidential election of 1948 became the upset of the century when Truman defeated Dewey. I was called to the White House to have an off-the-record meeting with the President and several members of his cabinet. They wanted to talk about Pan Am.

They talked first, and they knew more than I knew about the deceit and manipulations of Trippe, and his machinations to try to monopolize foreign air travel. I never would have admitted anything voluntarily, but now I had no choice but to tell them the truth. Evidently, I was the first executive-level employee who could confirm all of Trippe's duplicity firsthand.

After I left, Truman's committee compiled a report on Pan Am that went to all government agencies. Eventually, Pan Am was charged with excessive competitive aggressiveness, sharp business practices, and bringing undue influence to bear both on the U.S. government and on governments abroad. The committee recommended a sweeping investigation of Pan Am to determine if any antitrust laws had been violated, and threatened Trippe with possible criminal indictment for monopolizing international air routes and bypassing CAB and FAA regulations.

The result was a sweeping reform of the airline industry, providing competition between U.S. carriers operating on domestic as well as international routes. On August 1, 1949, the CAB denied Pan Am's application for domestic routes. Henceforth, all domestic routes were to be subject to presidential review. The CAB embarked on a wide course of issuing permits to other air carriers to serve U.S. cities and foreign routes. Thus, Air France would have New York and Chicago; KLM, New York and Miami; El Al, New York via London and Paris. Years later, the CAB would accommodate the State Department as it traded off landing rights for political advantage.

Pan Am was not restricted to landing rights in New York or Los Angeles like the foreign carriers, but it was not allowed to operate between the cities or have any cabotage rights therein. The CAB also denied the merger between Pan Am and TWA, thus denying Pan Am any domestic routes.

The Civil Aeronautics Board made it plain that there was no substitute for healthy competition as a stimulus to progress and efficiency. TWA was awarded the plum, the routes to serve Paris, Rome, Madrid, Athens, Cairo, Jerusalem and Mediterranean Europe, North Africa, and the Persian Gulf. But as a final blow, the CAB gave United and Northwest Airlines routes to the Orient.

Pan Am finally ended up with six terminals in the United States: New York, Boston, Philadelphia, Chicago, Washington, and Detroit, with no air service between these ports—that is, no cabotage rights. For international routes, Pan Am had certificates for Ireland and England, and was forced to share routes with other U.S. airlines in other markets. It put an end to Trippe's grandiose plans to have Pan Am as the chosen instrument.

In early 1949, I went for an interview at the State Department accompanied by Bill MacCracken, who felt I was too valuable as a troubleshooter to go back to flying for the airlines. He thought I should be part of the FAA. Suddenly, there was a buzz in the corridors as President Truman came by, flanked by Secret Service agents. He stopped to talk to us and wanted to know what we were doing there. MacCracken told him.

"I think it's a helluva good idea," said the President with a twinkle in his eye.

Which is how I started working for the Federal Aviation Authority— a job that over the years would get me into more hot water.

CHAPTER 21

Learning How to Fly a Desk

AT AGE FORTY-ONE, in the prime of my life, I went to work for the State Department. Having worked for Pan Am for eighteen years, from 1930 until 1948, I now signed on for a new job with the government. I couldn't possibly imagine it would last twenty-eight years.

The first thing they did was to verify my family history, check my citizenship (I had become a citizen at age eleven, when my father became an American), our family roots, and my religion. Many photos were taken, my fingerprints as well, and all scars on my body were recorded. My physical exam was extremely thorough and included my height and weight.

Then, for the next two days, I had to take language tests to prove my ability to speak, read, and write all the languages listed on my résumé. To qualify, a passing grade on each language was necessary. For the following two weeks, my wife and I attended diplomatic classes on how to work and associate with foreigners, attend embassy socials, and make foreign business contacts. Finally, we were taught the ethics of behavior in a foreign country.

The next two months were a concentration of intense courses near Washington given by the FBI, and the CIA. During the following three months, I had to demonstrate my ability to defend myself against a physical attack by a foreign agent, to fight and kill if necessary, or disable a human being. This was taught in the FBI and CIA training schools for overt and covert work in enemy territory. I was also shown how to keep in shape physically and how to continue to keep my skills honed. The indoctrination into the FAA required another six weeks of study.

On February 16, my forty-second birthday, I was called to the State Department and informed that the FAA wanted to send me to Argentina to set up the Argentine airlines. Apparently, the present airline was in chaos due to work stoppages and slowdowns, which were being masterminded by local Communists. My job was to reorganize the Argentine airlines into a trouble-free, world-class operation.

My wife was my great joy, and it was lucky for me that she enjoyed traveling, meeting people, and going to new countries. Summer was just setting in (south of the equator, summer comes at the opposite time of the year).

After a few days in Argentina, it was obvious that setting up a national airline there was not going to be easy. To start with, there were few properly trained people, so where would one get pilots, engineers, and maintenance staff? The Communists also recognized the problem and were trying to smuggle in trained Party members from other countries to infiltrate selected airlines. The British, who were also trying to prevent the infiltration, joined forces with us.

Under the Perón dictatorship, it seemed as though Argentina was patterned after the democratic life in the United States. But this was just a surface perception. Perón, like all dictators, took care of himself and his friends a lot better than the citizens. This led to unrest and demonstrations by the poor against the government.

Eva Perón, a woman of the streets in her early life, set out to help the disadvantaged. It was rumored that she suffered bitter reprisals at the hands of her husband. However, this didn't stop her from helping the poor while still enjoying the good life.

Working with the top management of the existing Argentine airline was next to impossible, and "impossible" was the word they used for every suggestion I made. The second most used word was *mañana* (tomorrow). The unions were so saturated with recalcitrant workers that everything was near a standstill. The situation was divided between people who didn't want to try anything and people who didn't want to do anything.

If that wasn't bad enough, there was an even more critical problem with the airline. Several important executives, whom I considered the core of the airline, suddenly disappeared. We got no help from the police, who took down the information but never called back. These men were difficult to replace, and what made it even sadder were the furious wives and relatives who blamed the airline for their disappearance and threw stones at us. It was a long time before someone whispered in my ear that the missing officials were victims of Perón's execution squads.

I was caught in the jaws of a giant nutcracker and, after a while, concluded, "What's the use of a dictatorship if you can't put it to work for you?" While I have no use for dictators, I have even less for Communists. It was not my purpose to get anyone killed, but in order to get some action, I put pressure on our U.S. and British embassies to exert their influence on Perón's government to break up the gridlock. I wanted permission to fire some workers, which was against the law in Argentina. Permission was granted.

Buenos Aires was a beautiful white city with many boulevards and wide plazas. Its subway system was luxurious, with the stations made of brick and marble. To emerge from the underground to get to the plazas above, you used an elevator. Argentina was a rich agricultural country, a leading oil exporter as well as an importantt cattle country. The two million–plus people in the capital were as sophisticated and cosmopolitan as those in Paris, London, or New York. Life in Buenos Aires was lived in very high style.

Argentineans were a very united people—a mixture of European immigrants and Indian stock. They all spoke Spanish and the more educated spoke Castilian Spanish. The people had one common interest—the love of sports, particularly soccer. But there were also hunting, fishing, sailing, skiing, mountain climbing, horseback riding, and more.

The Ezeiza International Airport in Buenos Aires was twenty-six miles from the city and was not served by taxis. Private cars driven by entrepreneurs provided this service, and at the time I was there, a ride from the airport cost 40 pesos. The finest hotel then was the Hotel Bolívar, a large, elegant establishment.

I was allotted an embassy car, but I needed a second car for Maria to get around in. As she couldn't drive, I needed a driver, but chauffeurs were not expensive in Buenos Aires, and the car we purchased was an unexpected pleasure for Maria. The British economics minister was returning home and he sold me his two-year-old Rolls-Royce for $7,000.

After much negotiation with the various embassies and many government departments, it was finally decided to have an Argentine national airline. It would be an instrument of international commerce and national security along the lines of the other world airlines.

Our base was a poorly functioning, poorly maintained airline that needed more than a swift kick in the pants. The first order of business was to get rid of the incompetent managers and supervisors and replace them with new people. We had to find intelligent and able Argentineans and train them in running an airline. The problem was where to get them?

Supervisors had to be people who would set an example by arriving at work promptly and maintaining regular hours. Meanwhile, the workers and their unions were constantly complaining of poor treatment because no one addressed their needs. The result was ongoing demonstrations. By posting regular work schedules for supervisors as well as for workers, tempers cooled off. The next problem to tackle was economic security for the employees.

Workers had to be treated fairly and honorably and receive adequate wages. Next came emotional security. Workers had to feel they trusted their supervisors and that the work they did was worthwhile. Like most workers, they wanted to enjoy the pride of accomplishment.

Much of what I suggested was not on the Communist agenda, as Communist workers were obliged to accept whatever they were told and not question authority. I then set up a system of rewards for those employees who came up with worthwhile suggestions.

Training supervisors in a classroom was the toughest job of all. Some trainees responded well and enjoyed getting things done quickly. Others resisted and had to be weeded out. We set up programs for pilots, flight engineers, and mechanics. To do this, I imported some out-of-work American pilots and other personnel who were fluent in Spanish. I asked the pros to help prepare a curriculum for supervisors to follow. I lectured to classes as well.

The system finally began to work, which left me with more time to go sightseeing with Maria—in her car, of course. We always ended up on Avenida Santa Fe, where the finest shops were located, as Maria never lost a chance to go shopping. Because there were more holidays celebrated in Argentina than anywhere else in South America, it created more shopping days for Maria.

One day in July, I received an emergency call that the city of San Juan, Argentina, had suffered a very destructive earthquake. The city fathers were pleading for assistance. San Juan is located five hundred miles northwest of Buenos Aires in the Andes mountain chain across from Chile. Pilots were scarce and the captains and co-pilots on the airline were obliged to stick to their schedules. I decided to jump in and help. I needed a co-pilot. Searching the records, I found one on sick leave. I recruited him for the emergency and I commandeered one of the four-engine Argentine military DC-4s. Working with emergency crews, I made four round-trips almost nonstop, flying relief equipment to San Juan and bringing out orphaned children and old people who had lost their families and homes.

As July is the winter season in Argentina, the upper air can register between 20 to 40 degrees below zero. Wing defrosters often malfunctioned at these freezing temperatures. The only incident happened on my fourth round-trip, when I was exhausted and two engines conked out. I was obliged to feather the outboard engines, i.e., the numbers one and four engines. I landed safely with my human cargo, using just the two inboard engines. A ground inspection revealed that the oil radiators on the outboard engines had frozen.

Eventually, we got the airline functioning smoothly. Now it was necessary for me to make numerous trips to Europe to set up reciprocal agreements with other airlines, including landing rights, interchange of maintenance, and other operational matters. The Argentine government was very pleased when it began gaining recognition for its international airline.

That just about completed my work. I managed to get some additional flying time in by personally checking out pilots and flight engineers, but it was different from flying a regular schedule for Pan Am. In the end, we sold our Rolls at no profit. Maria and I were named first-class citizens of Buenos Aires, and we were recognized as *porteños*, as the residents of Buenos Aires are called.

We returned to Washington for reassignment. At my debriefing at the State Department and the Civil Aeronautics Administration, I was told our household goods were being shipped directly to Pôrto Alegre, Brazil. "You're to help the Brazilians set up a national airline called Varig [Vicão Aerea Rio Grandense]."

We had some home leave due, so we visited my family in Miami, then decided that instead of flying to Brazil, we'd get permission to travel to Pôrto Alegre by ship. It was a second honeymoon. Luckily,

Maria never tired of traveling and thoroughly enjoyed meeting people. All I had to say was we were going to such and such a place, and she'd say, "How much time do I have to pack?"

The Moore-McCormick Line brought us back to Buenos Aires, then cruised up to the Rio Grande. From there, we took a small ship to the Logos dos Patos to Pôrto Alegre, a city in the province of Rio Grande do Sul. The trip took all day. On our arrival, we were met by the officials of Varig, an airline founded in 1927 by Otto Ernst Meyer, a German, and his nineteen-year-old Brazilian secretary, Ruben Martin Berta.

Varig was originally granted permission to serve Brazil's southernmost state, Rio Grande do Sul, and its single aircraft was a German Dornier WAL, a seven-passenger seaplane. It was a two-engine plane with a puller propeller in the front and a pusher propeller in the rear. The fledgling company had 550 shareholders.

In 1939, when World War II broke out, Brazil sided with the Allies and Otto Ernst Meyer was forced to resign and Ruben Martin Berta was elected president. After the war, Varig added six DC-3s to the line and Berta talked the shareholders into allowing the employees to own and operate Varig. Today, it is called the Ruben Berta Foundation and it is the company's largest shareholder. In 1952, Varig purchased Aero Geral Airline, a small, defunct company in northern Brazil, enabling Varig to service the entire country.

As part of our welcome to Pôrto Alegre, the airline gave us a special barbecue, prepared by genuine *gauchos* (cowboys), so our first dinner in Pôrto Alegre was a marvelous treat. A beautiful city, it is located on a two-hundred-mile-long peninsula that has no name, but the bay between the peninsula and the mainland is called Lagoa dos Patos.

Next morning, I visited Varig's headquarters to watch it function. Its maintenance record and reputation for courteous service were second to none. I began to wonder what I was doing there.

As I was an invited consultant of the airline, I began to poke around at the bottom and at the top of management. My impression was that though Varig was an important instrument for world trade and national security, it was stagnating. There's an old business adage that says, "If you're not going forward, you're going backward."

For the next month, I flew their airplanes and made en route inspections of their major and minor way stations. It was soon apparent that everything needed upgrading from pilot training and night flying to engineering training and maintenance.

Newer, more efficient planes were needed. At the small way stations, the employees were feeling neglected; I could see that a new promotion policy and merit wage structure were needed. Because the line was employee-owned, the top managers should be made to look on airline workers not as employees but as partners.

I revised the school curriculum to improve training, but progress was slow in coming. Varig management said there were some radicals in the union who were creating the problems. When I commented, "But these people are owners of this airline," the answer was a shrug.

There was a strong group of Polish refugees who had emigrated to Brazil during and after World War II. Most of them spoke or understood Russian and detested Communists, so we made those who were eligible security guards. I had been around Europe too long to ask questions about what happened next, but before long, the airline was expunged of all undesirable troublemakers.

Varig accepted my recommendation that they purchase Douglas DC-4s and Lockheed Constellations. With a firm date set for future deliveries, I made arrangements for the chief mechanics at all the way stations to take turns going to engineering college in San José de Campo near Lão Paulo.

While Varig's standards were quite good, they still didn't meet aviation rules in accordance with international standards, so we prepared a new set of rules. In all, it took a year to get Varig on track and running smoothly. Soon, I was getting urgent letters from Washington to wind down the job, as there were other assignments waiting for me.

As a token of their appreciation, Varig flew us home to Washington. We were the only passengers on the plane.

CHAPTER 22

A Three-Ring Circus
Called TWA

FROM PERSONAL EXPERIENCE I must say that the State Department was always on the ball. Upon my return, I was obliged to attend a course for an updating of FAA matters, after which I was sent to Oklahoma City Institute for two weeks of advance work on the CAA.

It wasn't long before my next assignment came through. The head of the CAA called me in and said, "Henri, for this particular job you're our most experienced officer. TWA is a mess. Howard Hughes seems to have a love-hate relationship with his airline—sometimes he works at running it and sometimes he simply vanishes.

"You have experience running airlines. See if you can figure out how to get this one on the ball and make it profitable—then try to get Howard Hughes to sell his shares to a new company of airline executives."

The whole airline industry was a small community. If you were in it long enough, you knew almost everybody, and if they didn't know you, they had certainly heard of you. This time, the language wasn't Spanish as in Argentina, or Portuguese, as in Brazil, it was American. But that doesn't mean the problems were any different.

So Maria and I bought a new car and drove off to Kansas City, home of TWA. Surprisingly, I was welcomed there, and after we settled in, I spent the next three days poking around. Just as a plan began to form in my head, disaster struck. There was a torrential rain that didn't seem to stop, and before long, the Kaw River threatened to overflow and inundate all TWA facilities just where the Kaw enters into the Missouri.

The rain just kept pouring down. As the river waters started to crest, I volunteered to help fly as many planes as possible to Wichita, Kansas. Suddenly, it was an around-the-clock operation, the newer planes first, the older ones after that. One plane, a Constellation, had only three functioning engines. Nevertheless, I took off in the rain with a light load of fuel and made it. On my return, the only planes remaining were in poor or unserviceable condition. There was a DC-4 sitting there, one of my favorite aircraft, with only two operable engines. In training, we learn to fly four-engine planes on three and two engines. I had done it before. The DC-4 looked so helpless on the runway. If it stayed, it would be demolished by the waters that were rapidly rising at the airport. Its tanks were about a third full, so I hunted down a volunteer TWA co-pilot to help me. The takeoff took forever, as we couldn't get enough airspeed to lift off; somehow, we got airborne, and managed the flight successfully, but I needed all the available Wichita runway to land. It was delicious. Deep down inside, I understood what was lacking in my life—the good old days of crisis flying.

Eventually, the rain stopped and the floods subsided. What was left were tons of mud and more mud. All the airplane logs were gone. Those logs recorded the number of hours each engine had flown (a necessary rule to enforce the overhaul of engines after a certain number of flying hours), tests for metal fatigue, the maintenance records, the tracking of replacement parts, etc. Decisions had to be made on how to figure out the hours each engine had operated. It couldn't be calculated with any margin of safety, so I ordered each plane overhauled and brought up to new airplane standards with new logs set at zero time.

TWA had to wash off the mud on all machines, tools, benches, cabinets, and spare parts. Most tools could be salvaged, but delicate instruments such as gauges and electronics testing equipment could not be saved. The only records that could be re-created came from the manufacturer as to when each plane was built and when it was turned over to TWA.

Temporary headquarters for the airline was set up in St. Louis. As I represented the State Department and the CAA, I was the official on the spot. I had to certify each plane and spare part after overhaul and issue airworthiness certificates, enabling them to carry passengers and be engaged in international commerce.

When I visited the New York office as part of my investigation and looked through corporate papers, I discovered that Howard Hughes owned 45 percent of TWA's stock through the Hughes Tool Company, yet his name did not appear on corporate stationery. However, TWA was Howard Hughes's toy and he played with it as such.

Back in 1946, TWA was showing signs of postwar depression as business plummeted. To inaugurate new international routes, heavy expenses would be incurred, but TWA was losing $18.6 million annually. The stock, which once had a high of $71 per share, had dropped to $18, making it virtually impossible to borrow the capital to pay for the new Lockheed Constellations ordered by Howard Hughes before the war.

Despite Hughes's being a lone wolf, Juan Trippe could never best him in a deal. Still, the other airlines were not exactly friends of Hughes's. He was always busy with other matters and spent far too little time with the company, despite his pride in it.

We were finally able to negotiate a deal with Noah Dietrich, managing director of Hughes Tool Company and Howard Hughes's alter ego. He managed to borrow $40 million from Equitable Life Insurance Society to be applied to new equipment and other capital expenditures.

To be honest, TWA's future and Lockheed's were connected like Siamese twins. Lockheed, builder of the Constellations and the P-38 Lightning pursuit plane during World War II, had the eighteen Constellations ordered by Hughes sitting on a runway ready for delivery. If they weren't bought, both companies would go into bankruptcy.

The government felt it could not allow TWA to go out of business. At the start of World War II, TWA was a leader in airline technology: it was the first carrier with planes to rise above bad weather with high-altitude flying; it was the only airline operating four-engine transports, and if it went out of business it would eliminate several valuable international airline routes from a postwar, security-conscious nation.

Juan Trippe, through inside sources, heard about TWA's plight and tried to buy the company. He approached TWA directly, as well as trying one of his famous end runs by going to Equitable, which had loaned TWA $40 million. Neither ploy worked.

About that time, I was recommending new training methods for

TWA personnel in maintenance, engineering, and flight training, as well as the training of the stewardesses. The international pilots needed more training as well, because they had insufficient training in international law, foreign languages, navigation, and communication techniques. I got Howard Hughes to personally agree to fund new training establishments to the tune of $10 million.

Over the years, Howard Hughes and I didn't see each other often, but we kept in touch ever since I had helped him win his first air race. Now that I was assigned to TWA, we saw each other at meetings, the good ones and the tough ones. So it was no surprise when he called one day, asking me to come to New York. He hinted a little and it was apparent that he was going to offer me the presidency of TWA.

We had a congenial meeting, but I wasn't sure that this was what I wanted to do. While Howard Hughes was certainly not Juan Trippe, he had eccentricities of his own. As a billionaire, he could do anything his heart desired. I saw the job as a challenge, which I'd enjoy, but it was loaded with pitfalls, particularly the one of absentee ownership. I told him I would think about it. This was in early 1952.

On the TWA flight for my return to Kansas City, I was given VIP treatment and seated next to another VIP, Dwight Eisenhower, then president of Columbia University. He was going to visit his home in Abilene and as we spoke he remembered that we had met once before. It happened at a military base at Atkinson Field in Georgetown, British Guiana, while I was on Pan Am business, I was given royal treatment and occupied the executive suite available for visiting VIPs. When General and Mrs. Eisenhower arrived with all their luggage, I offered to move out of the suite, but he insisted I stay. We laughed about that and had a fine chat all the way to Kansas.

No sooner had I returned to work than I received a call from Hughes. "Henri, we just concluded the deal with Lockheed for some newer-model Constellations with longer range, more power, and larger passenger capacity. I want you to gather up your pilot and flight engineer groups, as well as hostesses, and bring them with you for special training. Then when you're through here, go to New York and train the international pilots."

I didn't work for TWA and I didn't like that kind of imperious attitude. However, I did it, recognizing that I could never be president of a company where someone else made all the decisions and called the shots. The training went well and the new Constellations were a dream to fly.

Back again in Kansas City, I began to take a hard look at the personnel and management teams. It was apparent that it was Pan Am all over again. The vice presidents and other high officials were busy being busy, accomplishing little, and receiving high salaries and bonuses. This was causing a drop in morale and a general malaise among the employees.

The deadwood had to be cut out. It was absolutely necessary. So we hired new, knowledgeable people capable of running an airline. The next item on the agenda was to make certain the employees were receiving competitive wages and that they were happy on the job. I stipulated that each one go through a training program to help instill personal pride.

Subsequently, a lot of what I did was checking out routines, the handling of passengers and freight at the foreign destinations, and passenger service. When I had been there five years, the State Department and the FAA called me back to Washington for a conference. I was called on the carpet because of numerous complaints that I had been too rough with the employees and had fired top executives.

I said, "You can't run an airline with incompetent executives who create morale problems. Also, it's not in my reports, but we found some executives with their hands in the till. To make the body whole, you have to cut out the cancer."

I got a kiss on the cheek and a kick in the ass for my work and told to go back to TWA and do more of the same. When I returned to Kansas City, Howard Hughes asked me to come to California. He was taking a special flight from Los Angeles to New York and he wanted me aboard to inspect the operation.

TWA was nicknamed the "playboy airline," because Howard Hughes was the president. He was an extremely wealthy man and a big shot in movies, with Hollywood stars for girlfriends. The trip turned out to be a playboy's dream (or nightmare). The plane was loaded with movie stars as well as champagne and caviar. They tried getting me to drink, but I rarely do and, besides, I was there on an inspection flight. At one point, to escape the frivolity, I went up front and flew the plane.

It finally came to the point where the company was running efficiently and I was told by the State Department and the FAA to back off and let TWA run the airline with its new management team. Next on the agenda was to monitor the operation with regard to domestic and international safety.

By now, Howard Hughes was getting into a financial bind with his many activities. His investments in Nevada gambling casinos were taking an enormous amount of his time and money, as were his Hollywood investments. TWA needed an additional $200 million and he wasn't willing or perhaps able to come up with the money. At the peak of the crisis, Noah Dietrich, who had run his business empire since 1925, suddenly quit. I was supposed to convince him to sell, but Hughes was not willing to sell his interest in TWA for less than $546 million. It never came to pass.

Toward the end of my assignment, I recommended the building of a new overhaul base away from Kansas City, as one more flood would destroy TWA. At the end of the year—1952—Eisenhower was elected President of the United States. I was also called back to Washington for another slap on the wrist. The New York FAA office was complaining that I was checking out pilots for overseas flying instead of leaving it for the New York office. Luckily, after a long talk, HQ wrote back that if New York officials would attend manufacturers' flight schools and graduate with the airline pilots the way Henri had, there would be fewer complaints.

TWA was now running smoothly, so Washington had me checking out other airlines in the Midwest, as well as inspecting the two existing flight schools in the territory. One was Parks Air College in St. Louis, Missouri, and the other was the Miami University air school in Cincinnati, Ohio. I also lectured at these schools, trying to instill in the students what a pilot's proficiency should be.

My final inspection was checking the TWA operation from Los Angeles to Ceylon. Maria and I thought that in Kansas City we had finally found our permanent home, but it turned out not to be. In early 1954, I was recalled to Washington and informed that this time my assignment would be the biggest challenge of my career.

CHAPTER 23

Japan

WE RETURNED to Washington in 1954 to prepare for my next assignment. The first order of business was to attend a State Department/ FAA conference with manufacturers of advanced jet aircraft being readied for airline operations in 1958/1959. This was interesting as we all got a glimpse of the future.

Then the State Department finally set up a review and evaluation of my five years with TWA. As the department received excellent ratings on the work I had accomplished, the conclusion was that my stay with the airline had been successful. I was shown several letters from other airlines requesting that Henri Keyzer-André personally check out their pilots because of recommendations from TWA.

Just as I was allocated a beautiful new office in Washington, the secretary of state received a call from John M. Allison, our ambassador to Japan, requesting help for the Japanese airline industry. This required someone with expertise in operations, engineering, and manufacturing, plus technical experience in all phases of aviation. Knowledge of Japanese preferable. The secretary of state submitted the request at a White House conference and it was granted.

My name was being painted on the door to my new office when I was summoned by Secretary of State John Foster Dulles. He had reviewed the files of the eligible officials available for the Japanese assignment and I was given first choice. He outlined everything that had to be accomplished and ended with, "You fit the job description to a T, except you don't speak Japanese. But you do speak thirteen languages, so a fourteenth should not be a hurdle. Now to the nitty gritty. The big problem in their aviation industry is this; what wasn't destroyed in the war was dismantled. So this is a sensitive assignment. Because of the complexities, you'll have to agree to stay a minimum of four years."

"Mr. Secretary, I like the challenge, but I have to discuss it with my wife." That night, when I examined the pros and cons with Maria, she agreed that Japan would be an exciting assignment. I could not possibly know that the decision to live in Japan would have an enormous impact on my life. It eventually allowed me to unravel the Amelia Earhart mystery, a secret I shared with no one until this writing.

At our second meeting, Mr. Dulles added some sober comments, reminding me it was only nine years since the end of World War II, when the Americans had dropped ninety thousand tons of bombs on Japan and virtually destroyed all major cities; this did not include the two atom bombs dropped on Nagasaki and Hiroshima. He added, "The Japanese are very conscious of 'face,' so your first job is to understand them while you gain their respect. Then it will be easier to help the country set up a productive airline. After you accomplish this, you would be responsible for training their air crews and personnel on how to operate an airline internationally." Then he laughed as he handed me a diplomatic dispatch from our economic minister in Japan, Ben Thebideaux:

YOU ARE REQUESTED TO BUY A NEW CADILLAC SEDAN AND BRING IT WITH YOU TO JAPAN. REGARDS.

After that Maria and I were rushed through health, security, and FBI checks as well as a personal financial investigation. During this time, I was given a diplomatic indoctrination course on Japanese culture and customs, and in between spent several hours a day studying the Japanese language. Maria had the task of selling our home, our automobiles, giving away our animals, placing her family jewelry in a bank vault, and placing most of our household furniture in storage. All this within a two-week deadline.

The big question was, Why the new Cadillac? I called the embassy in Japan and explained that on previous trips, I had observed that Tokyo's streets were so narrow it might be necessary to cut down telephone poles to allow the Caddy to pass.

First there was a laugh, then I was told, "Henri, the ambassador has a Caddy and has no problems with it."

About living accommodations, he said that because I would be working closely with the Japanese, trying to build a relationship, it would be protocol for me to be seen enjoying the life-style of a high-class Japanese businessman. Thus, Maria and I would live in a Japanese house rather than in the embassy compound. As it turned out later, this was sage advice.

Following a quick visit with my family in Miami, the State Department shipped our household effects along with the Cadillac, while we took a Pan Am Stratoliner to Tokyo with an overnight stop in Hawaii. Though I had been to Japan before, we suddenly encountered culture shock and discovered the meaning of red carpet treatment. Formally welcoming us was a high-level contingent from the U.S. Diplomatic Corps, as well as the president of Japan Airlines, the chief of Japan's Civil Aviation Board, and the general of Japan's Civil Defense Force.

Following the traditional introductions with flowers for Maria, we were all whisked away to the embassy for a second formal welcome by my department. There was an impromptu business meeting at which the Japanese aviation officials suddenly put me under interrogation with in-depth questions. This was followed by a tea ceremony in elegant Japanese style.

When it was over, Ben Thebideaux took me to one side and said he was pleased by the manner in which I had handled myself under fire while still showing proper respect to the Japanese officials. Then we were chauffeured by embassy car to our three-bedroom home, outfitted in Japanese style with a small, groomed garden and a roofed garage for our car. At 360 yen to the dollar, our rent came to 300 American dollars per month; our new address was *Ichi Ban Oyama Cho Shibuya Ku*, Tokyo, Japan.

In keeping with our new life-style, the embassy arranged to hire a cook for us, as well as a maid and chauffeur. All we had to do now was learn Japanese, the most difficult language in the world. This was one time my knowledge of Spanish, Dutch, German, Portuguese, and Russian would be of little use to me. Both of us were promptly enrolled at the embassy formal school to study the language. The funniest joke in the embassy was listening to my wife with her Zsa Zsa Gabor–type Hungarian accent trying to speak Japanese. Eventually, she got it.

I was informed that my new title was head of the Department of Transportation and my official offices would be at the embassy. The chief of protocol advised me to get engraved business cards and personal cards, and for Maria to get separate calling cards. Her first duty was to visit some of the other embassies and private homes of important people (we were given the list) and to leave our cards.

Humorist Stephen Leacock once made a comment that could have applied to me: "He jumped on his horse and galloped off in all directions." No one at the embassy knew anything about aviation, so I had to start digging to find out what my duties were and how to get going. It was finally decided that the best way to start was for me to be chauffeured around in an embassy car to pay my respects to the manufacturing companies, where I would leave my business and personal cards. Also on the list were visits to Japan Airlines, the Japanese Civil Aviation Bureau, and the Japanese Civil Defense Bureau, where I would also leave cards.

At the time, not too many Japanese people I met with spoke English. My progress with the Japanese language was so slow that communicating was a problem. I was cleared to hire a temporary translator and decided it would be more politic to get a Japanese national who spoke English rather than an American who understood Japanese. The embassy screened several prospects and I made the final selection, a twenty-four-year-old university engineering student in his last year. He was slated to go on to graduate work at MIT the following year and then return home to work in the automobile industry. He had enough technical background for my purposes and what he couldn't translate, he could ask one of his professors. I was hoping his Japanese/English translations would help me as well.

The first priority was to get acquainted with how the Japanese worked at manufacturing aviation products, as well as try to understand the relationships between employees and supervisors. As in most countries, the one thing that cannot be tampered with is tradition. I learned all too soon that most Japanese people were workaholics; hence, most supervisors expected them to work hard.

The next project was the study of their religions, Buddhism and Shintoism, and their reverence for the emperor, and to see how this affected their lives and work. This had been suggested by my interpreter. We worked at it and it gave me further insight into the Japanese persona.

Buildings in prewar Japan had been built with wood, but most were demolished during the war. Like the phoenix, the whole country had started rising from the ashes. Many industries that had been hammered flat left ten million people unemployed. The farm output had been cut in half, and there was a real threat of starvation. Inflation was rampant.

To counter all this, it was heartwarming to see the United States helping Japan get on its feet. The Japanese had been expecting to suffer anguish under the American occupation but were surprised when General Douglas MacArthur, after helping to create a new Constitution, said that Japan would govern itself.

An agricultural reform bill transferred ownership of most of the country's producing acreage from long entrenched landlords to the farmers themselves; then General MacArthur broke up the *zaivatsu*, the great industrial complexes. The new Constitution allowed for a Bill of Rights (amendments to the Constitution) similar to America's; it also lowered the voting age and gave women the right to vote. The Japanese Diet, a body similar to the U.S. Congress, was to be formed by popular election. The final act of good faith by the United States was to cancel all war reparations.

I spent long hours learning to speak the language and could speak it passably in less than a year. I visited twenty-five industries and, while getting acquainted, saw that they had salvaged the rubble from bombed-out buildings to rebuild again. The Japanese government had devised a five-year plan for national growth that included tariff protection and subsidies for key industries.

In a way Japan benefited from the destruction of World War II. New, more efficient factories were built, new steel plants were the last word in modernization, and the shipyards became a model of cost-efficient production. By 1956 Japan could boast of a gross national product about one quarter that of Great Britain or France.

To acquaint me with my new surroundings, the twenty-five Japanese counterparts I worked with arranged for me to tour their country, from Hokkaido to Honshu, Shikoku, the Kuril Islands, and Amami Gunto. The next indoctrination was the very hot baths they call *ofurros*, where whole families bathe together in the nude. Since American men have hair on their chests and the Japanese men don't, the Japanese ladies found it great sport to pluck a hair from an American man's chest, usually accompanied by giggles.

After a while, my Japanese friends would not let me use an interpreter as they preferred I speak Japanese. My interpreter eventually left for America, and I was on my own. Now our maid was my unofficial reading teacher. Each morning, at breakfast, she made me read out loud one complete newspaper story in Japanese. Often, before I finished struggling through my lesson, she would say in English, "Mistah, eggs getting cold."

Japan was rapidly turning from an agrarian society to an industrial one. The majority of the workers were college-graduate white-collar workers. Upon joining a company a man became a *moretsu shain*, a passionate company man. He arose at dawn, consumed a Japanese-style breakfast, and arrived at work punctually. He believed the company was feeding and keeping him. As one worker explained, "It's the least I can do in return."

Maria and I were invited to dinners and parties at Japanese homes, and we entertained at our home in return. In this male-dominated society, the usual form of business entertainment consisted of businessmen going out on the town. My hot-blooded Hungarian wife didn't like the idea of my spending evenings with Japanese friends, having dinner at cabarets, and being entertained by Geisha girls. But I didn't think it was such a bad idea.

When Japanese workers weren't being pumped up with pep rallies at work, they let steam off after work by playing *pachinko*, a sort of pinball game. It was a man's game and at the time, there were ten thousand *pachinko* parlors in Japan. Two other passions were golf and baseball. It took a long time before anyone would discuss the war with me.

The defeat in World War II, in the words of one writer, left the Japanese "dazed, tottering, dumb, and shocked." It was a disintegration of everything they believed in. I was inside postwar Japan and watched on a day-to-day basis, where a whole new philosophy was emerging as they began to come to terms with their past and future.

For the first year, I was three-quarters sponge and one-quarter worker. I was learning about Japan and absorbing its culture and I loved every minute of it. The only minor catastrophe that occurred during the first year was that the ship carrying my Cadillac had overturned in a typhoon. The embassy arranged for a replacement to be expedited to Tokyo. When it did arrive, I discovered that besides a chauffeur, I was expected to have a footman. The little Dutch boy who'd bitten his first American teacher on her rear end had traveled a long way. Finally, I learned the need for a big, flashy car. I had come to be regarded as a real honorable gentleman. On a visit to an airline headquarters or a manufacturer, the footman held the door open while the president came down to the car, bowed, then carried my briefcase. As I became more confident with the language, I began digging deeper, getting to observe the pilots in action, the machine operators, and then the bureaus that monitor each operation. From this, I could judge what international aviation standards were or were not being observed.

My biggest surprise was finding that most pilots who flew the scheduled airlines were not Japanese, but foreigners from many nations. Of the Japanese aviators, some were former kamikaze pilots (those war pilots who volunteered to fly on suicide missions by crashing their planes into targets). The engineers and skilled mechanics were ex-service personnel from World War II aviation units.

It was a shock to discover that each foreign pilot was following his own country's aviation laws. Although there were no common rules that applied to everyone, there were few mechanical mishaps during flights and landings. Fortunately, the program we were developing with the Japanese included radio facilities and landing and takeoff procedures, using tower and radio communications. Japan Airlines was operating DC-6s and DC-7s, and these were well maintained, since they had Douglas engineers to help them. Nippon Airlines had two Douglas DC-4s and six DC-3s.

Japan Airlines was desperate to acquire equal status with other international airlines. To achieve this, it required training programs so the people involved operated well-maintained aircraft. This meant efficient and quality maintenance crews to keep the planes in top condition.

Mr. Yanageta, president of Japan Airlines and also my neighbor, was delighted at my offer to set up programs to train more Japanese aircrews. We immediately set up classes for pilots, co-pilots, and flight engineers. Later, we set up courses for stewardesses. The next order of business was to develop an institute to train engineers, mechanics, and service people. I made it obligatory for all of Japan's civil aviation people to pass these training courses as well, so all those who monitored the operation had the same basic knowledge and training.

Everything didn't run smoothly all the time and occasionally there would be a terrible flare-up like the one at Hanada Airport. Hanada had good, long runways. The only obstacle came during the completion of the Tokyo Tower, which had been deliberately designed to be taller than the Eiffel Tower in Paris. Though the tower was seven miles away, it was on a straight line with Hanada's most-used runway for take-offs. All the airlines considered the Tower to be an obstruction. I attended meeting after meeting with the group constructing the Tower and made numerous suggestions as to color of the Tower and the safety precautions that could be made so it would not be an obstruction.

The local group wanted to paint the Tower silver, so it would stand out and become a world landmark like the Eiffel Tower. I pointed out that silver blended with the sky. In a meeting that included all the airlines, as well as the Tokyo mayor and the council, it was forcefully brought out that regardless of airline objections, the Tokyo Tower had to shine. And the mayor added, "Tokyo will not spend a single yen for any other color of paint."

I never learned what the Japanese word was for "brouhaha," but whatever it's called, this was it. Simply put, Tokyo wanted a silver Tower, while the Civil Aviation Bureau and the airlines wanted safe, visible international aviation colors. It finally ended up with the Japanese version of a town meeting, attended by management officials of all the airlines, including Pan Am, Northwest Airlines, Lufthansa, Air France, KLM, as well as the Japanese. It was suggested that each airline try to come up with a solution that might please the mayor and the council. Then one person was singled out to handle the problem.

Me!

So the airlines met and caucused and tossed suggestions around by the dozen. Finally, Northwest Airlines agreed to furnish the international orange paint while Pan Am agreed to pay for the painting if the mayor agreed. Lufthansa, KLM, Air France, and Japan Airlines said they would furnish bright lights to make the Tower shine at night. Though I didn't believe the politicians would buy it, it was necessary to convince the mayor and the council. One person was selected to make the presentation.

Me!

All I had going for me was the fact that I was now fairly fluent in Japanese and I was respected. But I needed more than language skills, I needed the wisdom of a Solomon or a Hungarian. There's an old maxim that Hungarians love to tell about themselves to prove how shrewd they are: "In a revolving door, if a Hungarian gets in behind you, he always comes out ahead of you."

The only Hungarian in Tokyo that I knew was Maria—besides she was a natural blonde, which made her twice as smart. "I need a gimmick," I told her. "Something that will make them accept this concept."

"Let's take a walk and I'll think about it," said my resident Hungarian.

Earlier, I had promised to take her to a new exhibit at a museum, so we wandered off in that direction. She kept coming up with ideas, but they were pretty much what we had hashed over in our meetings.

There's nothing like looking at Japanese silk paintings to take your mind off your problems. We spent a pleasant afternoon and returned home for tea. "So that solves your problem," said Maria.

"What does?"

"Figure it out for yourself."

It took me a half hour to figure it out, and I thought with a little hype it just might work. I set up a meeting for everyone involved and told them we had the solution. Then I went to work on a presentation. It was elaborate and definitive and I got an artist to do a rendering of the Tower.

At the meeting, I made a long, formal speech stating that Tokyo Tower was truly an edifice unparalleled in the world, not only a symbol of great Japanese architecture but something that would stand for culture, signifying that a new era of Japanese structural art had arrived. I then unveiled the painting of the shining Tower done in the ancient Japanese style, delicately painted on silk.

I said the Tower would be an art symbol of aviation safety. It would no longer be an obstacle. Everyone, including our opponents, agreed and the project was accepted. And so I learned that life is made up of small victories. Eventually, when the Tower was completed, we invited all the foreign ambassadors, airline executives, the mayor and the council, to a monster party in the Tokyo Tower. A certain Hungarian got the painting and a mink jacket.

Now that I was getting more fluent in Japanese, I was putting in longer hours. Next on my agenda was tackling the rules and regulations that monitored civil aviation and scheduled airlines. Japan's rules were not strict enough to comply with international laws. When completed, the new rules would not be put into place piecemeal, but all at once, so as not to confuse the people who had to work under them.

Though I had become "one of the boys" and was more or less

accepted by the Japanese business community, it was still difficult to get them to change methods of operating. They found it easier to accept something new only if it fit into their personal or cultural philosophy. From my point of view, because of this caution, progress was hampered by the old problem of two steps forward and one step backward.

The growing acceptance by my Japanese associates rested mainly on the fact that I was openly giving of myself and sharing my knowledge and expertise. I asked nothing in return. This generosity, of course, was courtesy of the U.S. government, but a government is amorphous and I was a specific human being to whom they could relate. It worked in my favor and helped the progress of my assignment.

On my agenda was an inspection tour of Nippon Airlines, accompanied by my counterparts from the civil aviation group. It was unbelievable how this airline maintained and overhauled its equipment with so few inspection tools, such as a magnaflux, go-or-no-go gauges, string gauges, and metal crack limit gauges, to name a few. Worn engine cylinders were farmed out to special machine shops, where they were chrome-plated, then reground to fit new pistons. Parts from wrecked planes were used to repair and overhaul airline equipment.

I made survey trips by riding the commercial planes and watching cockpit discipline. Though improvements could be made, there was a level of excellence that I found gratifying. Performance levels of ground personnel were not as good. What required change was the poor communications between the workers and management.

Once they began to trust me, some of the Japanese pilots brought up the subject of World War II and showed me craters in the ground where Zero fighters had zeroed in. Because they are such proud people, they were concerned about how the Americans felt about them. I often thought about it and came to the conclusion that many Americans carried around a burden of guilt for having dropped the atom bombs on Japan, hence this postwar effort to help Japan despite what had taken place at Pearl Harbor. But I never spoke my thoughts aloud.

Many phases of manufacturing were new to the Japanese, and even after working for a year and a half with the airlines and manufacturers, it became obvious that better quality control was necessary. We devised new training systems and explained that the fine art of management was to communicate with the workers without being unpleasant, and at the same time show personal interest in their projects while being quick to act on good suggestions.

In this line of work, you are never far from paperwork and finances. The world of aviation was entering the jet age, so it was necessary to check into the financial status of Japan Airlines and prepare it for the future. To be competitive, Japan would have to buy a fleet of the new American jet airliners that would soon be coming off the assembly lines.

But money was a problem. The country was reluctant to commit itself to new aircraft. Other airlines around the world had already placed orders for jet planes, and when Japan belatedly made its decision, it was placed on the waiting list with delivery expected in 1960. This frustrated the Japanese, but it was not a matter of favoritism as manufacturers worked on a first-come, first-served basis.

The aviation community was a small world with few secrets, and suddenly the Russians came forward with a proposition the Japanese could not refuse. It invited a large group of Japanese VIPs to Russia to inspect a modern jet airliner, the TU-104. Then, on September 17, 1957, a delegation of Russian aviation experts flew into Tokyo on a TU-104 aircraft filled to capacity with Japanese military officers, Japan Airlines executives, and the secretary of transportation who had gone to Russia to inspect the TU-104. It was a great public relations coup for the Russians.

The TU-104 was a two-engine jet capable of flying across the Pacific to Los Angeles with an intermediate stop in Hawaii. It caused great excitement with the management at Japan Airlines when the Russians offered twenty-five TU-104s to Japan for immediate delivery.

The plane had low-mounted, swept-back wings with a span of 113 feet, 4 inches, two Mikulin RD-3 or AM-3 turbo jet engines set close to the fuselage, developing 881 pounds of thrust. The pressurized cabins seated fifty passengers, and the plane had a top load of 156,528 pounds. Its cruising speed was just under 500 miles per hour.

The Japan Airlines executives had no qualms about asking my help, suggesting I take a close look at the plane firsthand. Then the executives let me borrow one of the two looseleaf books of specifications the Russians had presented to them, while the other one was being translated into Japanese. They were well aware I understood Russian.

It's impossible to determine if there are any serious flaws in an aircraft by reading the manual, but I did spot one major problem. The

Mikulin engines had to use a special fuel in order to meet the international safety requirement to keep the plane aloft in case one engine failed. The Russians intended to arrange to have special fuel tanks stored all over the Pacific, so the operation of this aircraft by Japan Airlines could commence almost at once.

I made notes and photographed the manual with my Leica, then wrote out an emergency report and passed it on to the embassy, which relayed it posthaste to the State Department, where it was certain to create shock waves. Rumor had it that President Eisenhower might fly over. Subsequently, we were notified that an ad hoc committee made up of five senior officials in the State Department was en route to Tokyo.

By the time they arrived their sudden trip was camouflaged with diplomatic language. This was a State Department inspection committee convened to check out U.S.-Japan relations and to check on progress in aviation.

The first meeting was extremely tense as I knew very little about these men. I expanded on my report and told the committee, "The Japanese Government is very excited about the deal and is one hundred percent for it because this coup would make JAL the very first airline to have jet service across the Pacific." It was not surprising that everyone on the committee was upset. There wasn't a quiet ulcer in the room.

One member of the committee said, "Russia is desperately trying to expand its sphere of influence in the Pacific. Our policy, and that of our friends (Russia, though an ally, was not considered a friend) is not to allow it. Think about it. For a number of years, these planes will have Russian pilots, engineers, technical and other advisers flying across the Pacific and into our backyard. We can't have that. Now what was that about a special jet fuel you mentioned in your report, Henri?"

"The special fuel comes from a source in Indonesia and is processed within the country and stored in fuel cells [tanks] near its largest city, Djakarta."

"What about the plane's performance?"

"Because I speak Russian, and I serve as a consultant to the airline, I have been asked by Japan Airlines to fly with the Russian instructor tomorrow morning to check on the plane's safety, but it's only a limited flight."

"When you're through, get back here as quickly as you can."

The next morning, to bring up the gross weight of the Tupolev TU-104, we had the ground crew load the plane with sandbags and shotbags (bags of lead pellets). Meanwhile, the Soviet pilot, having learned I spoke Russian, kept praising the TU-104. When everything was ready, I strapped myself in the co-pilot's seat and the instructor took the captain's chair.

To take off fully loaded required a runway longer than five thousand feet. The climbing rate of five hundred feet per minute was slow, so it took a long time to reach thirty thousand feet and level off. Next, we were to test-fly the TU-104 on one engine. The instructor shut off one engine and the plane struggled to maintain altitude.

The wing deicers and the pressurization systems worked well and the radio was excellent. I unbuckled my seat belt and walked back for a closer safety inspection. There were no facilities for emergency passenger evacuation and the exit doors had no safety on the positive locking device. More important, it had no fuel-dumping facilities in case of emergency landings, making it dangerous to land on one engine. In addition, the TU-104 could not get airborne on one engine on a six-thousand to seventy-five-hundred-foot runway.

After we landed, I met with the executives of Japan Airlines to discuss my findings and report on the safety flaws. Then they revealed more about the Russian offer. In return for routes between Tokyo and Moscow, the airline would receive an easy purchase plan, a pay-as-you-go deal out of the profits. So the Japanese government, strapped for money, had jumped at the proposition.

How was it possible to convince them that these particular Russian planes could not give them the same high quality of service as American jets? I pointed out, "Quality is never an accident. It's the result of intelligent efforts by many people." The Japanese agreed that American piston aircraft had given them excellent service. I promised them that if they turned down the TU-104, the American government would help Japan Airlines obtain American jets quicker, so they could offer quality service across the Pacific.

Another important consideration would be to see if the Japanese were required to buy the special fuel from the Russians or get it directly from the cracking plant in Djakarta. I also pointed out to them that if they were to fly all over the world, Russia might not be able to guarantee a continuous supply of the special fuel everywhere. They might be obliged to purchase, pay for, then ship and store fuel in numerous facilities around the world. Not only would this be expensive, but Japan Airlines could be held hostage by a single supplier, Russia, or Russia's source. It would be wiser and more economical for a commercial Japanese airline to use a universal jet fuel.

I knew that my arguments made sense, but logic isn't always an answer. The thinking was split. The Japan Airlines executives, accepting my arguments and concerned about safety, were willing to wait for U.S. aircraft, but the politicians in government were overwhelmed with the idea of having twenty-five commercial jets immediately available, no cash down. All my work, my training programs and maintenance standards, could be thrown out the window with a single signature.

When I met with the committee at 1:30 P.M., I was surprised to find that we were alone in a secure embassy office that had no windows, just a table and six chairs. There was a coffee urn and some *petit fours* on the table. As we drank coffee, I reported the results of my flight and my discussions with the Japanese.

I said, "In the long run, this isn't a good deal for Japan. There's a split on this; the airline people want U.S. jets, the politicians are bullheaded and want the deal."

"Everyone knows about bullheadedness," said the chairman, "and it's not only a Japanese trait. All politicians thrive on it."

"So do generals," said another committee member, a former general himself. "During World War Two, President Eisenhower had to deal with three of the orneriest, most bullheaded guys of the twentieth century: General Charles de Gaulle of France, General Bernard Montgomery of Great Britain, and General George Patton."

The ex-general paused for a moment as if reflecting on World War II, then he added, "I read your file, Henri. You've proven time and again that you're a very resourceful man. You were trained by the CIA, the FAA, the FBI, and other military and government agencies. You're our aviation expert. We'll back you in any effort to supply American jets to JAL. But you are going to have to be responsible for finding some answer to this problem. Either convince the Japanese to turn down the Russian offer, or arrange for some bolt of lightning to strike those special fuel tanks."

We talked some more but we were simply going around in circles so I took my leave. It was time to think, so I took the afternoon off replaying the committee's words in my mind over and over again as I drove home. I had been given no explicit instructions, but it seemed I was left with very few options.

Now where in hell could I find a bolt of lightning?

CHAPTER 24

How to Make Lightning Strike!

FOR ME, the best way to tackle a problem had always been to put all the facts on paper. This I did. Then I reviewed them carefully. There was no question that the Soviets had designs on Asia in general and Japan in particular. Obviously, this was behind the "instant" friendship offer of twenty-five commercial jet aircraft at bargain-basement terms.

However, the Japanese reaction to the offer was divided into two groups. One group, mostly prideful, ambitious politicians, wanted the Russian jets because it would thrust Japan into the forefront of the world market. They could be the first to offer jet travel in the Pacific while other airlines stood in line at U.S. manufacturers. This group registered little concern about the serious matters of purchasing special fuel, the plane's safety flaws, its efficiency, and replacement parts.

The other group, comprised mostly of flying personnel, was worried about the lack of safety features on the aircraft, the lives of their passengers and their own lives. They were willing to be patient until the delivery date of 1960. Although Americans had shown themselves to be generous in helping this war-ravaged country, Japan was a proud nation, and my instincts told me that in the end, Japanese pride would win. And so would the Russians.

Aside from the weather, the only method of producing lightning was to have it man-made. It was clear to me that some sort of action was necessary and the matter was in my hands. I dared not involve other U.S. personnel. I dispatched a confidential letter to the committee via diplomatic pouch informing it that I would be working on a research project "on my own," which would not involve embassy or other government personnel.

Luckily, the Russian fliers had turned over a blueprint of the Djakarta fuel cells located at the water's edge to show how large tankers could sail right up to the tanks and load up with fuel. My next step was to obtain a large marine map of Southeast Asia that included Malaya and Indonesia. Then I spent hours working on the best strategy for a covert foray into Djakarta. When I had figured out what would be needed and the means of getting there, the next hurdle was how to go about recruiting some men to assist me.

Among my Japanese friends was a most vocal anti-Russian jet pilot, one I knew could keep a secret. I explained that I needed four men, preferably ex-marines of the Japanese Imperial Navy. He told me to contact a cousin at the Japanese Naval War College. Arrangements were made for us to meet. It turned out I had met this man on a fishing trip on the General Electric ship owned by its president, Mike Sadona. We talked, and once I felt comfortable with him, I outlined the bare bones of the expedition. He knew exactly what I needed and he also knew three bored, Japanese marine veterans looking for some action, any kind of action, who might be willing to join us just for the hell of it.

It was not going to be a picnic, as the typhoon season was approaching. I met with the three men, and I went into greater detail without specifying when or where. The fact that I spoke fluent Japanese made everything more acceptable. They asked hard questions. As I didn't want to compromise the plan in case one of them backed out, I answered without indicating what type of target or mentioning Djakarta. When I said that I thought the fishing trip required five men in all, they said four were enough if I was the fourth.

One of the men, the self-styled leader, had been an armaments sergeant and he immediately made some positive suggestions. "The bazooka you suggest is not accurate and does not send a missile high enough or far enough. A limpet mine might be attached to a target, but if the target is combustible, it might be discovered by a guard or bomb-sniffing dogs. A mortar would be more accurate. I would suggest a delayed-action, explosive projectile delivered by a mortar."

Military equipment of this nature was not readily available from Japanese sources. I presented a requisition order to the top Army man at our embassy. While in the process of investigating me, he was mysteriously informed to assist me in any way he could and ask no questions. Also, to destroy any paper trail. The equipment was obtained from the U.S. Army base in Japan, with all serial numbers and identification filed off, no questions asked. As requested, they were newly stenciled: DUMMY MISSILES. PRACTICE PURPOSES ONLY.

Through a CIA source, arrangements were made to rent a small land plane, to be ready and waiting for us in Singapore. We took off as passengers on a Japan Airlines plane to Singapore, four friends on a fishing trip. The luggage was heavy, but we sidetracked customs as "special" well-paid baggage-handlers moved our bags onto the rented plane, a British two-engine De Havilland. The rental agency sent a pilot, an Australian, again no questions asked, to check me out on the aircraft's performance and the controls. When he finished, he lit a cigarette, said, "G'by, mate," stood up, and departed. In the captain's pocket was a maintenance manual, and in the rear of the plane was a tool locker, complete with tools, as requested.

After checking the weather, I filed a flight plan to Tanjungkarang, Sumatra, and a tentative one for our return trip to Singapore in one week. Before Sumatra, as part of Malaysia, got its independence after the war, the dominant colonial power there had been the Dutch, and many still spoke the language. The Japanese had occupied the country from 1942 to 1945, so I didn't know what kind of reception my three Japanese fishing partners would get from the locals. Our aim was to keep a very low profile.

Luckily, the universal language was still money. We arranged to have the plane anchored down to a revetment in case of a storm. We hired a van and driver to take us and our luggage to the dock site. My CIA source had checked earlier and told me small motorboats were available as rentals. We settled on a forty-foot cabin speedboat with a low profile that slept four, which my three marines and I could handle when we crossed the Krakatau Strait to the village of Serang, very close to Djakarta. I would do the navigating.

We carried very light tents and fishing gear, but it was still nervous time because of the many ships in the area and the numerous police patrols, mostly fast cutters with wailing sirens. I had brought along the marine maps of the area, so we made our trip leisurely. Our boat was a wooden craft and looked old, but the motor was in tiptop shape, hinting that it might be used from time to time to haul contraband.

We moored at a desolate spot near Serang to wait for a rainstorm to use as our cover. The islands received plenty of rainfall, so it was merely a matter of time until the next storm. For three days, we fished in the Java Sea. We caught lots of fish, including some small sharks, and my Japanese companions were in heaven, as they loved to eat raw fish.

Small fishing vessels passed and occasionally someone would wave to us and we waved back. Only once did I have my proverbial heart in my mouth. A snappy-looking powerboat zipping along the bay spotted us and came scooting alongside the place where we had anchored for our day's fishing. As I was able to converse with him in Dutch, he became extremely pleasant. It turned out he was a patrol officer looking for smugglers. Because we had a dozen fish on a line sitting in the water, I offered him and his crew a half dozen freshly caught fish. They were delighted to have them.

It had crossed my mind to bribe him, but I realized it might be a foolish move. Fishermen offering the catch of the day was simply a gracious gesture. A bribe could bring an inquiry. Two days later, some foul weather turned out to be more than ideal for our project. A severe electrical storm had come up full force. Though we knew that these types of storms were common in the area, we didn't think it would be wise to depend on one in our plans. But here it was, and the fuel cells were located right on the water, making it ideal for us. The rain came down in a deluge.

The three marines were in their glory. Hugging the shore, we got as close as we could, unwrapped the mortar and the missiles in the cabin, opened a can of grease and waterproofed the projectiles. Then we wrapped them in a thin oilskin. We moored next to a jutting rock, dropped the anchor, and carefully moved the mortar and shells to shore, walking across the shoal. We lugged our armaments close to the fuel cells, which were illuminated occasionally by a flash of lightning.

When we came within range of the cells, we set up the mortar. I was nervous, but my friends weren't. Nevertheless, we worked swiftly. The sergeant took out his range finder and waited for the light from a streak of lightning to measure the distance. He moved us another thirty feet closer. About three o'clock, we lobbed four of the nine-hour-delay missiles onto the two fuel cells.

We left posthaste. After we had cruised about a quarter mile, we deep-sixed the mortar into the bay, along with two spare missiles that we had rendered inoperable. We returned to our camp, cleaned up, and thoroughly inspected our wet camp, after which we boarded the boat and headed into the choppy waters. The ship pitched and rolled all the way as we headed back to Tanjungkarang, Sumatra. When we arrived, we awakened the boat owner, returned the fishing gear, and settled payment. All we had with us was our luggage, so we paid the boat owner to drive us to the airport in the heavy rain. Then we carried our equipment onto the De Havilland.

It continued raining, so we slept inside the plane. By 10:00 A.M., the rain stopped, but it was overcast. We refueled and took off for Singapore. The flight was uneventful. I paid for the use of the De Havilland in cash and we boarded a commercial airliner for Tokyo. I was too hopped up to sleep, but my three marines had no problem.

Though this was an adventure for the ex-marines, I later arranged for each one to receive a gift of $1,500 in U.S. funds, a considerable sum at the time. Subsequently, there was a story in the newspapers telling of a freak accident in which two large fuel cells near Djakarta had been destroyed when struck by lightning during a severe electrical storm.

In a diplomatic pouch, I sent a clipping to the committee and a report that the Japanese had decided to turn down the Russian offer. Then I added, "Sometimes it pays to talk things out."

I didn't expect a reply, but I could surely visualize the smiles on the President's men.

CHAPTER 25

Entering the Jet Age

No ONE had missed me. Maria thought I looked more relaxed after my fishing trip and even suggested I do it more often. At work, the great debate was subsiding. The controversy over the TU-104s became academic once the fuel supply vanished. Japan Airlines had no choice but to turn down Russia's offer. It was agreed that the DC-8 had become the plane of choice.

As part of its preparations for the new jets, tanks to store JP4 and JP5 fuel were installed aboveground in Kyushu, in the southern part of Japan. This universal type was used in nearly all international jet aircraft. Ironically, this new fuel would be supplied by the cracking plant at Djakarta.

When word finally came through that McDonnell Douglas had set a date in late 1959 for delivery of the DC-8s, Washington arranged for me to fly to the McDonnell Douglas plant at Long Beach, California. I would be accompanied by the chief of Japan's Civil Aviation Bureau, as well as a select number of pilots and engineers to attend flight, engineering, and jet-maintenance schools.

For me, the transition from flying slow, piston-powered aircraft to high-speed jets would prove to be difficult. The school had a reputation for being rigorous and strictly all business. Flight training was continuous from 8:00 A.M. to 4:00 P.M. In addition, I was obliged to participate in the engineering classes from 5:00 P.M. to 9:00 P.M.

To top off my day, from 9:00 P.M. to 11:00 P.M., I assisted the repairman on the DC-8 flight simulator, where every move in the air could be duplicated on the ground. Each day, after heavy use by the students, it was necessary to make adjustments or repairs. Then I hopped in and tested it. It was my way of learning more about the behavior of the plane.

By coincidence, I attended classes not only with the Japanese, but also the French, Portuguese, and the Swedes. I was often called upon to explain technical expressions and aircraft components in their own language. When the day arrived to make my first jet flight, I was comfortable with the plane. After my first takeoff, I asked the instructor to let me do a pass over the runway to see how fast it would disappear. He agreed, and I was amazed to see the runway vanish as fast as I could turn my head to look at it.

Douglas gave me very intensive DC-8 training. Once I was qualified as a DC-8 pilot, I was hungry for ways to acquire more jet flying time, as there would be no opportunity to do so in Tokyo. With a little research, I found that because of the influx of students, most McDonnell Douglas pilots didn't have many weekends off. So I asked the company if I could handle production flights on weekends, i.e., test-fly planes coming off the assembly line. They agreed. I got in lots of jet flying time while becoming totally familiar with the aircraft.

Because of my fluency in languages, I was invited to everybody's parties, which is how I discovered that United Airlines, Sweden, and Portugal had placed their DC-8 orders early, overbought, and each had at least one extra plane. I called Fred Keck, president of United, explained my position in Japan, and asked if he had an extra DC-8 for sale. He said, "Yes, I'll sell it to Japan Airlines at cost, provided we get the contract to service and overhaul their DC-8 fleet engines." I told him I'd check it out.

At the request of McDonnell Douglas, I stayed three extra weeks to continue testing planes and logging hours of flying each day. Flying was my life. I loved it. Finally, I returned to Tokyo and met with the Japanese officials involved in procuring new aircraft. I explained the availability of the three DC-8s, and said that if they wanted a jump on the competition, they should make some quick decisions. They gave me the green light.

SAS, the Swedish airlines, agreed to sell its extra DC-8 at 20 percent above cost, and TAP, the Portuguese airline, said they would sell one at 10 percent above cost. United agreed to sell its extra plane at cost, after coming to terms on a contract for overhauling and servicing all engines of the three planes. By the time Japan jumped into the world market with quality international jet service, it had gained a year.

I still hammered away at the importance of proper training schools for every phase of flight—overhaul, maintenance, and engineering. The DC-8s were being worked hard. The next phase was setting up quality controls on repairs, but we ran into a major problem. As more and more world airlines bought jets, there weren't enough spare parts being produced to service everyone's needs. Due to delayed shipments, it was difficult to operate at full capacity.

In the maintenance department, a constant problem was trying to keep parts for different aircraft separated. I suggested a method that had served me well in South America—color-coding. The jet parts for the DC-8s were color-coded white; the DC-7s, piston aircraft, were color-coded blue. Because United Airlines was overhauling the jet engines, all parts on the DC-8s manufactured by Pratt & Whitney were color-coded red.

There were factories in Japan, like Mitsubishi, that had designed and built planes, helicopters, and parts in prewar and in wartime Japan and were still functioning. Once the DC-8s were operating smoothly, I decided to check on the aviation plants again. Of course, I couldn't do it alone, because I had to take along my usual quorum of twenty-five counterparts from Japan's Civil Aviation Bureau and the Civil Defense Bureau.

But it was a diminished aircraft industry in Japan. We traveled to most of the nation's islands visiting plants and having manufacturers entertain us royally. Most of them had been reduced to making panel instruments like turn-and-bank indicators, altimeters, and radio equipment. Some were recapping aircraft tires and still others were producing plane seats or paneling. For the most part, their work was excellent except for the odd example where more quality control was needed.

Quite unexpectedly, I was electrified by a situation of high drama. While visiting Shin Meiwa Industry, I was shown the "Emily," the seaplane that was the pride and joy of Japan's Imperial Navy. This aircraft was almost an exact copy of the Pan Am Hawaiian Clipper, the Martin M-130, considered the finest airliner of its time. I had spent an enormous amount of time on the development of the Clipper and knew it intimately.

Though the Japanese designers tried to disguise the profile, they hadn't succeeded. It was as impossible to hide the graceful lines of the Clipper as it was to change the profile of an eagle. As the Pan Am pilot/ engineer assigned to the project, I was familiar with the original drawings and specifications of the plane. I had pored over these plans a thousand times. I had taken the plane apart a hundred times.

Now I was staring at a clone of the Clipper, replicated for the Imperial Navy by Kawanishi Aircraft, which was controlled by Shin Meiwa Industry Ltd. The Emily could only have been built after a close examination of a Clipper—the missing Hawaiian Clipper! I was now positive the "lost" plane had been hijacked. During the war, those who had seen the plane from a distance reported similar observations. And now here was the proof in front of me.

Our guides prattled on proudly about the creative design and the seaworthiness of this amphibious aircraft, innovations created by the genius of Glenn Martin. As I inspected the plane further, I even spotted other changes that had been lifted directly from the Sikorsky S-42. There was little I could say other than to praise them politely for making such a nice plane. The war was over and I was now a diplomat. That fact didn't remove the knot in my stomach when I thought of the missing Pan Am crew I had known so well, particularly my close friend Captain Leo Terletsky.

Partway through my tour of duty, the embassy gave us a cocktail party so I could meet the heads of industry and banking in Japan, as well as officials of other embassies. Along the way, I was introduced to the deans of Tokyo and Waseda universities. The deans asked me to speak to the students of their respective institutions, which I did shortly thereafter. This developed into a regular job of teaching two classes in Japanese: the first, a course in philosophy to a class of young ladies; the second was to explain the principles of atomic energy to a group of young engineers, a subject that had interested me since my days at MIT.

I found out something curious about Japanese students. The university students were studious and eager, while at the airline training schools at Hanada Airport, the students, also eager to learn, showed little interest in becoming pilots. It turned out that being a pilot was not considered a prestigious position in Japan, while a teacher's position was considered the highest because it dealt with knowledge. Flying was also dangerous. It took a lot of perseverance on my part to glamorize the pilot's position so we could attract students.

The stewardesses were obliged to learn foreign languages, particularly English, while trying to adjust their thinking so that they could become members of an international community. I taught them table manners, which led me and my wife to become TV stars. We were invited to host a TV show at 12:30 A.M. Maria and I would show the Japanese how to use a knife and fork instead of chopsticks, how to use their fingers for finger food, and how to sit and eat at the dinner table in different countries. Unexpectedly, this show became popular, so I became a TV personality as well as a *sensei* (master) at Tokyo and Waseda universities.

In the midst of running around Tokyo in twenty different directions, I received an urgent call from Washington to fly to Korea and see what I could do about helping them start an airline. I was so exhausted by my running from one job to another that I was looking forward to a Korean vacation.

On my arrival in Korea, there was the usual reception followed by a big dinner in a fancy restaurant. I didn't speak Korean and discussions were through an interpreter. By the time we finally got down to business, they threw me one line that almost had me in hysterics.

"We wish to start an airline, but we have no money."

With a little prodding I learned that not only didn't they have money for planes, they also didn't have money to train crews. The big question was "How do you start an airline without money?" So the Koreans, who asked the U.S. ambassador to ask Washington for help, were simply hoping to find a prize in the Cracker Jack box. I asked for some time to think.

After forty-eight puzzling hours, I came up with a prospective answer. I decided to call friends at the World Aircraft Company in Burbank and presented the problem to them. They were a leasing company that could also make provisions to train crews. After a long, involved chat, World asked me to come to Burbank personally to check their available planes, equipment, and facilities. I reported to the Koreans and the ambassador, who checked with Washington, who in turn authorized my flight. I returned to Tokyo to make arrangements for my work and classes and took a JAL flight with a captain I knew well.

There was a saying that you never get anything for free, and my efforts to get planes for nothing almost cost me my life. The trip to Los Angeles was by way of Hawaii on a four-engine, JAL DC-7C, a regular commercial flight with a Japanese crew. Always the *sensei*, I would occasionally sit in the observer's seat watching how the crew performed. We were less than two hours out of Hawaii.

With the plane on automatic pilot, everything was functioning normally when suddenly an unseen object smashed into the plane with terrific impact. It was as though an antiaircraft missile had sliced through the fuselage behind me and into the steward's station.

Vibrating uncontrollably, the plane then began to shake. The alert captain took the plane off automatic, shouted to the co-pilot to put on the seat belt sign, watched the erratic engine revolutions on the flight control panel, looked at me, and pointed to the two right-hand throttles. I agreed. He immediately shut down the number-three and number-four engines (the two on the right side).

Due to the hole in the plane, the cabin was beginning to depressurize and there would soon be little oxygen in the cabin. The co-pilot lowered the oxygen masks and ordered everyone to put one on. We all did. Then we began to descend until we leveled off at eight thousand feet. We no longer needed the masks. A young stewardess, with blood on her hands and clothés, ran onto the flight deck reporting that whatever hit the airplane had killed the male attendant.

The captain announced in Japanese and English that we had an emergency and asked everyone to remain calm. The no-smoking sign was on. The captain and I discussed the situation. We knew that if we were to reach Honolulu, the plane would have to be lightened.

Most of the passengers were Japanese. I had greater experience in emergency situations, but I could not have the captain lose face by asking him if I should take over. So I suggested that it might be more comforting if the Japanese captain walked down the aisle calmly and told the passengers that everything loose had to be thrown overboard by the crew. He agreed and immediately suggested that I take the captain's seat.

After a few minutes, the aircraft began to shudder again. It was imperative to start broadcasting a Mayday to alert ships in the vicinity in case we had to ditch. Meanwhile, radios and electronic equipment, along with the luggage, the plane's serving carts, and magazines were being tossed out of the cabin door. All our rigid training for emergencies was operating very well.

A scramble of U.S. Air Force fighter jets from Honolulu came alongside to help guide us in. One jet jockey rolled around us to observe and report on the plane's damage. He gave us a thumbs-up for luck. As we approached the lights of the airport, I negated the Mayday to the ships. The tower and I stayed in constant radio communication. By the time the controllers saw us, we were given immediate clearance for an emergency landing. Fire trucks and ambulances were zipping across the runway just like in the movies. The captain returned to the cockpit but opted to sit in the co-pilot's seat. Between us, we agreed it was necessary to rev up engines one and two to full throttle as we approached the runway. Earlier, I deduced that something had flown off one or both engines and then hit us. I prayed that whatever blew off the other engine would not come off the ones we needed so badly.

After surviving so many accidents and near mishaps, I had learned to expect the unexpected, and to never really be unprepared. But the last-minute information from the Honolulu tower was totally unwelcome: "Prepare to encounter crosswinds." Struggling to control a lopsided plane, trying to keep it level, and fighting dangerous crosswinds made the landing difficult. The plane, leaning to one side, pushed added weight on the undercarriage and we blew a tire. It wasn't pretty, but the bottom line was that we made it. If there is a good part to any crisis, it's thinking about it *after* you're safe and it's all over.

The accident had been a fluke. The investigation revealed that Northwest Airlines had sold the DC-7C to Japan Airlines in 1957. It had four Wright R3350 supercharged engines; each engine was equipped with three turbines that utilized exhaust gases to generate additional horsepower. It had four square-tipped Wright propellers made by United Aircraft.

The airplane, its engines set to cruising at 2,500 rpm, carried a full load of passengers and cargo. Its speed was 380 miles per hour. Suddenly, a three-inch tip had snapped off the number-four propeller; traveling with dynamic force at lightning speed, it became a high-speed missile. It severed the blade of the number-three propeller, then sliced through the fuselage, causing decompression in the cabin. The steward, standing near the forward cockpit, was struck and killed instantly.

The medics removed the body of the attendant, and all the passengers, though shaken, were glad to get off the plane safely. The JAL dispatcher at Honolulu notified us that another plane was en route from Tokyo so passengers could continue their flights. The plane would bring an investigative crew. I wired back that all DC-6 and DC-7 propellers should be inspected for integrity and metal fatigue. A similar report went to the FAA and Douglas for world distribution.

After checking out the various World Aircraft Company planes and facilities at Burbank, I wired a report to the U.S. ambassadors in Japan and Korea. A deal was made swiftly and this became the start of Korean Airlines. Because I was due for two months' home leave, I asked Maria to meet me in Washington. While I awaited her arrival, I was debriefed about my activities in Japan and Korea. Finally, Maria and I took off for a vacation in Europe, then returned to Japan.

It was the right time to be away from Japan. On our return, we were confronted with the results of an earthquake. Japan is shaken by more than a thousand perceptible tremors annually, but every few years, a serious earthquake occurs somewhere in the country, destroying buildings and killing people.

Our home suffered some damage. The main freshwater line coming into the house was broken, so I had to turn off the water. The cesspool, which gathered all the waste from the house, had cracked and had to be repaired. My Cadillac, which had been parked on the driveway with the hand brake on, had traveled backward about ten feet.

It wasn't the worst quake to hit Japan. That one had occurred on September 1, 1923, when a quake registering 7.3 on the Richter scale hit Tokyo. Charcoal stoves, red-hot in preparation for the lunch hour, had turned houses into raging conflagrations. Many people fled into Sagami Bay and drowned. In all, 130,000 perished. Japan experiences two types of earthquakes—one moves vertically, the other moves horizontally. The vertical ones do the most damage.

As Japan began to make progress on the economic front, more and more aviation companies came to Japan to either set up businesses or arrange to have products manufactured. Japan was also licensing many products to be manufactured there. This would be costly at first, but it was calculated to save time and money in the long run. Japan was eager to become an export nation.

An old colleague, Igor Sikorsky, came to sell helicopters to the Japanese. He demonstrated the ability of his helicopter to lift heavy parts from the ground to the tops of buildings. When he was told that the Japanese had great difficulty placing heavy air-conditioning units on tall buildings, he showed them it could be done with his machine. He did the same with the Civil Defense Bureau regarding rescue operations. He sold several helicopters immediately.

Cessna Aviation Company was trying to have some aircraft parts manufactured in Japan by making use of the technical assistance program. Eventually, the idea was to build Cessnas there. The Kawasaki Company was interested, as they were planning to manufacture small trainers, as well as larger passenger aircraft. However, the assistance program specified only the hardware of the aircraft, not the instruments or the engine, which were made in the United States by Continental Engine Corporation.

The Japanese were having a difficult time getting their aircraft industry off the ground—this from a country that had built ten thousand Zero fighters during World War II.

The Japanese were working furiously to develop a jet engine. One experimental engine they demonstrated for me blew apart—a complete fiasco. General Electric Company and Pratt & Whitney, manufacturers of jet engines in the United States, would not agree to send technical assistance. I didn't have enough manufacturing know-how, but when they asked for assistance, I agreed to help them as much as I could. The principle of a jet engine is simple. The problem was they could not manufacture a metal compound hard enough to withstand the rigors of extremely high temperatures generated by a jet engine. It was difficult and expensive.

CHAPTER 26

The Amelia Earhart Story, Part 2: Unraveling the Puzzle

MY COUNTERPARTS in the Japan Civil Aviation Bureau invited me to visit the Shin Meiwa factory with them.

As an accepted colleague, I was given the freedom to study all Shin Meiwa archives, including all the old and new specifications for the planes and engines they were trying to build. I looked at sketches, blueprints, and artists' renderings. As I started going back over the years, out of sheer curiosity I leafed through the 1930s file.

It was quite heart-wrenching to suddenly come across original specs on the old Zero fighter plane built before World War II. There, before me, was the progression of the early Zeros. To my horror, I thought I was looking at sections of the plans for Amelia Earhart's plane, despite the fact the Zero was a single-engine and Amelia's a twin-engine aircraft.

The people escorting me were mostly of a different generation and had no idea that what I saw in the files had any bearing on Amelia Earhart's disappearance. I flipped back through the files to the early plans of the Zero, to integrate it with my personal knowledge and history of that time period.

The prototype had crank wings so head-on it looked like the letter W. By the mid-1930s, the Zeros had great success during the Sino-Japanese War. While the Japanese take pride in the air conquest of

235

Manchuria, the northeast province of China, little is said of the opposing forces.

The Chinese pilots, trained by an Italian military group and flying antiquated Italian aircraft, were no match for the Japanese "Claudes" (early name for the Zeros). Because Chinese pilots came from upper-class families, many graduated even though they couldn't fly a plane. Whoever went up came crashing down.

A frustrated Chiang Kai-shek then invited Russia to send several squadrons to help repulse the Japanese. The Russians jumped at an opportunity to have their pilots gain experience in combat. They fared much better but were soon overwhelmed by the large numbers of Japanese Zeros.

The early Zero was successful, but in truth, it had flaws and was prone to crashing, mostly because of its underpowered engine. It had maneuverability equal to that of any fighter in the world, but it needed vast improvement in handling and rate of climb to match the world's best fighters. But it wasn't far behind.

The Zero, despite its wide wing, was a compact flying machine, and its head Japanese designer, Jeri Horikoshi, was improving the aircraft rapidly, often by the hit-and-miss method. I could see where he worked feverishly, turning out many improved prototypes. Two aircraft companies, Mitsubishi and Nakajima, had worked zealously to create a state-of-the-art fighter plane, but Nakajima bowed out, leaving Mitsubishi to develop this advanced fighter alone.

The plans revealed change after change to update the plane, particularly with the selection of the power plant. There were three engines developed: The Kinsei 64, with 1,070 horsepower, was too heavy for the light plane. The Sakae-12 was developed by a competitor and was rejected for that reason. The 12-Shi's Zuisei 13, a lighter, though less powerful (875 horsepower), radial engine with fourteen cylinders, was finally selected by Mitsubishi. The greatest innovation was the first constant-speed, three-bladed propeller ever used by the Japanese.

From my discussions with the ex-pilots, it was the emperor who demanded that the Zero be the supreme fighter plane in the world. The man on the throne had all-encompassing power, which made him sacred and inviolable. He was also the supreme commander of the armed forces. It has been argued and reargued that the Japanese are not warlike by nature, yet a militant group of hawks, spurred on by an ambitious emperor, could drive the people to war.

Horikoshi was trying to please his emperor. Hirohito was well aware of Amelia Earhart's exploits and her preparations to circumnavigate the globe. His embassy in the United States kept him abreast of the latest developments; it also had intelligence agents, borrowed from the German network, nosing around the country, seeking more detailed information about Amelia's publicized route. Thus, the Lockheed plane was well tracked, while the Pan Am Clipper ships were becoming the targets of sabotage.

It was Emperor Hirohito who demanded that his intelligence services capture these advanced aircraft and he offered all kinds of rewards. The Imperial Navy, in obedience to their emperor, agreed to capture these two planes. Hirohito knew that Amelia's plane had become the most advanced aircraft in the world, especially since the U.S. government had contributed $5 million to guarantee her success (building a runway and facilities at Howland, positioning warships along her route, plus contributing advanced radio and other technology). Her aircraft was a flying laboratory.

I thought back to the time I flew over the Gilbert Islands with members of the Japanese defense forces during routine visits to their naval base, Koror. It was becoming clearer to me how capturing the Hawaiian Clipper or Amelia's plane could take place.

All this was going through my mind as I continued to check the progress revealed in the aircraft plans. In 1937, when Japan was plunging farther into Manchuria, the emperor began demanding a higher degree of performance from the scrappy little fighter, the Zero. Earhart's plane disappeared in July of 1937. By January of 1938, two aircraft companies, Mitsubishi and Nakajima, were handed the Navy's new, more-advanced specifications.

Then Nakajima withdrew, supposedly because it did not believe the specifications could be met. The real reason could have been that Amelia Earhart's Lockheed had already been put at the disposal of Mitsubishi. Soon, advanced features of Earhart's plane and engine were added to the A5M, and, gradually, the A6M, the new, advanced Zero, emerged. Its speed and endurance had increased. To give him credit, the brilliant Horikoshi was able to adapt the best of the aircraft's engines and features, while removing many flaws on his own.

The result was that by the winter of 1940, one year before Pearl Harbor, Japan had one of the world's best fighter planes, if not the best.

It exceeded the emperor's wildest dreams. Japan also had a large cadre of pilots, battle-tested in China. And to improve the plane's performance still further, at the insistence of the emperor, no body armor was placed behind the pilot's seat, making it lighter and faster, but not safer. Actually, it was decreed as part of "policy" in accordance with Imperial Navy tradition. And, as a sign of courage, most Japanese pilots refused to wear parachutes.

How much was adapted from Amelia Earhart's airplane is hard to estimate exactly. The improved Zero included navigation instruments similar to the U.S. Navy's, many top secret in 1937, the year Earhart disappeared. To an engineer, reading a specification chart is like reading a newspaper. Looking at the plans, easily identifiable parts of Amelia's plane were staring up at me.

The earlier A5M featured a carburetor (which supplies an internal combustion engine with an explosive vapor mixture of air and fuel) that had to be controlled manually by the pilot as he started climbing from sea level to gain altitude; the same was true as he descended. For a fighter pilot in an intense air duel, time was of the essence; each second that was lost adjusting the carburetor or waiting for engine response might be a matter of life or death. Earhart's was automatic, and an identical automatic carburetor was now incorporated into the newer A6M Zero. This dramatic change enabled the Zero to climb or dive faster without constant pilot adjustment. Amelia had retractable landing gear, and this mechanism had been copied. I found a propeller governor that had been duplicated. Each one of the two Pratt & Whitney engines on Amelia's plane was a single radial. The Zero, before Amelia vanished, was also a single radial engine: after she vanished, it became a double radial, incorporating the best features of her engine, the Hawaiian Clipper's, and the Japanese model. This improved its performance and made the air cooling system, which had long stymied the Mitsubishi engineers, more efficient. All these changes were in the Horikoshi plans.

Before the Earhart disappearance, the A5M suffered from ignition leaks, which led to ignition failure; post-Earhart, the A6M had a new ignition harness to prevent failure. It was right out of Earhart's plane.

Too identical to be accidental were the completely new wheels, new brakes, and new type of tires—the same as Amelia's. Even the tail skid (wheel) was now identical, which if not locked in the fore and aft position for landing and takeoff, you were riding a wild horse. Add to the list the new oil pump for the hydraulics, the new type of magneto, and the new generator for electricity.

While not a radio technician, it was obvious to me that what I was looking at in these specifications was the same radio equipment that was in Earhart's Lockheed when I upgraded her plane in Florida in 1937.

It suddenly jolted me to realize, for the very first time since she vanished, that I had been harboring deep guilt feelings in the pit of my stomach. I had been afraid to ask myself the question, Could something I did at the time have contributed to her disappearance?

During the next few weeks, I traveled around the outer islands with Japan's civil defense units and was shown air bases that had been protected during the war. It seemed to be a good time to start asking questions, hoping I was masking inquisitiveness behind my open Dutch face. The pieces were coming together. I was determined to solve the Earhart riddle, recognizing I would have to be patient, very patient. I dared not become antagonistic.

Prior to their preparations for an invasion of China, the Japanese had long been fortifying their small outlying islands. Involved in these preparations was the Imperial Japanese Navy. Aerial superiority was the centerpiece of their plan. By 1941, with its super-Zero poised like a *Ninja's* sword, Japan's military leaders and the emperor had confidence that their hunger for conquest could consume the Pacific.

Back at work, because of my indignation, I became more focused. I continued to poke and probe and ask questions of my Japanese colleagues. Each night, I tried to recall everything I knew about Amelia Earhart's last flight. I dug up my Pan Am files, which I had brought to Japan—information collected from Pan Am air stations across the Pacific. As part of Pan Am's own investigative and evaluation team, I had kept every scrap of paper concerning her disappearance. It was also imperative to remain objective. I wrote out an outline of important points:

1. U.S. Navy commander Clarence Williams, in an article in the *Oakland Tribune* on July 2, 1937, revealed there were southerly crosswinds, plus heavier headwinds, than were forecast.

2. Approaching her destination, Howland Island, her D/F (direction finder) was not functioning. She could not send or receive on the D/F frequency with the U.S.S. *Itasca*.

3. If her aircraft had been blown off course, Noonan, unable to use the drift meter at night, would be unaware.

4. Amelia's radio skills were surprisingly weak.

5. At 2:00 P.M. Western Pacific Time, she left Lae with 900 gallons of fuel (though her tanks were topped at 964 usable gallons, it was estimated there would be an evaporation of 50-plus gallons in the hot sun and from venting). The grassy runway at Lae ended at a shallow cliff above the beach. On her 72-degree, northeast flight path, the plane lifted off the runway, then dropped below cliff height but remained airborne. I was certain that if I hadn't suggested more-powerful engines, she'd have crashed into the ocean.

6. There were reports (unconfirmed) that instead of flying directly toward Howland, she flew a secret U.S. intelligence mission at high speed over Japan's extensive naval facilities at Truk, which was en route to Howland. It is located on the northern tip of the Solomon Islands.

7. Noonan was a superb navigator who had invented his own "advanced sunline," an improvement on the old mariners' method of "running down the latitudes" (the mariners could obtain the latitude with a simple astrolabe at high noon).

8. There were rumors that Noonan had too much to drink the night before the flight, overslept, and did not set the plane's chronometer (a superbly accurate timepiece) with the international radio broadcast. In navigation, exact time is essential when used with a sextant (a refined angle meter used in conjunction with a chronometer to determine longitude at sea).

9. After landing at Lae, Amelia reported her fuel pump was malfunctioning. When the spare did not work, the original was repaired. This delayed the flight one day to July 2, 1937.

10. What about the allegation that Amelia Earhart suspected Noonan to have been drunk, thus lending belief to the theory the plane had been "lost"? My own knowledge refutes this. Drunk or sober, Noonan was the best navigator of his day. Amelia spoke to her husband, George Putnam, at each stop along the route. George Putnam later told me personally that when Amelia called from Lae and said she suspected Noonan might be drinking, he warned her to "stick to him like glue." She did not let Noonan out of her sight before the flight. Even so, if he had been drinking, he certainly would have sobered up during the eighteen hours of flying. His navigating had been flawless up to that point.

In balance, knowing the Earhart/Noonan background, and after seeing the rapid improvements made on the Zero and the Japanese copy of the Hawaiian Clipper, my conclusion was that the Japanese had forced down Earhart's plane. I needed some missing pieces to determine the outcome of this complex series of events.

The finale simply happened. At Tokyo University, where I taught philosophy and atomic energy, a cocktail party celebration turned into an enormous bash. I found myself in conversation with some former Imperial Navy personnel on the university staff, along with a dozen of my Japanese chums from the Civil Defense Bureau and the Civil Aviation Bureau. Another group joined us, a club of some sort, consisting of eighteen kamikaze pilots who had not kamikazed. I brought up Amelia Earhart's name and asked if anyone could speculate on what happened to her. No one bothered answering. By Japanese standards and culture, this is considered rude.

One man, who identified himself as a former Navy commander, said, "We killed many Americans, and Americans killed many of us. It was war. Sometimes we had to destroy whatever was in our way to safeguard our own missions."

A kamikaze pilot said, "I believe that Earhart was lost in the Japan Triangle, which is more ferocious than the Bermuda Triangle."

For the first time since my arrival to Japan, the conversation turned to some of the atrocities committed by the Japanese forces. They quickly expressed deep shame. The talk then centered on some Japanese citizens who had been executed, people who were against the war. This had taken place, apparently, on some of the remote islands that were in Japanese hands.

About 9:00 P.M., too early for the party to end, I suggested to four friends from the Defense Department, ex-Navy types with whom I had worked very closely, to come over to my house where my cook would prepare *sushi* for them. It was Maria's obligatory bridge night at the embassy, and the house would be free, so the five of us piled into my Cadillac and my driver took off.

At home, the men continued to drink sake while I had a spritzer (wine and seltzer). They were getting bombed. I can honestly say that a drunken Japanese man is no different from a drunken American, Russian, or Frenchman. However, the Japanese are usually more polite. Before the food was ready, three of them were sleeping on the floor. One, to whom I'll give the pseudonym "Koshiro," for security reasons, was a former naval intelligence officer. He kept staring at me as if he were in a spell. I hadn't realized it till that moment, but Koshiro was as stone-cold sober as I was.

"When you were looking at the 'Emily,' you could not hide your dismay. You are not an impassive man, Henri. For many weeks, you have been flirting with us, asking questions about Amelia Earhart. No Occidental can be subtle in the Orient, where subtlety was invented. You have honor, *Sensei*, but you show your anguish. After many sleepless nights, I have decided to tell you some part of what you wish to know. You must agree that the source remains secret, to do otherwise would be to dishonor my family and my ancestors."

I bowed and said, "You have my word."

"Not many people in Japan wanted the war. Only the warlords in the Navy kept goading the emperor, filling his head with the dream of an Asian Empire. He read everything available on this famous woman aviator, and about the money being spent to outfit her plane with the latest technology. He wanted a way to seize it. At first, he wished to use members of the royal family to shoot her down. The warlords said that if that plot were discovered, it would disgrace the house of the emperor.

"To please the emperor, the warlords decided to select two of the brightest young graduates at the Japanese Imperial Naval University who were well schooled in intelligence. This they did. Lieutenants Matsui Nagamo and Toshio Abe were selected. They agreed to volunteer for the mission to capture Earhart's plane and execute the crew. They were told that there must be no evidence that Japan had a role in this attack. If caught, the government would deny complicity. Since Earhart was such a celebrated American, any mistake could easily have started a war.

"If successful, each man would be guaranteed to advance rapidly through the ranks to admiral, receive great honors and command great warships." Then Koshiro took a deep breath and closed his eyes as though in torment, as if the memory was hurting him physically. Suddenly, our cook came in and announced that the food was ready. The spell was broken.

When Maria came home, my friends were taken home by our chauffeur in the Cadillac. She went to bed, but I stayed up all night thinking. What could I do with this information? I knew from previous discussions that Koshiro had been involved in naval intelligence work.

I saw Koshiro a week later at one of our regular meetings. I suggested lunch, and we went to a quiet restaurant nearby. He didn't want to drink, and though I pressed him, he avoided the subject of Earhart. With nothing to lose, I said, "Koshiro, you were in intelligence. Supposing you planned to capture a land plane. How would you go about it?"

He looked at me for a long time, then said, "First, I would find out the radio frequency of the target plane and monitor its transmissions. I would have available a radio operator who spoke flawless American English to give out false information. At the right moment, we would transmit a single decoy radio transmission to pull the plane south over the lower portion of the Gilbert Islands.

"By the time it has exhausted its fuel, it would be forced to land in shallow waters off the coast of Nonouti, a Japanese-controlled base in the Gilbert Islands, some five hundred to six hundred miles away." (At the time, direction finders at Howland and Pan Am's Pacific stations pointed toward Gardner Island, but the U.S. Navy discounted it.)

We said little after that. By phrasing the question the way I had, it enabled him to narrate this information without dishonor and without personal involvement.

In the afternoon, I had difficulty concentrating on my work, so I let one of my embassy pals talk me into playing three sets of tennis. That night, there was a new American movie showing for embassy personnel, but I begged off and Maria went alone. I needed time to think.

Lieutenants Matsui Nagamo and Toshio Abe had set the trap to capture the plane at Nonouti. In all probability, Earhart and Noonan had been interrogated and executed, their plane, or what was left of it, was pulled ashore, dismantled, and shipped to the Mitsubishi factory.

The following day, I did some research on my own. Toshio Abe, a highly decorated combat officer, had reached the rank of admiral and was assigned to the largest aircraft carrier in the world, the *Shinano*, a seventy-two-thousand-ton ship that had been commissioned on November 19, 1944. Not completely fitted out, the *Shinano* had been ordered out of Tokyo Bay to escape Allied bombing. It was sunk that very day by the American submarine *Archer-Fish*, south of the mid-island of Japan called Hanshee. There had been 2,515 crewmen on board. Only 1,080 survived. The ship's Captain, Toshio Abe, a survivor of Midway, went down with his ship. The *Archer-Fish* was honored by being present in Tokyo Bay for the surrender ceremonies, which officially ended World War II.

His brother officer, Matsui Nagamo, also a star graduate of the naval academy and a much-decorated combat officer, reached the rank of vice admiral. He, too, commanded a newly commissioned ship. During the sea battle at Cape Enjano off Leyte in June 1944, his aircraft carrier, the *Zuikaku*, was sunk by an American destroyer. Admiral Matsui Nagamo went down with his ship.

I frequently mulled over what I had pieced together and what I should do about it. I was part of the State Department and bringing up this kind of revelation was not in our government's best interests. It would stir up old animosities. The United States was doing its utmost to put Japan back on its feet, which was the reason I was there in the first place. Deep down, I had a suspicion that the U.S. government was aware of what happened to Earhart, Noonan, and Lockheed number NR16020. If the government knew sometime between 1937 and 1940, it could cause the kind of explosion that might trigger a war at a time the United States was totally unprepared for it.

After the war, trying to mend a shattered Japan and fashion it into a democracy was of prime importance to America. In other words, there never was a good moment to bring the Amelia Earhart matter to light, despite all the articles, books, and speculations about the missing aircraft. My decision finally was not to report immediately what I had unearthed but to prepare my personal dossier of the aircraft plans I had seen with my own eyes, what I had been told by a former Japanese naval intelligence officer, and dovetail this information with my old files.

THE DOSSIER

The following maps and detailed notes are adapted from the Pan Am files. I was part of the team that collected and evaluated them. They show Amelia Earhart's much-publicized route, her activities up to reaching Lae, New Guinea, her departure and her subsequent disappearance. Based on what my Japanese informant revealed, it shows how the Lockheed was brought down, including fake radio messages, which diverted her to Nonouti in the Gilbert Islands.

Her last radio transmissions were noted word for word in the *Itasca* log, along with the times. One of the most gripping unanswered questions is: At sunset, why did Amelia insist on changing transmitting channels from 6210 kHz to the lower frequency, 3105 kHz, after the radio operator at Lae, Harry Balfour, advised against it? The following information shows she may not have had a choice.

Amelia didn't know Morse code, so she couldn't communicate by that method. I can attest that she had her aerial antennae when she left Florida; the long trailing wire for long wave, and the short one on top of the fuselage for short wave. It was subsequently reported that she may have lost her long-wave antenna during her landing at Lae, because the trailing wire was not reeled in.

It was difficult for investigators to understand why, from the moment she changed frequencies to her last voice transmission, she carefully avoided two-way communications. Also, during her transmissions, she was not on the air long enough for the *Itasca* or Howland radio direction finding equipment to get a bearing on her position. Ultimately, Amelia Earhart and Fred Noonan disappeared into history. What are the missing pieces to this puzzle?

By putting together all the known preflight and postflight facts, everything suddenly comes into focus:

1. Evidence indicates that strong headwinds and crosswinds were blowing across her flight route. Noonan, unable to see waves at night in order to use his drift meter, was unaware of the drift. Heavy clouds prevented his getting a fix on the stars by sextant.

2. Harry Balfour, radio operator at Lae, had clear, two-way radio communications with Earhart and asked her not to switch frequencies from 6210 kHz (daytime) to 3105 kc (nighttime). Inexplicably, Earhart disregarded advice.

3. When Balfour received an updated weather report showing headwinds and crosswinds in her path, he was unable to relay this information to Earhart.

4. The trailing aerial is the paradox. She had it when she left Miami. She used it consistently on her trip until she reached Lae. What happened to the aerial? One speculation is that it was lost at Lae when it wasn't reeled in for the landing. But this would have been discovered on a thorough maintenance check before taking off for Howland.

My contention is that as part of the sabotage plan, the trailing antenna was not removed, but the reel was tampered with at Lae so that at some point in the flight, it simply unraveled and dropped into the ocean. This left her without a long-wave antenna in mid-flight and she was unable to communicate properly.

5. At sunrise, 1800 hours GMT, weather and atmospheric conditions created a blinding sun glare (attested to by *Itasca*'s officers). By the time Noonan could take an advanced sunline, he would discover they were at least one hour, possibly two hours, behind schedule.

6. The flight plan called for a seventeen-hour, twenty-minute flight. But this made no allowance for a wind factor. Strong winds, the plane's heavy weight, and the weather slowed their cruising speed of 150 statute miles per hour to about 125 miles per hour.

7. Earhart and Noonan were novice radio operators; 4800 kHz was the top limit of her direction finder, yet she asked *Itasca* to transmit on 7500 kHz. But was it Earhart or someone else on the air?

8. Howland Island is a sandbar two miles long and a half mile wide. When Earhart and Noonan were due, the waters around the island were calm, so *Itasca* sent up dense smoke to attract their attention; the smoke didn't rise, instead it clouded and hid the island.

9. The two Japanese naval intelligence officers and the radioman who spoke colloquial American English were on Nonouti. Contact was made with Earhart and false signals were being sent to U.S. naval vessels. This accounts for the confusion. Earhart started circling, searching for the speck on the ocean that was Howland. *Itasca*, out of radio range, heard only Earhart's alleged short, unclear signals, some of which were undoubtedly false.

10. At 2014 GMT, Earhart (or the saboteur) spoke for the last time: "We are on the line of position 157–337." Experts have stated there was a two-hour discrepancy. Noonan should have had no problems getting an accurate fix, and Earhart should have had no problem keeping on track. The only possible conclusion is

that she was misdirected by the instructions of the Japanese radio operator.

11. The Lockheed, low on fuel, landed on the water close to Nonouti's shore. The empty gas tanks would have kept the plane afloat. As my informant stated, Noonan and Earhart were captured and slain. The plane was crated and sent back to Japan.

12. The emperor's instructions to the two naval officers included the complete destruction of all evidence.

13. Severe electrical storms were reported in the area of Howland. This would create static and affect radio signals.

14. The next day, on July 3, 1937, a large U.S. naval flying boat set out from Honolulu on a nineteen-hundred-mile rescue search. The pilot, Lieutenant W. W. Harvey, was forced to return to base after encountering "heavy snow, sleet and lightning storms."

15. The U.S. government asked Japan for help. Two Japanese vessels, the survey ship *Koshu* and the Imperial Navy's plane tender, the *Kamoi*, did join in the search. It is mind-boggling to try to understand why their search was not conducted near the Phoenix Islands, the suspected crash area, two hundred miles south of Howland. Instead, the two ships checked the area around the Marshall Islands, about 750 miles northwest of Howland. Coincidentally, their search pattern was about one hundred miles north of Nonouti.

THE LAST WORD

The following are Earhart's final radio messages on July 2, 1937, as listed in the log of the Coast Guard cutter *Itasca*, the ship that was placed near Howland by the U.S. government at the request of Amelia Earhart for the specific purpose of sending her weather reports and acting as her homing ship:

2:45 A.M.: Recognized Earhart's voice. Message not clear except "cloudy weather, cloudy."

3:45 A.M.: "Itasca from Earhart. Itasca, broadcast on 3,105 kilocycles on hour and half hour. Repeat, broadcast on 3,105 kilocycles on hour and half hour. Overcast."

4:43 A.M.: Heard Earhart's voice. Signals unreadable with five listening.

5:12 A.M.: (from Earhart); "Want bearing on 3015 kc. Will whistle in microphone."

5:15 A.M.: "About 200 miles out. Whistle briefly in microphone."

5:45 A.M.: "Please take bearing on us and report in half hour. I will make noise in microphone. About 100 miles out."

7:30 A.M.: "We must be on you but cannot see you. Gas is running low. Have been unable to reach you by radio. We are flying at 1,000 feet."

7:57 A.M.: "We are circling but cannot see island. Cannot hear you. Go ahead on 7,500 kilocycles with long counts either now or on schedule. Time on half hour."

8:03 A.M.: "Earhart calling Itasca. We received your signals but unable to get minimum. Please take bearings on us and answer on 3,105 kilocycles." Earhart made long dashes on [for] brief period, but emergency high frequency direction finder could not cut her in on 3,105 kilocycles.

8:14 A.M.: Earhart called Itasca. "We are on line of position 157–337. We will repeat this message on 6,210 kilocycles. We are now running north and south."

There were no further messages received from Amelia Earhart. Earlier, when she had been asked by the ship's officers on the *Itasca* to transmit on the emergency frequency of 500 kHz, Amelia did not reply—or something had prevented her from doing so.

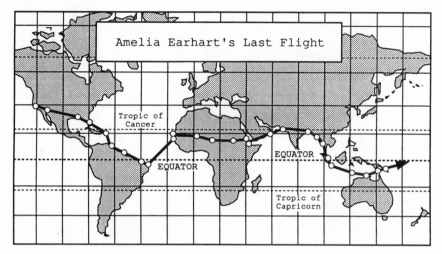

Here is the route they followed until they left New Guinea. They had made a few minor changes in their flight plan while en route and were slightly behind the schedule originally announced to the news media.

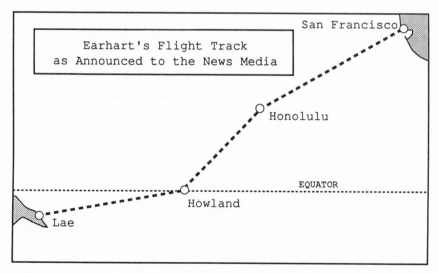

Here is the route Earhart had announced she would follow on her way back to California. Supposedly, she would make a triumphant arrival at her starting point on the July Fourth holiday.

┌───┐
│ ┌───────────────────────────────────────┐ │
│ │   Three Radio Direction Finders   │ │
│ └───────────────────────────────────────┘ │

Electra
Standard Aircraft
Direction Finder

Itasca   Howland
Standard Ship   Modified Military
Direction Finder   Direction Finder
└───┘

There were three radio direction finders available when Earhart flew to Howland. None of them led her in — why? The *Itasca* had a standard ship's direction finder, but it did not cover the two frequencies she carried. Actually, the engineers had originally provided a third frequency, 500 kHz, that did fall within the tuning range of the *Itasca*'s direction finder. However, Amelia could transmit on that frequency *only* if she reeled out a long antenna wire below her plane while in flight. But her trailing antenna was sabotaged.

Without the long antenna, not only would Earhart be unable to transmit on 500 kHz, but the strength of her signals on 3105 kHz would be extremely weak.

The special, modified military direction finder set up on Howland by the Coast Guard could take bearings on 3105 kHz. In addition to her signals being weak, Earhart never stayed on the air more than a few seconds at a time. As a result, Radioman Ciprianti, manning the Howland direction finder, complained bitterly that he never had an opportunity to get a bearing.

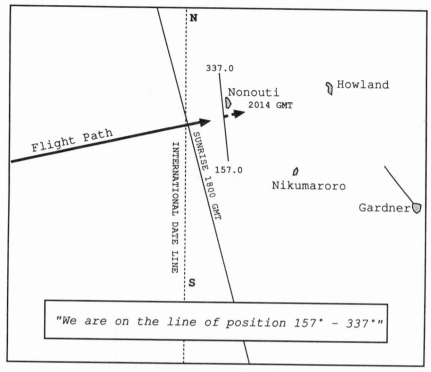

"We are on the line of position 157° - 337°"

At 2014 hours, Amelia came on the air for the last time. Investigators have long puzzled over her declaration, "We are on a line of position 157°-337°." If Noonan had taken a sight on the sun at sunrise, this is the bearing on the line he would have obtained. But it was more than two hours later and the sun's angle would have changed by several degrees. "Why had Fred been unable to get a bearing with his sextant since sunrise?" they asked.

Today we know she was not referring to a sunline but to a geographic line between Howland and Gardner as plotted on her chart. Her announcement only served to further confuse the crew of the *Itasca*.

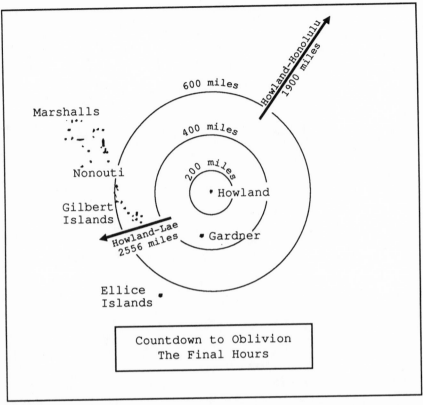

Countdown to Oblivion
The Final Hours

Earhart made only brief, hourly broadcasts before sunrise. At 1415 hours, 1515 hours, and 1623 hours (GMT), radio operators aboard the Coast Guard cutter *Itasca*, laying off Howland, were able to pick up only a few words. But after 1745 hours, some of her signals improved rapidly. This led them to believe she was much closer than she actually was. Author has shown the messages were decoys.

Although the ship called her all night, and continued to do so long after her last transmission, Amelia was careful to avoid any two-way communication with the crew. Finally, at 2014 hours, she announced she would change to 3105 kHz. The *Itasca* never heard from her again.

During the first seven hours of the flight, Earhart navigated by reference to the islands below them. During the night, Fred navigated by the stars. After sunrise, the only guidance they had was radio bearings and sextant sightings on the sun.

CHAPTER 27

I Don't Think the KGB Liked Me

I DIDN'T have time to dwell on Amelia Earhart, as a series of events occurred that were quite disturbing. Out of the blue, the Russians began playing mind games with me. It took me awhile to figure out why.

One day, the minister of politics at the Russian embassy invited me to lunch. It was generally understood that Russian political officers were KGB agents. I didn't particularly like the man, and so I was leery about accepting. Discussing it with our embassy intelligence officer, he suggested that I go if only to find out what he was up to.

The restaurant he had selected was in *Shinjuko*, the area where they served live, poisonous snakes as a delicacy. Movie actors and actresses went there simply to get the high, aphrodisiac effect one got from eating this particular snake, *doku mamushi hede*. The high lasted about four days. Obviously, the intention of the Russian was not to feed me but to embarrass me in public if I refused to eat the snake.

The waiter produced a pair of tongs while my host selected a particular snake. The art of preparing a poisonous snake is gruesomely fascinating. The first thing a waiter does is cut off the snake's head and place it on a plate. The head keeps opening and closing its mouth, biting all the time. Then the waiter cuts out the liver and heart, drains the snake's blood, and puts liver, heart and blood into a small glass bowl. As you drink the blood, you can feel its heart beating all the way down to the stomach.

Next, the waiter grinds up several pieces in a hamburger grinder. While this is going on, the pieces of the snake left on the plate keep

253

jumping up and down. The customer takes his *hashi* (chopsticks) and
catches all the wiggly pieces and eats them. The only seasoning one
may have is dried snakeskin ground up into fine dust and sprinkled on
like salt.

My host watched as I went through the ceremony and ate every
blessed piece. This was not part of the scenario. My host's stomach was
churning, so he was unable to eat anything. All he did was drink vodka
while his face turned white watching me. I thanked him for lunch and
he departed a very sullen man. I don't think we spoke ten words to each
other. And for four days afterward, I felt I could do anything and I did.

When I discussed lunch with our intelligence officer, we speculated
on why the Russians had picked on me. The conclusion was that the
Russians had seen my reports telling the Japanese to cancel the
TU-104 because it was too unsafe and that getting special fuel would
create severe problems.

About six weeks later when I was invited to lunch by another
Russian embassy official, I became certain something was bothering
the Russians. Lunch was to be at a particular restaurant in *Kyusha*, to
sample the world's deadliest delicacy, variously known as blowfish,
puffer, swellfish, or *shimonoseki fugu*. One of the most unusual crea-
tures of the sea, it is perhaps the world's deadliest fish. However, in
Japan, it is considered the height of elegant gourmet dining. Over one
hundred species of the killer puffers can be found around the world,
and these include an astounding variety even among the same species.

They share one characteristic, which is their uncanny ability to
expand from a normal fish shape to a globe size two or three times
larger. When frightened, a blowfish gulps water or air into a sac in its
belly that expands like a balloon. This discourages hungry predators
and intimidates rivals. When the fish feels safe, it deflates into its
normal size.

In Japan, eating *fugu* is a gastronomic version of Russian roulette.
Not infrequently, someone eating the fish will lose his life. A hush
descends over the area when chopsticks clatter onto a table from
lifeless hands, the diner a victim of its deadly poison. Dying of *fugu* is
often the subject of *Sayonara*. The Japanese have a verse that trans-
lates into English like this:

> "My friend and I eat *fugu* often.
> Today I carry him in his coffin."

When we first arrived in Japan, we were warned about the deadly gourmet fish at an embassy lecture. Fascinated, I did some piscatorial research on my own and became familiar with this deadly fish. So why was this Russian official, whom I didn't know, willing to take me to this expensive gastronomic treat? Once again I conferred with the embassy intelligence officer, who said this time, "Tell him to go to hell and refuse." But curiosity got the better of me. It ended up with a decision to accept despite the warning.

The restaurant was beautiful and I remember thinking that if you have to go, you couldn't depart from a nicer spot. The Russian turned out to be a tall, thin man with a serious demeanor and eyes that kept glancing all over the restaurant. He spoke through his teeth without opening his mouth. I don't know how he did it. His English was fair, so I began speaking to him in his mother tongue. We talked about flying and airplanes, and though he might have been a technical expert, he didn't know aviation.

He ordered the fish for me which was prepared to perfection. Then we looked at each other. On a hunch I said, "Have you been stationed in Tokyo very long?"

"About one month," he said.

"Are you familiar with Japanese etiquette?"

"Well, not really, except for the little I read."

"Don't you know it is the accepted tradition in Japan that the host takes the first bite?"

"No—I—that is—" Then he excused himself and walked rapidly out of the restaurant. I didn't eat the fish but picked up the tab. It was worth it.

Once more, I reported the incident to our intelligence officer. He came up with a new morsel of information that confirmed our suspicions. "Henri, I checked it out and it seems the Japanese did show the Russians your extremely negative report on the TU-104. I was also informed the Russians were upset." I couldn't divulge to my associate the ramifications of what he had told me.

Back in my office, I did a little objective soul-searching on my own. If the Russians knew I was opposed to the TU-104 because of poor safety features and the difficulty in obtaining special fuel, they might have alerted a sharp-eyed agent to nose around Djakarta. While the Indonesians might accept lightning as the source of the fuel explosion, a cynical agent might not believe in coincidence. He would have at his disposal local Communist friends to question people in the area. A tall, blond American who just happened to speak Dutch and who just happened to be fishing in the area would certainly stand out, particularly one who was accompanied by three Japanese fishermen. In addition, I had chatted with the patrol boat officer. He would certainly have kept a record of it.

It wasn't much of a jump to link me with their suspicions. It never once dawned on me that I could possibly be traced back to Tokyo. Henceforth, I would have to be very, very careful.

Unexpectedly, General Dynamics of San Diego offered JAL three beautiful 880 jet airplanes. The offer was advantageous, but it required a new program to be set up for training pilots, engineers, and crew at the General Dynamics school.

The procedure was pretty much a replay of what took place at McDonnell Douglas. Maria and I were due for our home leave, but this would be cut short because I had to return to Tokyo to help JAL set up its own program for the 880 aircraft. The biggest requirement was the need for me to study the advanced technology.

I was back in Tokyo only a few days when I was invited by Japanese friends to several performances at the Fujiwara Opera Company, as well as the Missei Theater over the period of a week. I stopped at the embassy in my formal wear, and as I was leaving the compound to locate my Cadillac, some sixth sense warned me. I turned my head. Bearing down on me out of the gloom was a large black car without lights, noiselessly accelerating. It was coming right at me. For a millisecond, my body was paralyzed. But my instincts made me dive to my left and the car, a diplomatic Mercedes-Benz, sideswiped me, roughly scraping my right arm and leg, spinning me to the ground.

Shaken, I stayed down to make sure the car was not coming by for a return engagement, then I checked my banged up body. Nothing was broken. When I got up and inspected the damage, my pants leg had a fifteen-inch slash and the arm of my jacket was ripped off.

By now, embassy Marines had come to help, escorting me inside. I was given first aid while someone contacted my wife in the car. When told what happened and that I was okay, she went home to get my spare tux. I replayed the incident in my mind and concluded it was a Russian embassy car. Some vodka-swilling SOB didn't like me. The feeling was mutual.

Just to keep everybody honest, an indignant diplomatic note was sent to the Russian ambassador on the carelessness of one of its drivers. It was simply our way of putting them on notice that we knew what they were up to and to quit fooling around.

It was quiet after that. The second class of *tetsugaku* (philosophy) for ladies was about to start, and once again I was *sensei*. The class limit was forty, but the university was deluged with three hundred applications. The first class of young ladies had been handpicked, exceptional students, so many graduates were able to get good jobs in industry. All the others got married. As a result, my class had become very famous.

At the same time, I started a new class of *genshiryoku*, (atomic energy), with six new male students. Because most Japanese have a powerful drive to succeed, the students' efforts need constant acknowledgment. Their enthusiasm is fueled for reasons of their own rather than someone else's. Then there is the matter of pride, or face. For these reasons, I was always aware that a Japanese student usually accepts an idea more readily if he discovers it for himself. Whenever it was necessary to criticize a student for a mistake, I referred instead, to my own earlier mistakes, while being careful to make my point. I found it was always good to practice principles of positive reinforcement when students were genuinely trying hard.

As time passed, most of the challenges in aviation were overcome. JAL had become a truly international airline with jet service. I knew that my time in Japan was winding down. In 1961, Edwin O. Reischauer was appointed the new ambassador to Japan. He not only spoke Japanese but also was married to a Japanese woman. He received the country's immediate acceptance.

And, finally, when my second class of forty ladies graduated, all of them also found jobs or got married. It became one of the most famous classes at Tokyo U. The students in my second atomic energy class all graduated with honors. The ambassador, on hearing about the famous girls' classes, called me to his office. "Henri, what in heaven's name are you teaching these young ladies?"

His wife was present so I told them about the philosophy class. It was Mrs. Reischauer who said, "If only we could teach Japanese ladies with such famous results at all the universities." The Reischauers then began to work with great energy to solidify the bonds between the United States and Japan.

Looking back over the years I spent in Japan, I think we did a considerable amount of good work in helping the Japanese people get

back on their feet by improving their industries, airlines, and universities. Most of all we helped them regain their pride and dignity as
they found their place among the family of nations.

Ambassador Reischauer deserves the major share of the credit.
During his tenure, he strengthened postwar relations between the
Japanese and American governments. Among his accomplishments,
he helped establish hospitals in Hiroshima and Nagasaki to study the
effects of radiation on the survivors of the two atom bombs. He pushed
new technical assistance programs to increase quality control in Japan.
The list is long and includes: guidelines for territorial fisheries; the
building of schools; he backed my efforts in aviation; shipbuilding,
the railroad system; atomic reactor plants to furnish electricity, and
the import-export industry.

Japan gave him many awards, but the most wonderful moment came
when Tokyo University was to bestow on him a doctoral degree. A
large group of Communists were demonstrating just outside the embassy, making a terrible din and snake dancing down the street. He
walked into their midst and bowed to them. They stopped, all bowed
back, and then they returned to snake dancing. It was clear he was
telling them that only in a free society can you do anything you damn
well please.

One of the fun tasks I had in Japan was to play the role of Santa Claus
at the embassy and around the country. I think it started on my TV
show. I didn't mind as I loved kids and didn't have any of my own,
except at Christmastime when I had thousands. The children nicknamed me *Ojjisan*, meaning old man.

Inexorably, my tour was coming to an end. In appreciation for my
work, Tokyo University honored me with a doctorate. For a while,
there was a party every night. It was heartwarming, and we were
finding it more and more difficult to leave the country. At a meeting
with the top officials of the Japanese Diet, they were kind enough to
mention many of the things I had accomplished, but they had one
more favor to ask of the U.S. government.

The Japanese Diet had purchased a new DC-8 at the Douglas plant
for its own use. Instead of leaving Japan for good, could Henri fly
them, their associates, and people in the aviation industry everywhere, opening the eyes of the Japanese to what existed in the rest of
the world? They also wanted to visit the earth's great natural wonders.

The United States government said they could borrow me as long as they liked. So I went to California, picked up the new jet, and flew my many friends to places in the world few people have a chance to see, including the Vinson Massif in Antarctica, 16,864 feet high. That was the first trip.

The second trip was to fly over all the great mountains of the world: the volcano, Mt. Etna, Italy, 10,902 feet high; Mt. Ararat, Caucuses, 16,946 feet high; the Matterhorn, Swiss Alps, 14,688 feet high, and, of course, Mt. K2 at 28,250 feet, and Mt. Everest, 29,026 feet high, in the Himalayas.

Though I was supposedly attached to Japan indefinitely, President John F. Kennedy requested that I wind down my trip while training a Japanese crew for the job. I was to return to Washington for my next assignment.

CHAPTER 28

Can a Concorde Do a Barrel Roll?

By THE TIME I left Japan in 1962, I had written their aeronautical statutes, plus a complete set of regulations for their air carriers. This included minimum standards for aircraft operating certificates, plus everything from how to conduct civilian accident investigations and accidents involving military aircraft, to airport operating certificates.

The Japanese were very pleased with the rules and they expressed their satisfaction to my superiors. As no good deed goes unpunished, I was asked to amend Washington's files and bring them up-to-date for the Civil Aviation Administration. This may sound somewhat dull, but actually it served as a cover for my real job.

Under very strict, high-security conditions I worked for four years on the atomic-powered airplane. In fact, the concept of a nuclear-powered plane began during the late years of the Roosevelt administration.

The work started in 1948, and at the time was given the code name Lexington Project, being established at MIT by the Atomic Energy Commission. This was to be a feasibility study. The study urged the undertaking, which would take an estimated fifteen years to develop at a cost of $1 billion.

Major General Donald Keirn was selected to head the project and direct the U.S. Air Force portion of it. Others were Brigadier General Irvin L. Branch; Captain (later Admiral) Hyman Rickover; Dr. Herbert York, director of the Defense Department Office of Engineering and Research; Dr. Vannevar Bush, vice president of MIT but working at the time with the Carnegie Institution on the study of plutonium; C. L. Kelly Johnson, Lockheed Aircraft vice president for advanced development projects; General Leslie R. Groves, head of the Manhattan Project; and I, the aeronautical engineer. As the work continued, some members left, others were added. Rickover, of course, channeled his efforts toward nuclear submarines and surface craft.

Because it was a long-range undertaking and expensive, it became a political football, and thus an on-again, off-again project. Every time it was on again, I would have to refresh my knowledge, study new aspects of nuclear propulsion, and get myself up to speed. While in Japan, I taught a less advanced course in atomic energy to engineers, but on my return to the FAA, I was drawn into the fray once more.

No one, other than administrator William Langhorne Bond and his co-workers, knew of my involvement, which functioned under tight security orders. In its later life, the Lexington Project became the Aircraft Nuclear Propulsion (ANP) Project. I was sent regularly to several universities for the highest level of advanced training in atomic energy. Eventually, this led to my being asked to be the liaison between the FAA and the Atomic Energy Commission.

While I wore two hats, I was later assigned other duties. Because of my languages, I handled all foreign students designated by their governments to study at the FAA. Between 1964 and 1977, young men from nearly every country in the world participated.

Much of the work to build the atomic plane is still secret, so I can say little about it other than it featured two different nuclear engines: one was being built by General Electric, the GE-N-211, a direct cycle nuclear turbojet; the other, by Pratt & Whitney, was an indirect cycle nuclear engine. Because of mounting costs, work on the plane was suspended in 1961, revived again, and finally shelved in 1966.

During this program, I met many wonderful and brilliant people. Those of us in government all got an extra step in our pay structure through the Department of Schooling and Achievement in Science. Because of all the work we did and the schooling we went through at various institutions, we all received an equivalent of a Ph.D. in physics—nuclear physics.

Through it all, I was merrily rewriting the FAA statutes. Upon completion they were called: "Aeronautical Statutes and Related Material: Federal Aviation Act of 1958. Revised June 1, 1970."

The next assignment was to Oklahoma City, where the FAA operated an aviation school for new aircraft. As part of a four-week course
on general aircraft aviation and helicopters, I had to successfully fly
each model, including the Douglas DC-9 and the Boeing 727. After
familiarization, I wrote the rules thereto.

In order to continue to issue certificates for these planes, it was
obligatory to continue to fly *each* aircraft for twenty-five hours per
year. This forced me to take trips to places I didn't want to go. To get
all this flying time, after dinner I'd take my wife flying for a four- or
five-hour jaunt that would end at midnight or later.

Another one of my jobs was to monitor Air Force One, the President's plane. This required checking and rechecking the pilots on
their ILS (instrument landing systems). On the side, while coordinat-
ing the FAA and the Department of Agriculture, I wrote the rules for
travel with animals.

During 1969, Pan Am bought the first two 747 Boeing jumbo jets
on provisional certification. This meant the plane was certified only to
train pilots and could not carry passengers. Because I was amending
and writing detailed air carrier rules for the FAA, I was assigned to a
six-week training course on the 747 in conjunction with the Pan Am
pilots. I found it to be a pilot-friendly plane.

I had been back from the 747 training in Seattle for three months
when it was announced that the First Lady, Mrs. Pat Nixon, was slated
to pour red, white, and blue water over the first scheduled 747 flight
from Dulles Airport to Paris. Boeing had two more 747s in Seattle about
to be certificated for carrying passengers; it would use company pilots
and FAA co-pilots to test them. Depending on weather conditions, it
takes a minimum of ten days of testing to certificate a plane for carrying
passengers—unless you run into problems.

The two available 747s ran into problems. The first occurred during
a landing in bad weather. The 747 hit an obstacle on the runway and
the number-four engine broke off. Next day, again while landing, the
remaining 747's rear landing strut and gear broke off. It was suggested
that the inaugural flight, scheduled eleven days later, be postponed.

On hearing about the two accidents, President Nixon, using his
usual abusive language, called the FAA administrator and commanded
him to get a 747 passenger-certificated plane to meet the schedule.
The photo opportunity was too good to miss and the FAA was ordered
to find a qualified test pilot to certificate it on time.

President Nixon was noted for his terrible temper and he was apparently seething. Which is why the administrator beseeched me to do him a favor. Using a 747 Pan Am pilot-training plane, I was to test and certificate it for passenger flying in ten days; a backbreaking effort, but I agreed. The administrator called the President and then he called back: "Henri, you just received a special citation from the President of the United States."

"What did the President say?"

"Get that son of a bitch up to Seattle and get that damned plane ready."

My wife was having lunch at the Turkish embassy at the time. I told her we were going away for ten days and to come directly to FAA Hangar 6. She asked about clothes. I told her not to worry. Just to take along a checkbook and buy what she needed in Seattle. The phone call cost me $3,000.

I commandeered an FAA Jetstar and a return crew and on to Seattle we flew. Upon arrival, I expected to get a good night's sleep and then to start the next morning, but it was not to be. On direct orders from you know who, everything was being expedited. I was scheduled to fly from 6:00 P.M. that night to 10:00 A.M. in the morning. The plane had no interior furnishings except for one hundred oil drums (fifty-five gallons each) filled with water to approximate the weight of the passengers.

Situated in strategic places around the inside of the plane were twenty-one engineers preparing to make tests; they were hooked up with TV cameras so I could observe each one from a monitor in the cockpit, by switching from one spot to another. To certificate an airplane for passenger carrying, the FAA is very strict. The following tests must be performed:

1. Takeoffs, landings, and turns under gross weight.
2. Over a six-to-eight-hour period, check for twists in airframe, stress sounds, wing flexibility, steering systems.
3. Check fuel flow, hydraulic oil flow, air pressure, landing gear up and down, redundant flight systems.
4. Check radio frequencies, radar scope for bad weather detection, operate the antennas.
5. At forty-five thousand feet, check cabin pressurization for six hours, check cabin cooling and heating systems.

6. Check engine power maximum climb; fly aircraft cutting one engine, then two. Check drop in altitudes.
7. In a storm at high altitude, check wings and engine cowls for ice accumulation; time it takes to free aircraft of ice, including coffee-makers, food-warmers, toilets.
8. Check auxiliary unit (small jet engine) in rear of plane that starts generator in case of electrical failure.

The ice test was the most dangerous, as we had to perform the test under storm conditions. Our meteorologist searched and finally spotted one in Canada. After getting the necessary clearance, we took off into a 45-knot crosswind. We didn't find the storm, the storm found us as we kept climbing through clouds until we hit snow and sleet and leveled off. Crystal ice began to form on the wings. It accumulated until we could no longer maintain altitude. Sluggishly, the plane started to descend, then I turned on the deicers. The system worked perfectly.

At a lower altitude, we ran into rime ice and let it accumulate on the wings. Again the deicers worked well. The deicing system was using 500-degree heat that flowed from the engines and then blew out through the leading edges of the wings and leading edges of all the surfaces of the empennage (tail assembly). It was an ideal system. Meanwhile, the inside of the plane remained comfortably warm.

Flying through so much rough air, the aircraft had been shaken violently, and we could see the wings flexing up and down. On the monitors, I could see that the engineers, nonflying types, were becoming concerned. I ordered my dinner, and when the stewardess in the rear came forward to the flight deck with my tray, they calmed down. I couldn't spare the time to eat it.

We'd land at night to refuel to keep our gross weight up, then we'd fly over the Pacific or north to Alaska or return to Seattle, depending on the weather. Then we would have to bring the plane down in Seattle for servicing from 10:30 A.M. to 6:00 P.M. This gave us a chance to sleep and move around. Then we'd fly all night.

Finally, I completed the tests and the paperwork and signed off the plane with a certificate for passenger flying. Now the interior had to be completely furbished for carrying passengers. Two Pan Am pilots, waiting for this moment, came aboard to fly the plane from Seattle to Dulles Airport in Washington for the scheduled departure to Paris the next day.

All that work under extreme pressure so that the First Lady could pour tricolored water on the 747. I didn't bother to watch the inaugural flight take off. I was too busy writing some rules for the 747.

In the interim, Pan Am asked to purchase twelve and Braniff Airways six of the new Concordes, the supersonic transports (SSTs). With extra engines and spare parts, this amounted to a $2.5 billion purchase. The Commerce Department and the FAA wanted an estimate of the cost to operate the machines for air carrier operation. They also wanted to know of its reliability in regard to maintenance operation and overhaul. Finally, it had to be certificated for passenger carrying in the United States.

Which is why the FAA requested that I attend the Concorde School at the British Air/Space Facility in Filton, England. It was a six-month project; three months to learn construction and maintenance and overhaul engineering, studying the intricate systems of the plane. Then I had to receive sixty-five hours of training in the simulator, plus actual flying time on the Concorde itself.

When I got to Filton, I learned that the Concorde was a technologically new dimension in aerodynamics with very sophisticated systems. The planes flew faster than the speed of sound. Out of each four airline captains of jet aircraft who took the course, one was unable to complete it—in other words, the failure rate was 25 percent.

As the FAA representative, I was given an additional hurdle. It was expected that I would have to get perfect scores. Each wrong answer, written or oral, whether on the simulator or in actual flight, would cost me a quart of the best Scotch.

The power plants, called Snecma, are manufactured by Rolls-Royce and require constant attention. Each engine develops sixty thousand pounds of thrust, and burns nine thousand gallons of fuel per hour. The intake air must be kept subsonic when the plane is flying at speeds of Mach 2.*

One curious aspect of the plane is the heat factor. Because of the speed ranges, it must be flown within temperature limits for structural integrity; 127 degrees Celsius at the nose and 91 degrees Celsius at the wing tip. As a result of this friction heat, the Concorde increases nine inches in length during flight. There are four air-conditioning units to

---

* Mach 1 = the speed of sound, which varies due to weather and altitude; Mach 2 = twice the speed of sound.

keep the plane cool. If just one unit fails, the airplane must be slowed down until the nose temperature drops to 100 degrees Celsius. If three units fail, the plane must be flown below the speed of sound (subsonic).

The plane carries 205,000 pounds of fuel. The wings have no flap to slow the machine. Takeoff, landing, or flying the plane is all done with the plane's attitude. As the plane approaches Mach 1, the captain must turn on the afterburners as well as turning on the autopilot to take the plane through the first shock waves as the speed reaches Mach 1.7.

Finally, the day of my test flight arrived, and because of foggy weather, we had to go to London's Heathrow Airport, where we had category 3, ILS, runways 28 and 29, left and right. My British instructor said, "Okay, Ace, the moment of truth has arrived."

I was reminded constantly that this plane flew faster than any bullet shot from a rifle. It flew faster than the U.S. Air Force F-16, or F-18. The greatest distraction was the warbler/barber pole in the cockpit. The pole came up and warbled when the pilot diverted from standard temperature, standard airspeed, angle of attack, angle of the droop snout (nose) and the fuel transfer when the afterburners were not turned off.

The tower worked everything by light. When my checklist was complete, I taxied to position. The weather was bad, with a 150-foot ceiling. With the throttle forward and the afterburners lit, the airplane tracked straight. You didn't have to use levers to guide it. The nose steering affected the action of the rudder.

Acceleration started slowly, as it was an extremely heavy machine. Suddenly, 100-knot speed was announced, then 162 knots. I brought the nose up 14 degrees at 200 knots. When I set the speed at 450 knots to climb to thirty thousand feet, the fuel automatically transferred from the front tanks to the rear tanks. The afterburners were turned off, and the flight attitude was increased to 19 degrees. The climbing rate was 6,000 feet per minute until we reached thirty-five thousand. I had to make another change in power, and suddenly the barber pole came up and warbled and I knew I had made a mistake. I would have to buy the first round of drinks that evening. When we got near Mach 1, I had to turn on the afterburners again and the automatic pilot. This I did, and we awaited the first shock wave at Mach 1.7.

When the afterburners were turned off, we were approaching sixty thousand feet. I now had to take the fuel out of the tip tanks so the wings could rise and get into proper position to reach Mach 2. When the afterburners and the automatic pilot were turned off by hand, I was asked to make one emergency descent by turning on the reverse thrust to see how fast the plane would come down. It came down like a rock.

I had to make two ILS landings at Heathrow. Before I was through, the barber pole came up and warbled again. I finished with two errors, which I was told was excellent for the first test flight. I was treated to a glorious dinner and given a British certificate that stated I was qualified to fly the Concorde.

Because the Concorde was a joint venture between the British and French, I was obliged to fly the French Concorde for one hour in Paris. As I spoke French fluently, the instructors and I got along fine. Near the end of my hours flying, which went along perfectly, the instructor said to me, "Henri, would you like to roll her over?"

I said, "You bet." After slowing down to subsonic speed, I rolled the plane over twice. What a sensation to roll over a huge machine the size of the Concorde.

The French officials also threw a party for me, followed by a gourmet dinner. I received a certificate saying I was qualified as a first-line captain to fly the French Concorde. Next day, I was flown back to New York on the French Concorde at Mach 2, around 1,200 miles an hour. It took three hours, twenty-four minutes. Some difference from my days of flying the Pan Am Clippers at 125 miles an hour.

The Concorde is a technological marvel, different from anything I had ever flown before. So I was a little sad that because of my report, we had to turn down this multi-billion-dollar program. It costs twice as much to fly the Concorde as a 747. The British and French will only fly the Concorde for one thousand hours per year—because of the way the plane is built, it cannot be inspected in the center section. After thirty thousand hours of flight time, the plane has to be taken completely apart and overhauled. When I did my computations, I discovered it was more expensive to overhaul the Concorde than build a new one. After reading my report, Pan Am and Braniff decided against purchasing the plane.

CHAPTER 29

Why Does Death Keep Knocking on My Door?

MY LAST five years at the FAA were relatively quiet. I was writing regulations and acting as a senior adviser to younger staff members. My life, which had experienced its share of danger, was growing steadily quieter. The last exciting thing to happen to me was flying a Concorde at twice the speed of sound (approximately 1,200 miles per hour), then topping it off with a barrel roll. That should have been enough of a final thrill for any man. As Yogi Berra might have said about my life, "Quit while you're ahead."

In February 1977, upon reaching the compulsory retirement age of seventy, they threw me a retirement party. I wasn't ready for a pipe and slippers, but you can't fight government regulations. In retrospect, it didn't seem as though there was much left for me to do. I should have slowly faded away. There wasn't a place in the world I hadn't flown to, flown over, or visited. Retirement meant going back to playing the organ, or writing my memoirs. But the big pilot in the sky had other plans.

The departure party kept getting bigger and bigger until it had to be held in the main dining room at the Washington Sheraton Hotel. Heading the list of guests was the secretary of transportation, William T. Coleman, and the head of the FAA at the time, John L. Lucas, a former secretary of the Air Force. Many embassies sent representatives. As they say on Broadway, "It was a smash."

For an unemployed old geezer, I had led too active a life to retire, so I thought about my options. Other than flying, I had expertise in one other area, nuclear energy. While sitting around and cogitating about what I might do to keep occupied, I came to understand the truth of the old adage, "The hardest thing to do in this world . . . is nothing." No one should ever retire.

A group of nuclear scientists, of which I was one, fully understood the nature of this rapidly growing, complex technology. But there were too few knowledgeable people to utilize this science for peaceful purposes. So I joined the Society of International Concerned Scientists and attended the Nuclear Energy Symposium at Helsinki, Finland, in 1974; then the next one in France, in 1976; and, after my retirement, in Geneva and Vienna in 1978.

It was at the Cern Nuclear Institute in Geneva that I met former President Ford, who was also attending the Geneva symposium. There were very few Americans there, so he invited me to lunch to talk about fusion energy and the nuclear fission plants being constructed in many countries. This included Russia, which was expanding its nuclear power rapidly. He considered this a threat and suggested I meet with him in Washington on my return.

I went on to Vienna, where I gave a speech at the Nuclear Fusion Symposium entitled, "U.S.A., Progress in Fusion." After the speech, I was approached by three young Russian scientists whom I had met in Geneva and earlier at Helsinki: Paul Andrei Zhavoronkov, B. P. Venikolapov, and Vladimir Goldansky, all brilliant young men. I learned from them that Russia intended to lead the world in nuclear fusion reactors for domestic use and create a mammoth nuclear industry worldwide.

When I returned to Washington, I contacted Gerald Ford. He had checked on my background and knew about my overt and covert missions and also that I spoke Russian. He thought it might be a good idea if I could take a trip through Russia to gain firsthand knowledge of just how advanced the Russians were.

I told him that my days of derring-do were in the past, and I left, not expecting to see him again. Unexpectedly, a major tragedy occurred in my life. My darling wife, Maria, died suddenly of a massive coronary at our home in Arlington, Virginia.

After many wonderful years together, it was a devastating blow. Living alone in an empty house intensified a difficult period of mourning for me. I had no regular job to obliterate the lonely hours. All I had were fond memories, with too much time to endure grief. Friends encouraged me to occupy my time. I acquiesced.

So once again I met with former President Ford, who told me he had discussed the matter with President Jimmy Carter, himself a former U.S. Navy nuclear submarine commander, who agreed to the trip as long as it was "unofficial." I could go as a civilian and, believe it or not, pay my own way as a member of the Society of International Concerned Scientists. I was to ascertain just how good Russia's nuclear plants were. And if this nuclear power could be used for military purposes.

U.S. intelligence sources informed me that there was some unhappiness about the nuclear program in Russia, and that Secretary General Leonid I. Brezhnev, assisted by KGB head Yuri Andropov, had targeted the nuclear program for a complete managerial overhaul.

As I had my own consulting firm, I suggested a letter from the President to Kulov, head of the USSR Nuclear Regulatory Agency. It would invite three young scientists, to be selected by me, to visit the United States to study nuclear power for peaceful purposes. The President thought the idea of the three scientists was good, but he didn't want to involve the government in my trip.

President Ford came up with the idea of contacting his pal, Armand Hammer, the American industrialist whom the Russians considered a good friend, and asking for his help. He was contacted in Moscow, told of my proposed visit in December 1979, and that I was a nuclear consultant, a concerned scientist, and that my expertise would be put at the disposal of the Russian nuclear program.

Letters on my behalf were sent to several leaders in Russia, while I wrote to the young Russian scientists advising them of my visit. I sent letters to such people as Anatoli Alexandrov, one of Russia's leading academicians, and G. L. Budkev, head of high energy physics at the Institute of Physics at Georgia Academy (Russia's MIT).

Not quite sure what kind of reception I would get, I boarded a KLM flight on December 10, 1979, at 6:00 P.M. and was in Holland at 6:30 A.M. The following day, I flew to Vienna. There I took a train to Budapest, where I was met by the American ambassador to Hungary, Harry E. Berkhold. At lunch, he passed on some information, and a large bag containing cold weather clothing, then took me to the airport where I boarded an Aeroflot plane to Moscow.

Armand Hammer had really scored. Waiting for me at Sheremetyevo Airport in Moscow was Boris Kadomtsev of the Moscow Korkachov Atomic Institute. I was taken to the staff house of the institute, where he and his family lived, and given accommodations.

Taking nothing for granted, Kadomtsev had a KGB agent present to check my luggage. Spotting my carton of Alka-Seltzer, he asked what it was. I told him, so he helped himself to some packets. He was also interested in the Gillette tilt razors that I had brought along as presents. He took one.

Next day, I was Kadomtsev's guest at the Party Congress of the Soviet Union held at the Kremlin. I listened with rapt attention. After some discussion, the Congress adopted a five-year plan for an economic strategy to develop their nuclear power industry. Its theme was: "To raise labor productivity, increase per capita energy throughout Russia and help agri-industrial complexes."

The bottom line was to phase out the use of coal, peat, and all fossil fuels, which together generated half of Russia's electricity. Target date was the year 2010. The coal and oil would be exported to European countries for hard currency.

Russia had two shoddily built, fast breeder reactors; the United States had none. President Carter did not want breeder reactors, which reprocessed uranium into plutonium, and plutonium is a radioactive element used in making nuclear bombs. As a nuclear specialist, I knew the President was right. Breeder reactors produce more fuel than they burn, making it possible to extract fifty times as much energy from uranium as with conventional reactors.

Russia's need for change was brought about because of the drop in productivity from a five-year growth rate of 36 percent between 1971 and 1975 to 24 percent between 1976 and 1980 (though the five years were not yet over). The new watchwords in Russia were "efficiency" and "urgency." Thus, more and more nuclear power plants were being built hastily and inefficiently. Scientists blamed the builders, and the builders blamed inept scientists.

At the institute, they were handing me technical problems to solve. Just being there, made me an unpaid consultant. In Washington, I had been thoroughly briefed about which areas I should stay clear of, but I was free to discuss anything else. I told them I hoped to take three selected students back with me to the United States for training on operational maintenance and problems of fission and fusion reactors.

Armand Hammer paid us a quick visit and emphasized that it would help advance Russia's peaceful use of nuclear power.

Subsequently, I was given special permits to travel around the various nuclear plants in Russia and Siberia. Accompanying me would be a group of advanced students to be trained as a team. They were: Paul Andrei Zhavoronkov, V. I. Goldansky, A. G. Movosyelona, S. P. Velikhov, S. N. Belyaer, A. N. Yagorov, B. P. Venikolapov, N. Z. Styrizkovich, M. K. Krosovsky, A. N. Yarnov, and N. A. Nekrason.

The official chaperon was to be Boris Patton, president of the USSR Academy of Scientists. But, before we started, I was to be given "a severe test of knowledge," that is, they wanted to see if I knew what I was talking about.

The assignment, by Gennadi A. Veretennikov, head of the National Corporation for Nuclear Power, was to find out what was preventing one of their breeder reactors, based on the Caspian Sea at Shevchenko, from working. As word of the test spread, the military suddenly became interested in me, and S. L. Sokolov, minister of defense, furnished us with their most modern aircraft, a new Ilyushin 76 Candid transport. This particular plane normally made four trips a year to transport military equipment from Archangelsk to Vladivostok. It was temporarily diverted to our use. The results of the litmus test were obvious: fail, and go home; succeed, and stay to complete the survey.

On the trip were twelve nuclear scientists, including me, two KGB agents, several senior military scientists, ten soldiers with automatic weapons, two baggage handlers, and the aircrew.

We left Moscow for Volgograd (formerly Stalingrad). There we took on fuel and headed for Astrakhan at the mouth of the Volga River. After a short stop, we went on to Shevchenko, a military installation where we were segregated and quartered. It gave me a chance to get better acquainted with everyone in the group. We discussed the disadvantages of the fast breeder reactor; they were more costly to build, more complicated, and more hazardous than conventional reactors.

Then we were taken to the reactor for the inspection. The dialogue was mainly between myself and the senior scientists at the plant, whose noses were clearly out of joint. To make a fuel rod, it must be used with fissionable uranium 235 up to 0.7 of the total uranium; the balance of the rod must have uranium 238, which is not fissionable. If unstable at first, about 3 percent of uranium 235 should be added. Breeders must never be cooled by water, but by liquid sodium, which melts just below 100 degrees Celsius, its boiling point.

Liquid sodium is a soft, silvery metal that will burn on exposure to air. It reacts violently to water. I got them to agree to flush out all the water from the cooling pipes and then make certain all the joints were tight. I recommended that they clean them by blowing them out with hard air pressure for forty-eight hours. I reminded them all that liquid sodium can sift through small openings and burn on exposure to air. It also reacts violently to water left in the cooling pipes. (I was certain this was where the problem was.)

Finally, we lowered the fuel rods into position, and the breeder started to heat up to its operating temperature (critical temperature). When the uranium 235 had largely burned up in the reactor, the nonfissionable uranium 238 remained as waste. But if this waste 238 was placed around a new fuel core and eradicated by fast neutrons, it converted to uranium 239, which is fissionable and could be used as fuel. This is how the breeder can extract fifty times as much energy from the remaining uranium 238 and can be used over and over again.

When the breeder reactor began to function smoothly, everyone, including me, breathed easier. Each aspect is so critical that the slightest flaw can cause horrendous damage. After the successful "test," the scientists were much warmer to me.

From Shevchenko, the first leg of the flight back was to Tbilisi on the Kura River. It is located in the mountainous section of Georgia, forty miles from the Turkish border. Tbilisi is a beautiful city whose plants produce rare chemicals.

The next morning, on the second leg, we flew over the Caspian Sea, crossing the plateau of Ust-Urt to Tashkent, known for its production of tractors, excavators, and electronic equipment. The city has the tallest TV tower in continental Asia, 375 meters (over 1,200 feet) high. I was told it symbolized a jump in education from illiteracy to high technology in sixty years.

From Tashkent, we flew to Astrakhan to refuel and then on to Volgograd. Situated on the Volga River, it was called Stalingrad until Stalin's fall from grace. This is where the Russians stubbornly refused to surrender to a superior German army in World War II. As a reminder of the street-by-street fighting, many buildings still retain the pockmarks of bullet holes and shells.

We visited the three-and-a-half-mile-long dam of the Lenin Hydraulic Power Station, which holds back the largest reservoir of water in the world. Our next city was Donetsk, to visit the Institute of Physics at Georgia Academy, which boasted a small, high-energy cyclotron capable of colliding beams. We looked over the apparatus and discussed it with the teachers. From there, we went to Kharkov, stayed overnight, then on to Kiev to visit yet another polytechnic institute.

We returned to Moscow having learned little of Russia's nuclear operation that I didn't already know. I was asked to meet with Defense Minister Sokolov, who told me, "Because of your success, you may check the other plants. Now you must do something for me. I am responsible for the transport fleet. You are a pilot and an engineer of aeronautics. I wish for you to evaluate the Candid plane. For this, you will be permitted four round-trips to Vladivostok. I know it is a good craft, but I need someone objective to point out its flaws." I agreed.

One of the things that amazed me about the country was the presence of one hundred ethnic groups who speak eighty different languages and write five different alphabets. I would be touring most of them.

They took me to a sick reactor at Obninsk, near Moscow. It was a 5,000-kilowatt plant and it looked as though it was suffering from starvation. The reason was simple enough to diagnose. Like a mule, if you don't feed it properly, it won't work. The problem at Obninsk was that it produced poor results from its atomic pile.

This was a good opportunity to discuss the situation with the students at a symposium, letting them assist in pointing out the problem and the solution. Under our direction, the corrections were made and we stayed until the reactor came up to operating capability.

At a sick breeder reactor, I was informed by the plant's scientists that it had a few technical problems to overcome, but I could see the same problem existed. I inspected the plant itself and found it had been put together in a shoddy manner. Because of the increasing costs of shielding devices used for backups, I recommended that they use standard parts in all their reactors to reduce costs so there would be no need to skimp on quality. For some reason this comment caused some resentment.

At the Byeloyar-Skaya plant in the Ural Mountains of Lithuania, they were building a 1.6-million-kilowatt unit. We were allowed to see the plans for the buildings but not the reactors themselves.

The largest nuclear plant in the world was being built at Lenin-Gradskaya, with a four-channel type of reactor capable of developing a million kilowatts. The construction was poor. Of all the plants we saw, Ignalinskaya, in Lithuania, was the best. Proper materials were used and they instituted good safety measures.

For the most part, most high-power plants had inadequate safety measures regarding the cooling systems. There was constant danger of contamination, despite the efforts by the Russians to prohibit disposal of nuclear waste in the soil, the seas, oceans, or lakes. All residue containing radioactive elements was mixed with cement bitumen and formed into blocks, then buried in concrete graves, though they were beginning to use glass blocks, which were insoluble in water. Some radioactive liquids were poured into metal tanks and buried in concrete graves; the tanks have to be changed every twenty-five years.

I noticed that in all their reactors, the cladding material that shielded the uranium fuel rods was protected with graphite. If the cladding material caught fire due to overheating, the smoke entering the atmosphere would be highly radioactive. When a reactor loses its cooling system, usually water, then the nuclear fuel rods overheat and melt. This is known as a meltdown.

The high dangers of radioactive emissions come from iodine 131 and cobalt cesium 135, as well as krypton, xenon, and strontium. When I pointed out that all their reactors were subject to these emissions, the answer was "There has never been any threat of radioactive contamination of the environment or the lives of personnel or the populations of nearby settlements."*

I replied, "But what about your nuclear waste disaster in Kasli in the Ural Mountains in 1957? It exterminated three villages, blew away part of a mountain, and rerouted a river." From their expressions, I could see the graduate students had never been told of the disaster, and the older scientists were grim-faced.

The Russians were slipshod because of haste. Herodotus said twenty-five hundred years ago, "Haste in every business brings failure."

All the members of our group were together again at the Korkachov

* This was before Chernobyl.

Institute of Atomic Energy in Moscow. Boris Kadomtsev, head of the
Physics-Plasma Department, gave a short lecture. In summary, he
said, "The Soviet leaders are driven by a burning sense of inferiority
and a determination to overcome Russia's historic backwardness. If we
slackened the tempo, we would fall behind. Russia will make any
sacrifices necessary to obtain equality with America. In Russia, if
something vitally matters to the State, it is done immediately."

After this talk, we were praised for our work on the reactors, then
our documents were checked to see if we were cleared to continue. All
members required special passes, which were blue and the size of a
cigarette case. Thanks to Minister Sokolov, my passbook looked as if it
had been made for a VIP, a small diploma prepared by a calligrapher. It
read *Kandeadah't Doktar Naook*, meaning "doctor of atomic sciences."

From my discussions, I realized that Russia could produce hydrogen
bombs. Russia was planning to construct a tokamak nuclear reactor
using plasma for fuel, controlled under high magnetic conditions.
Plasma is composed of deuterium and tritium (both isotopes of hydrogen), the same as in a hydrogen bomb.

We were shown the nuclear operation and power plant in the new
Sibir ice breaker. We saw a new class of aircraft carrier being built as
well as nuclear submarines under construction. They used nuclear
fission plants to create steam to propel the ships. They were proud to
show us the twelve Yankee ballistic subs removed from service as per
SALT I interim agreement.

We were being shunted all over the place before setting out on our
first trans-Siberian trip, but before returning to Moscow, we made a
stop at Novosibirsk to drop off some people and take on others. We also
made a stop at Perm. At the Kurchatov Institute of Atomic Energy, we
were told we would see the detonation of a hydrogen bomb on the
island of Novaya Zemlya.

We were also going to make a visual inspection of the atomic plant at
Volgodansk, where the small tokamak fusion units were to be manufac-
tured for worldwide sales. This was my main reason for going to
Russia.

Later, a military plane arrived carrying twenty-five people from
Siberian labor camps. Ostensibly, each one had been selected from his
respective camp for being outstanding. The plane ride and the opportunity to witness a nuclear explosion were their rewards.

One hour before the countdown, the twenty-five prisoners were placed close to where the bomb would explode. They were to be guinea pigs to absorb the effects of the fallout, something they never expected. These prisoners were considered expendable. I asked if people within a four-hundred-mile radius had been informed. I received no answer. Then the bomb was exploded. It was the most frightening sight of my life. The twenty-five men were rushed to Moscow by military plane to be used for medical research.

Russia was building a nuclear stockpile and it was fully expected that I would bring that message home to America with me. But it wasn't all work. I had time to walk around and talk to people. In Moscow, there was the theater, the ballet, the circus, and the opera. Gorky Park had its flea market and black market, and more hard currency changed hands there than in the local banks.

In January 1980, our first major trip began. We started at Archangelsk on the White Sea with a load of munitions and armaments and made a series of major and minor stops along the way to inspect nuclear plants: we flew 620 miles to Kirov; then over 600 miles to Omsk; 400 miles to Novosibirsk; 263 miles to Krosnoyarsk; almost 270 miles to Irkutsk; 388 miles to Cita; 450 miles to Blagoveshchensk; and 400 miles to Kharborovsk. Finally, we traveled the last 390 miles to Vladivostok to unload the military supplies. The next two trips were similar.

After completing the third round-trip, I sent my evaluations on the Ilyushin Candid Transport to Sokolov. Though it lacked the creature comforts of home, the plane was a real workhorse that withstood the rigors of some of the worst weather I have ever encountered. We had learned to make ourselves comfortable. Our group was down to thirty-six people: twelve nuclear scientists, five crew, a military contingent of fourteen soldiers and officers, two KGB agents, two baggage handlers, and myself. I was generally concerned because the plane was so heavily loaded there were restrictions on where we could land. The pilot was ordered to take on just enough fuel to reach the next destination, plus two additional hours of fuel for the safety margin.

By our fourth and final trip, the odyssey in Russia was becoming tedious. As the expedition began flying eastward, we continued to make scheduled stops to observe and evaluate the nuclear power plants. Parts of Siberia were so desolate that each city seemed like an oasis in a land of rocks, tundra, and mountains. Often, cities were receiving all their energy from nuclear plants—electricity, heat, industrial power, and a better way of life. Half a century ago, these were desolate outposts useful only for mining, hunting, or exile.

As we traveled farther into Siberia, the days started to get cold . . . then colder . . . then biting cold. This wasn't necessarily bad for flying conditions as it's generally 30 or 40 degrees below zero at thirty thousand feet. From what I saw, my main concern was the quality of maintenance on the plane and the quality of the jet fuel.

Serious problems started soon after we left Krasnoyarsk late in the afternoon en route to Irkutsk, near Lake Baikal. We ran into gale-force winds from the northwest at 90 to 100 miles per hour. This made it difficult for the captain to stay on course. The cruising airspeed of 590 miles per hour was a ground speed of 490 miles per hour. For a while, we followed the Angara River.

Suddenly, we ran into buffeting winds and were deluged with sleet and snow. It was suddenly very dark. We were 150 miles from our destination after passing over Cheremkhovo, Usolye, and then Sibirskoye, flying toward Angarsk, looking for an abandoned army airfield.

The plane began to shake. A giant hand had grabbed the plane and was using it like a baby's rattle. It was November 7, 1980, and I had a premonition we were going to crash and that this might be the last day of my life. . . .

. . . When I regained consciousness, I suddenly remembered the crash. I found myself on a bunk made of hardwood. It was agonizing to move my pain-racked body. The makeshift prison cell was a tiny room the size of a closet without a window. The only comfort was that I was no longer cold.

Trying to sit up was agony. My neck, back, and legs seemed to hurt the most. I was not comfortable in any position. Soon, the two guards came in and, using rough language, once again started questioning. They had brought me some worn work clothes to replace my tattered rags. I kept asking, but I couldn't get them to call Moscow. Other than my wallet, which contained some rubles, my driver's license in English, credit cards, and a couple of photos, they could not understand why I had no credentials. I kept repeating that everything was on the plane.

Two more men came into the room and seemed to take charge. They were KGB officials stationed in the area. They asked more questions. Soon a doctor came in and dressed the water burns and injected me with a syringe full of painkillers.

I had told them who was on the plane, but they acted as though they didn't believe me. Later in the afternoon, I was advised that the chief of the Soviet Armed Forces, K. U. Chernenko, was bringing a team of officials and investigators who would arrive the following morning. They were: Minister of Defense S. L. Sokolov; the deputy minister of defense; the chief of the air forces, and A. N. Yefimov. Later, Yuri Andropov, head of the KGB, was added to the list.

I asked the KGB agents if they could search the crash area for my luggage and briefcase with credentials. They went out to look, but the water had completely frozen over. I was given black bread and *chai*, which is tea without sugar. I drank the tea, but my face was too swollen to eat. I begged for another injection and this one mercifully knocked me out.

I awoke the next morning in great pain. Everyone who was supposed to come had arrived. Yuri Andropov came to see me and said, "I will get you to the hospital at Irkutsk to get your wounds attended to properly, then get you some better clothes to wear." He gave me *koumiss* to drink, which is fermented mare's milk.

"I will do what is necessary to get you a new set of credentials. This story of you being a saboteur—I know better, because I saw you at the Baikomur Space Center at Kazakhastan with the group of nuclear scientists."

I was taken by ambulance to the Irkutsk hospital, where they attended my wounds with salve and painkillers. No one checked if I had broken bones or torn ligaments as they did not take X rays. That evening, when I was more comfortable, the investigators, led by Andropov, came to see me. He introduced me to them as a person who had come to help Russia with its nuclear program.

The tape recorders were set up and I told them the story. I detailed the performance of the aircraft from the time we left Krasnoyarsk until the landing and crash. When I finished, they began to ask questions in a more civilized manner.

"Why do you think the airplane performed this way?"

I said, "It sounded like fuel starvation and a rupture of the hydraulic lines, which affected the landing gear extending, and it also affected the elevator systems—or the power of the elevators. Also, there was a collection of ice on the elevators because the temperature was way below freezing—perhaps fifty degrees or more below zero."

In all, they had me repeat the story eight separate times. I was told that the eighth tape sounded exactly like the first. The engineers inspecting the two engines on the left wing that broke off did find corrosion in the fuel metering systems to the engine. That would have caused the choo-chooing.

By the next day, my credentials from the United States had been wired to Moscow and then to Andropov. I now had two nurses who attended to me, Lyudmila Magiytz and Serafima Ladodrov. I was given quite a bit of *koumiss*, and by now I could eat, so I was given *swena* and *kapuska*, pork and cabbage.

In all, four or five days had passed, and finally Yuri Andropov brought me a packet of credentials. I was given a set of passable clothing. By now, my neck was paralyzed and I was unable to move it. I was being put on a plane at Irkutsk and flown to Hungary.

Leaving Russia was like leaving a nightmare. At Budapest, I called the American ambassador, Harry E. Berkhold. By now, not only couldn't I move my neck, I had sciatic pain in my legs that was so bad I couldn't take more than a couple of steps. The ambassador got me admitted to a hospital at Harkany, and I had to suffer a train trip to Pécs. As I couldn't get up or sit down, the ambassador was kind enough to send one of his aides to accompany me.

Dr. Béla Keszthelyi, head of Gryogyfurdo Korhaza Hospital, operated on my neck. After I started to heal and I could move my neck, he put me into the hot baths at Harkany, using physical therapists to examine my body.

My deceased wife's brother and family came to visit me at Pécs, then I went back to Budapest. By now, I could walk with the aid of a cane and a stick. I was anxious to get back to the States. The ambassador let me use a secure room to make a tape of my experiences, which would be flown by diplomatic pouch to Washington. I flew to Holland and transferred to a KLM plane to New York.

I arrived at Kennedy on a Saturday and was put into a wheelchair. I was out of Hungarian pain pills and I was suffering. On Sunday, you can get anything you want in New York—except a doctor. I decided the hell with it, I'll go where they know me. It took until Monday morning to contact the president of Air Florida, who held up the 11:00 A.M. flight for a half hour to allow me to get there by cab.

Finally, I arrived home in Palm Beach on Lake Worth. I was in great pain. It was Christmas week and again I couldn't reach a doctor. On the 24th I finally called up a close friend, a chiropractor, who came over with his wife and they carted me off to the Good Samaritan Hospital, where they sedated me and kept me overnight, then shipped me off to St. Mary's Hospital.

After a careful checkup, I was put into the intensive care unit, where I remained for a month. When I gained enough strength, they operated on the center of my spine to relieve the pain. It was helpful. Since then, every two years I have had two more operations.

I can now walk with the aid of a cane. That was the end of my trip to Russia.

CHAPTER 30

"One for the Gipper"

NEW YORK CITY, 1982. Two years had passed since the catastrophic accident in Russia, but I continued to have nightmares. The explosion was so vivid, I would wake up and find myself sweating and moaning. I could never, ever forget those wonderful young nuclear students and all those people who perished.

My condition would not allow me to forget. As a result of the crash, I had just undergone a second operation on my back and couldn't get around without a wheelchair. One Wednesday, while working on a problem relating to particle beam and laser beam technology for a client, the phone rang.

For no logical reason, I sensed trouble. It was a man whom I'll call Wilson, from the U.S. Foreign Service, a division of the State Department; "Henri, your trip to Russia was so successful that the volume of information you brought back is a must-read for every diplomat going to Europe."

"That's nice, but why are you buttering me up?"

"State wants to you take another trip—this time, to Israel."

"Why me, for heaven's sake? I just had an operation on my back. I'm in a wheelchair. Can't it wait until I'm more mobile?"

"No. This is imperative. Wheelchair or no wheelchair, you've got to get your ass over to Israel and do this job. It's very important. When you receive the coded letters of instructions, then you'll understand why you have to do it, what to look for, and what to do. The President [Reagan] is counting on you." He hung up.

The first letter brought me up-to-date with the reasons for the trip. The second letter arrived by diplomatic courier.

In effect, the first letter said that even though Mossad (the Israeli secret intelligence agency) worked closely with the CIA, there were some matters involving highly secret Israeli security measures that were never discussed.

The United States was interested in finding out if Israel had atom or hydrogen bombs ready for use, and if they had aircraft capable of delivering those bombs. Both these subjects were in my areas of expertise. The letter reminded me that a few months earlier, Israeli bombers had attacked and destroyed Saddam Hussein's nuclear reactor near Baghdad, because Iraq was capable of building nuclear weapons and Iraq was the sworn enemy of Israel. It was a preemptive strike, and Israel hadn't informed the American government until the raid was under way.

During Israel's war with Syria, Russia supplied Syria with SAMs (surface-to-air missiles). The Israeli Air Force knocked them out. In addition, Israeli pilots shot down twenty-five MIGs flown by Syrian and Russian pilots.

The Mideast is a hot zone. Israel is the first line of defense against any Russian nuclear threat and the United States doesn't want an ally with an itchy finger on the trigger. If they have nuclear toys, we want our own expert to obtain positive proof.

The letter by courier contained specific questions and stipulated that after reading it, I must seal and return it to the department immediately:

1. Does Israel have atomic or hydrogen bombs ready for use? What is the approximate stockpile?
2. Do they have aircraft capable of delivering these bombs? What is their range?
3. Do they have facilities to produce heavy water in the form of deuterium, tritium, or plutonium?
4. Do they have other types of atomic weapons ready for use?
5. Are they producing bombs for any other country?
6. Have they experienced malfunctions with their atomic equipment at Dimona?
7. Have workers had personal injuries or illnesses at their top secret nuclear reactor at Machon number 2, Dimona? Or at 8 Tier

Subterranean Structure in the Machon number 2 building,
where they produce plutonium?
8. Have they tested a hydrogen bomb?

I was very curious. Didn't State have all this information? The
Israelis had the bomb, the planes, and, probably, the best air force in
the world. It was an exciting mission, and while my mind was willing,
my body was in need of repairs. But like an old fire horse in pasture,
ring a fire bell and I would come out charging.

I was a consultant, wasn't I? So, consult!

The Mossad had guards at the El Al counter at JFK Airport in New
York. They checked my credentials thoroughly, and—would you
believe?—they took my wheelchair apart. They wanted to know the
exact purpose of my visit. That very night, El Al employees decided to
go on strike and I had to return home. It took three round-trips to the
airport before we took off at 5:00 A.M. on an alternative airline that
accepted El Al tickets. The Mossad reverified my credentials to make
certain that my trip was in line with their up-to-the-minute instructions from Washington and Tel Aviv.

After an El Al steward wheeled me on board and pinned a colored
identification ribbon on my lapel, I was seated up front, by myself, in
the first-class section while my wheelchair was stored. From then on,
the aircrew treated me like a VIP. While Hebrew is the official language of Israel, it is not one of the fourteen languages I speak. Luckily,
everyone in Israel speaks English. And since a couple of close friends
had taught me enough Yiddish to be able to rattle off some fancy
insults, I figured I would have little trouble communicating.

We had a two-hour layover in London, then took off again in the
afternoon. Dinner was excellent, and we arrived at Ben-Gurion Airport, outside of Tel Aviv, at 11:30 P.M. They wheeled me off the plane
very carefully, and at the exit, we were met by four military-looking
men in civilian clothes. Their identification ribbons matched mine.

In two minutes, I was whisked through immigration and customs
and into a van guarded by two motorcycle policemen. The van was to
accommodate the wheelchair, the luggage, and me. After a long ride
into the desert, I was finally deposited in my room at 3:00 A.M. Two
security guards checked through my luggage and camera again, and
then I was allowed to rest my exhausted body.

Next morning, I discovered we were in Dimona. After breakfast, I was wheeled around to the different plants. I was asked many technical and scientific questions by scientists trying to determine if I knew my stuff. Apparently I passed, as they were soon showing me the reactor where plutonium was being produced. A senior scientist confided that Israel practiced a deliberate policy of ambiguity on the topic of nuclear capability. During our first meeting, I was told emphatically, "Israel will not be the first nation to introduce nuclear weapons into this region."

They were so open that I wondered if the State Department was misreading the exchange of information between the two governments. I decided not to kid myself or the Israelis and I asked my questions carefully. The responses were:

The Arab world is well informed about what Israel is doing. They learned about Israel's nuclear capability fifteen years earlier when Prime Minister David Ben-Gurion announced to the Knesset that Israel's nuclear reactor was built for peaceful purposes.

In 1961, after hearing Ben-Gurion's speech, an incredulous President Kennedy sent a U-2 spy plane over Israel and confirmed the existence of the nuclear plant. All subsequent Presidents thought it prudent not to say anything further. After all, Israel was the only democracy in the Middle East and a close U.S. ally.

In 1970, General Moshe Dayan favored going public and integrating the nuclear capability into Israel's military posture. This suggestion was turned down. The government feared it would invite a demand for parity by the Arab nations.

The United States had no firm evidence that Israel had ever tested a nuclear weapon. However, on November 22, 1979, an American satellite recorded a double flash of light in the South Atlantic. The speculation was that Israel and South Africa had jointly tested a nuclear device.

The Israeli scientists held a discussion with me, then one without me. Finally, they agreed to show me everything, and one of them said, "Schlepp along with us." They helped me put on protective clothing and pushed my wheelchair on an inspection tour of the subterranean caverns of Machon 2, where plutonium was produced. They didn't hesitate when I asked if they had hydrogen warheads. The answer was "Yes." I was shown a stockpile of more than fifty.

"Have you facilities to produce heavy water in the form of deuterium and tritium?" I asked.

"Yes."

"Have you experienced any malfunctions at Dimona?"

"Yes. Three people were killed, some personal injuries, one man working on plutonium units died of sickness."

"Was that double flash in the South African/Indian Ocean in 1979 a hydrogen explosion?"

There was no direct answer, but the implication was that Israel did fire and test a hydrogen bomb. The U.S. government probably wanted verification to pressure Israel into signing a nonproliferation treaty.

Because the Israelis were so open with me, I brought something to their attention. "I want to compliment you on your efficiency—everything is so spick-and-span—but it's obvious a few of your people are getting a little careless." I pointed out that the reactor's cooling system had very rusty pipes. "I suggest you replace them instantly. It's a potential hazard."

The next day, I met with the energy minister, Yitzak Berman, and chief of the Air Force, Yitzak Rabin. They had learned from Washington that I was an aeronautical engineer and had been a troubleshooter for the FAA. They asked if I would take a look at their new fighter, the Lavi. I agreed, and we went traipsing off. We traveled through rolling hills and valleys and looked at the beauty of the cotton fields. But we also passed dozens of burned-out and rusting armored cars, a reminder of Israel's war with Egypt.

Their concern now was their present battle with Lebanon, and they wanted me to meet the hard-nosed, hard-line defense minister, Ariel Sharon, a tough-minded, former commanding officer of the armed forces of Israel. I met him at the military airdrome. He had a strong handshake and had a good word for the men who worked under him. I liked this man. We got right down to business.

I was impressed. The hangars were clean and the planes looked well maintained. As I was wheeled around, it was obvious that most of the planes were of American manufacture: bombers, helicopters, and modern fighters. All the aviation people I spoke with were dedicated and had an air of professionalism about them.

Next morning, the program was for me to see the insides of the planes. Everything was up-to-date in electronics, with attachments in readiness for bombing missions. I asked to look at their training program for the simulators. In the United States, these programs are created by pilots who've seen action and know what type of training is required.

Because of my condition, I could not get into an advanced simulator, nor was I qualified on any of these aircraft. I was knowledgeable enough to be impressed and I told them that ten years earlier, the U.S. Air Force accident rate was 3.16 mishaps per 100,000 hours flown. Now it was down to 1.6. Along with the decrease, combat performance increased remarkably. I credited this to hours of practice in the simulator.

At this point, I spotted the delta wing Dassault Mirage IV, France's strategic bomber that was capable of carrying free-fall nuclear bombs.

Finally, I got to where the Lavi (Hebrew for "Little Lion") was being constructed. Israel had overspent large amounts of money to develop the Lavi fighter, and the United States had invested in it as well, but it did not live up to expectations at this point. The machine itself was well constructed, but the engine was giving them difficulty. Some of the engineers on the project were foreigners, and I suspected many came from America. Apparently, the afterburner was not adequate enough to produce the speed they wanted.

Finally, the last meeting on the agenda was with Prime Minister Menachem Begin.

Because of the war, I had to wait over an hour and a half before I was admitted to his office. His greeting was cordial, but he was quite suspicious about why the United States would send me to inspect Dimona. He had been told of my safety suggestions, and on behalf of the workers there, he thanked me for making them.

The prime minister wondered why the United States wanted more information, as everything had been revealed by the U-2 overflight of Israel in 1960. He said it was President Carter's suggestion that Israel not acknowledge the testing of their hydrogen bomb.

During our talk, he kept receiving phone calls. His main concern was the U.S. attitude toward Israel's invasion of Lebanon and the clash with Syrian forces. He was most proud of the fact that the Israeli Air Force had now destroyed eighty Russian MIGs and all their anti-aircraft and ground-to-air missiles.

Then he stopped talking about the war and asked me if I liked the weather, which was not unlike Florida's, and the abundance of fresh fruit. Suddenly, he switched back to the purpose of my visit. He wanted to know what I had learned and I told him about the fifty hydrogen warheads, and planes capable of carrying nuclear bombs five thousand miles. We discussed the malfunction of one of their facilities and the reluctance of his people to discuss it.

He also explained the reluctance to boast of their nuclear ability, as it would start a nuclear arms race in the Mideast. He asked and I told him what I thought of the Lavi—that it would cost much more and still have less capability than a U.S.-made fighter.

Begin also admitted that uranium 235 and 238 came from the mines in South Africa, and I could draw any conclusions I wanted from that. On behalf of the U.S. government, I thanked him for his help in accomplishing my somewhat sticky assignment.

With my work completed, I took a trip to Jerusalem to visit the city with four thousand years of continuous history, a history revered by Jews, Christians, and Moslems.

In August 1982, the Israeli Ministry of Defense published a sixty-page report on its national security issues and warned that Jerusalem, Tel Aviv, and Haifa, as well as Dimona, could be attacked by Syria with Soviet Scud missiles, and that the Scud was capable of carrying nuclear and chemical warheads. This warning foreshadowed the Scud missiles launched against Israel by Saddam Hussein during Desert Storm.

I met later with John Lewis, the American ambassador to Israel. He told me how he was working to help bring about peace in the region and suggested that a UN force from France, Italy, and the United States supervise a peace treaty. He asked me what I had learned and I told him, as well as my comments on the Lavi.

Lewis commented: "The biggest problem in Israel today is inflation. People are confused and angry at these ongoing wars, which take a high toll in lives—and money that they don't have. I was never asked to look at Dimona and I've been very curious. Thank you for filling me in. It's information our government needs."

Because the strike was over, I flew back to the States on El Al and again I was treated like a VIP. At home, I spent a considerable amount of time preparing my report. It would be my last official duty, even though I was supposed to be retired already.

I received a nice letter for my efforts from Secretary of State George P. Shultz.

Nov 22 1982

Dr.Henri Keyzer-Andre
3755 Poinciana Drive Apt. 612
Lake Worth Fla.33463

Dear Dr. Keyzer-Andre:

I asked your department to write this letter
for my signature so that I may add my thanks
to you for an outstanding technical and
diplomatic performance in Israel during October
of 1982.

Yours sincerely

George P. Shultz
Secretary of State
Of the United States of America

Epilogue
by the Editors

ON THE PUBLICATION date of this book, author Henri Keyzer-André has recently celebrated his eighty-sixth birthday. As a result of the serious air crash in Siberia, he is obliged to walk with the aid of a cane. Nevertheless, he remains a dapper, swashbuckling individual, sporting the whitest Palm Beach suits in Florida.

After his wheelchair flight to Israel for the State Department in 1982, he finally stopped working for the government, though he remains a nuclear consultant and air crash specialist for private industry.

It was on his return from Israel that he was asked to accompany three sprightly widows to the Preservation Society's fund-raiser, a gala dinner/dance at Mar-a-lago. The ever-gallant Henri said he'd be delighted. After dinner, two of the ladies went dancing while the third, Mossette (also sporting a cane), continued talking with her escort. Henri was surprised to discover an attractive, sophisticated lady who was a painter, a world traveler, a gourmet chef, and a graduate of the Columbia University School of Optometry, who also found time to be deeply involved in the social and charitable life of Palm Beach. She had traveled to as many countries as Henri, so they continued talking far into the night.

The following week, they went as a couple on a "first date," to the Salvation Army Ball. Again, they both had so much to talk about that, as the old saying goes, "they started going steady."

But Henri's injured back was giving him a great deal of trouble. Mossette recommended that he switch surgeons, and together they discovered Dr. Benjamin Vallo, a professor of neurosurgery connected with New York University. After an operation, Henri moved into Mossette's apartment in New York to recuperate.

291

It was while Henri was telling her stories of his exciting past that Mossette suggested he write an autobiography. At this point, Henri proposed to Mossette. After being widowed twice, she was not anxious for a third marriage. Besides, she led a busy social life. But Henri persisted, and they were secretly wed in her apartment in Palm Beach on January 20, 1984.

Henri not only married a wonderful companion, he also discovered she was relentless in getting after him to work on his book. It turned out to be a ten-year project.

As neither Henri's nor Mossette's marriages had produced any children, this book is, in effect, their offspring. Between them, they have more energy than a couple of teenagers. While she is painting, Henri is playing music on his organ or listening to various language records in order remain fluent in the fourteen languages he has mastered.

As a member of the Kiwanis International, Henri chairs an annual program known as "The Golden Years," in which he takes senior citizens up to one hundred years of age on outings to various points of interest in Florida.

A popular guest speaker, Henri is often called upon to give talks or lectures on his colorful and heroic career. As a member of the Pundits, he also participates in programs that feature some of the best speakers in the world.

Together, Henri and Mossette are active supporters of numerous Palm Beach charities and artistic endeavors. These include the Wheelchair Sports Fund, the Raymond F. Kravis Center for the Performing Arts, and the Guild for International Piano Competition (which finances the winner's concert in Avery Fisher Hall in New York City). They also support the Norton Gallery of Fine Art, one of the finest small museums in the South.

Recently, Henri was commissioned commodore in the U.S. Naval Institute. Funds that come from commodore membership are used by the U.S. Naval Institute to support and expand their education forum.

The couple had traveled extensively in the early days of their marriage, and they now lead a quietly hectic life, supporting and donating financially to numerous charitable organizations.

Henri's study is covered with international honors and awards, including numerous honorary Ph.D.'s from many countries. He is actively working on his next book.

Index

293